Henry Lewis Thompson

**Henry George Liddell, D.D., Dean of Christ Church, Oxford**

A memoir

Henry Lewis Thompson

**Henry George Liddell, D.D., Dean of Christ Church, Oxford**
*A memoir*

ISBN/EAN: 9783337261337

Printed in Europe, USA, Canada, Australia, Japan

Cover: Foto ©Lupo / pixelio.de

More available books at **www.hansebooks.com**

# HENRY GEORGE LIDDELL

D.D.

DEAN OF CHRIST CHURCH, OXFORD

*A MEMOIR*

BY THE

REV. HENRY L. THOMPSON, M.A.

VICAR OF ST. MARY THE VIRGIN, OXFORD
SOMETIME STUDENT AND CENSOR OF CHRIST CHURCH

*WITH PORTRAITS AND ILLUSTRATIONS*

NEW YORK
HENRY HOLT AND COMPANY
1899

# PREFACE

THIS memoir has been compiled at the request of Mrs. Liddell, and has had the advantage of her constant encouragement.

Many friends of the late Dean have most kindly contributed to the volume their recollections of his life at various times and under different aspects. Their contributions have, as far as possible, been duly acknowledged.

The compiler of the memoir may himself claim, without presumption, to write with an authority based upon adequate knowledge. It was his good fortune to be admitted to Westminster School by Mr. Liddell in 1851. For four years he was under him there, and rose to be a member of his Sixth Form. From 1858 to 1877 he was a resident student of Christ Church, and as undergraduate, Tutor, and Censor, was brought into very varied and often very intimate relations with the Dean. The friendship which he was thus privileged to enjoy extended over nearly half a century, and was only ended by the Dean's death.

## Preface

The story of Dean Liddell's life, down to the year 1834, has been largely drawn from his letters to his parents, and from a MS. autobiography which he wrote in his old age for the instruction of his children, but which unfortunately terminates at that early date.

He was never a great letter-writer, and during his long residence at Oxford, where he was able to meet his chief friends in daily intercourse, his correspondence was not voluminous. There exist, however, a good many letters addressed to Robert Scott and H. Halford Vaughan, which have been courteously placed at the disposal of the writer, and from which quotations have been freely made. Sir Henry W. Acland, his oldest living friend, has contributed many charming reminiscences; and from the letters written to him by Dr. Liddell, when both had retired from active life, some interesting selections have been made.

The arrangement of the narrative is designedly unmethodical, especially in that portion which deals with the long period of his life as Dean. It has been thought best to mention subjects as they were naturally suggested, rather than to arrange events in a strict chronological sequence.

The writer desires to express his cordial thanks to the many friends who have given advice and help, and especially to the Rev. T. Vere Bayne, his former colleague as Tutor and Censor, whose uninterrupted residence at Christ Church for more than fifty years has made him an almost final authority on all matters connected with its history since 1848, and whose vigilant criticism has been most kindly and most usefully applied to the revision of the proof-sheets of a work in which he has taken a very warm interest from the beginning.

Thanks are due to Mr. Ryman Hall for permission to reproduce the crayon portrait by Mr. George Richmond, R.A.

OXFORD,
*April,* 1899.

# CONTENTS

### CHAPTER I.
CHILDHOOD AND SCHOOLDAYS (1811–1829) . . . 1

### CHAPTER II.
LIFE AT CHRIST CHURCH (1830–46) . . 13

### CHAPTER III.
THE LEXICON . . . . . 65

### CHAPTER IV.
HEADMASTERSHIP OF WESTMINSTER (1846–55) . . 86

### CHAPTER V.
DEANERY OF CHRIST CHURCH (1855–91) . 134

### CHAPTER VI.
DEANERY OF CHRIST CHURCH (*continued*) . . 166

### CHAPTER VII.
DEANERY OF CHRIST CHURCH (*continued*) . . 231

### CHAPTER VIII.
HOME LIFE . . . . . 249

### CHAPTER IX.
RESIGNATION OF THE DEANERY AND AFTER-LIFE (1892–8) 265

INDEX . . . . . . . . 281

# LIST OF ILLUSTRATIONS

PORTRAIT BY CRUIKSHANK . . . *To face p.* 28

„   „ GEORGE RICHMOND, R.A. . *Frontispiece*

„   „ G. F. WATTS, R.A. . . . *To face p.* 238

„   „ H. HERKOMER, R.A. . . . „ 265

THE CHAPLAINS' QUADRANGLE, CHRIST CHURCH . „ 16

THE MONSTER π . . . . . . . *p.* 75

CHRIST CHURCH CATHEDRAL IN 1813 . . . *To face p.* 149

CHRIST CHURCH CATHEDRAL (1856-1870) . . „ 154

CHRIST CHURCH CATHEDRAL AFTER RESTORATION „ 158

THE GREAT QUADRANGLE FROM A DRAWING MADE IN 1856 . . . . . . . . „ 161

THE GREAT QUADRANGLE AFTER RESTORATION . „ 164

BLOTTING-PAPER SKETCHES BY DEAN LIDDELL
  *Between pp.* 194 *and* 195

THE DEANERY, CHRIST CHURCH, FROM THE GARDEN *To face p.* 249

THE GATE IN CHRIST CHURCH CLOISTERS LEADING TO DEAN LIDDELL'S GRAVE . . . . „ 278

# THE LIFE

OF

# HENRY GEORGE LIDDELL

———◆———

## CHAPTER I

### CHILDHOOD AND SCHOOLDAYS

HENRY GEORGE LIDDELL was born on February 6, 1811. He was the eldest child of the Rev. Henry George Liddell, whose elder brother, Sir Thomas Liddell of Ravensworth, was created Baron Ravensworth at the coronation of George IV. This peerage, advanced to an earldom in 1874, was a revival of a barony created in 1745, which became extinct in 1784. He was thus a member, on his father's side, of an ancient and honourable family of the county of Durham, and his mother, Charlotte Lyon, was fourth daughter of the Hon. Thomas Lyon, brother of the eighth Earl of Strathmore.

He was born at Binchester, 'a good square stone house placed on an eminence facing the Bishop's Palace at Auckland, and distant from

B

that town about a mile.' It belonged then to the Lyon family, but was afterwards bought by Bishop Van Mildert and pulled down. Here Mr. Liddell and his wife lived, with his wife's brothers and sisters, serving his first curacy in the adjoining parish of Southchurch. He was soon promoted to the benefice of Redmarshall, near Stockton, and then to the Rectory of Boldon, a village on the high road between Newcastle-on-Tyne and Sunderland. Boldon was thus the home of the family during the childhood and boyhood of the future Dean. He describes himself as a studious boy, fond of the children's books of the day, such as Mrs. Sherwood's and Miss Edgeworth's tales, *Sandford and Merton*, *Robinson Crusoe*, and the *Swiss Family Robinson*.

'On my sixth birthday I was promised a great honour and reward. My father took me up into his study and inducted me into the mysteries of the Eton Latin Grammar. I remember the day, the place, and the fact as clearly as if it were yesterday. I continued to make pretty good progress under his kind teaching; but I fear that as I went on from day to day I did not regard the honour so great as I did on the first day.'

At the early age of eight, as was usual in those days, came the first great sorrow and separation in his life—his transference from the bright country home to the rough discipline of a private school. He was sent with his younger brother Thomas, who was but seven years old, to Bishopton Grove, a house standing a little distance from the road leading from Ripon to Studley Royal. The school was kept by a Mr. Weidemann, a choleric man and an indifferent teacher.

'In the course of a long life, I have not escaped several sharp and severe sorrows, though I have to thank God for blessings far exceeding the sufferings. But I do not think that any sorrow of youth or manhood equalled in intensity and duration the blank and hopeless misery which followed the wrench of transference from a happy home to a school such as that which received us in the summer of 1819. I remember, as if it was yesterday, the sinking of heart, the sense of desolation, the utter despair, the wish that I could die on the spot, when my kind and loving father parted with us in the Master's study, and passing out of the green gate of the little garden in front of the house, disappeared from sight. His heart, as he told me afterwards, was as heavy as ours. But we did not then know this.'

It was a rough place, with little kindness, unintelligent teaching, the frequent use of the cane, and the inevitable bullying.

'We little boys were made to sit at the long desks with our hands over our eyes; and certain big fellows, having needles fixed in little balls of sealing-wax, blew these missiles through peashooters, so as to pin our ears to our heads.'

In September 1823, at the age of twelve, Liddell was entered at Charterhouse School, where he remained till 1829. The long journey from Boldon occupied four days. His description of the school as it then was is worth recording, for at that time, under the famous Headmaster Dr. Russell, it occupied a leading position among English Public Schools, and in numbers nearly equalled Eton. On the night after his arrival in London, his cousin, Robert Liddell, afterwards the well-known Vicar of St. Paul's, Knightsbridge, took him to Mr. Watkinson's house in Charterhouse Square.

'Here I was turned into the 'Long Room,' a low, dark, dirty apartment, measuring (I should think) about 70 feet by 15, with an excrescence at the upper end, added to accommodate increasing numbers of boys. Here we breakfasted, dined, and supped; and this was our only sitting-room. The upper boys had cupboards between the windows, and a sort of table-desk in front of each cupboard, so that the doors of the cupboards being open they formed a sort of screen, and enabled them to read and write in comparative privacy. The lower boys sat on benches placed along the dining tables, and while the upper boys were at work were compelled, on pain of prompt punishment, to keep absolute silence. The upper fire was reserved for the upper boys. At the lower end was another fire, to which the lower boys were allowed to go; but the little fellows did not see much of it. Each boy had a small locker of two shelves, in which he kept his books and whatever else he chose. . . . The only place we had to wash in was a narrow room, with leaden troughs on either side, and cocks to supply water, which was caught in small leaden or pewter basins. Unless we found our own towels, we had nothing wherewith to dry ourselves but a long roller-towel behind the door. Considering that London was not much cleaner than it is to-day, it must not be wondered at if we boys, especially the little ones, were not remarkable for cleanliness. On Saturday and Sunday, however, when we went out to visit friends, we managed to make ourselves tolerably smart. I really wonder how this was achieved; the circumstances were not favourable.

'The bedrooms were small and crowded. In the room in which I was placed there were five beds, with not much space round them. Next me was a fellow named ——, who became the plague of my life. He delighted in teasing and vexing me in every way he could. One morning I woke and found my hair sticking to the pillow. Getting it loose, I found the whole pillow soaked with blood, and there was a boot (of the kind in those days called Bluchers) lying near my head. It turned out that I had been snoring, and —— had thrown his boot at me and hit me on the nose. However, it could not have been much of a blow, as it failed to wake me. I suppose it stopped my snoring.

'I do not retain so vivid a recollection of my early days at Charterhouse as of Bishopton. I only know I detested both. One of my letters preserved by my dear father is, after three years' experience, dated "Beastly Charterhouse."

'Dr. Russell was a revolutionary schoolmaster. He introduced what was called the "Bell and

Lancaster system" into the school; that is, the lessons were taught in the lower Forms by boys, and heard by the Masters. In order to rise from one Form to another, except in the lowest and the highest Forms, a boy had to serve as Praepositus or teacher of a Form for, I think, six weeks; and, as I have said, the Master came round and heard the lesson as it had been prepared under the direction of the boy-teacher, who was also responsible for the order and good conduct of the Form during school-hours. It was a system devised to save expense in Masters, and no doubt it was not without advantage to the teaching boys, though the benefit received by the taught was doubtful. But to a boy who was not physically strong, the office was a sore burthen; and to those who were not mentally strong, it was a waste of time both to themselves and to their Form. I served as Praepositus, I think, three times, and hated it extremely. One of the Masters, Andrew Irvine, a Scotsman (afterwards incumbent of a parish in Leicester, I think, and a notable preacher), used to go about the school roaring at the luckless Praepositi. "Liddell," I remember him shouting to me, " you're as saft as butter!" ... Every half-hour the Form was required to stand up, for change of posture, for a quarter of an hour (I think these were the appointed times). Old Watkinson—Watkey, we called him—came by and said, "Liddell, why is not your Form standing?" "I beg pardon, Sir," I said, "I did not observe the time." "You, Sir," he shouted, "*you* not know the time! You, who make more show with your watch than any boy in the school!" This was in allusion to a crimson silk watch-guard, which passed round my neck, and after meandering over my waistcoat was attached to the watch in the pocket. Rough treatment of this sort was not calculated to encourage shy or timid boys.

'When we got into the upper school, consisting of the two head Forms, one was delivered from this servitude of teaching. But Russell's tongue (he heard the lessons of these Forms himself) was not always under control. Many of us had a rough time of it even there. Once, I remember (I know not on what occasion), he told me "I was as lazy as I was long, and should bring down my father's grey hairs with sorrow to the grave." I was no doubt somewhat listless, having outgrown my strength, but I hardly deserved this reproach. It certainly did me no good. ... It was long before I shook this listlessness off, if indeed I have ever done so. Canning used to apply to me the words in Tennyson's *Miller's Daughter*,

"To be the long and listless boy,
Late-left an orphan of the Squire,"

though the last line certainly was inapplicable.

'One of Dr. Russell's rules was to constitute a Form between the Sixth and Fifth (or, as *he* would say, the First and Second), which he called the *Emeriti*, i.e. those who had served their time in lower Forms, and were entitled to be placed in the Sixth as vacancies occurred. Before joining the *Emeriti*, we were obliged to learn all the Odes and Epodes of Horace by heart, and to be able without book to translate them and answer all questions—grammatical, geographical, and historical. I achieved this task, but with much labour; for

I never had that facility which many others have of retaining in memory the actual words of poets or others. However, I succeeded at last in satisfying the Doctor. Then came a time of blissful ease and indolence. The *Emeriti* were supposed to learn the same lessons as the Sixth. They were, however, seldom called on to exhibit their knowledge, but were expected to sit in rapt attention, drinking in the wisdom displayed by the head Form, corrected as it was and amplified by the Master's turgid style. It needed, one would have thought, no great knowledge of boy-nature to predict the consequences. We did not trouble ourselves to prepare the lesson; and when, on very rare occasions, we were called on to produce what we had learnt, or were supposed to have learnt, great was the consternation, grievous the display of ignorance, and vehement the wrath of the Doctor.

'Before I rose to a place in this curious Form, it was my lot to sit next W. Makepeace Thackeray. *He* never attempted to learn the lesson, never exerted himself to grapple with the Horace. We spent our time mostly in drawing, with such skill as we could command. His handiwork was very superior to mine, and his taste for comic scenes at that time exhibited itself in burlesque representations of incidents in Shakespeare. I remember one—Macbeth as a butcher brandishing two blood-reeking knives, and Lady Macbeth as the butcher's wife clapping him on the shoulder to encourage him. Thackeray went to Cambridge, and I never met him after we left school till I went to Westminster as Headmaster in 1846. After that he often used to join Mrs. Liddell and myself when riding in Rotten Row. On one occasion he turned to her and said: "Your husband ruined all my prospects in life; he did all my Latin verses for me, and I lost all opportunities of self-improvement." It is needless to add that this was a pure fiction—I had trouble enough to do my own verses. At this time *Vanity Fair* was coming out in monthly parts in its well-known yellow paper covers. He used to talk about it, and what he should do with the persons. Mrs. Liddell one day said, "Oh, Mr. Thackeray, you must let Dobbin marry Amelia." "Well," he replied, "he shall; and when he has got her, he will not find her worth having." . . .

'As to religious instruction, we were not better off than boys in most of the schools of those days. On Sundays, an hour before church, we were assembled in the great schoolroom, and were called on to read parts of the Bible, each boy in his turn taking a single verse. The Doctor was very particular in requiring due emphasis to be laid on words and phrases, chiefly (I remember) by means of a pause before and after the word or phrase to be emphasized. Woe betide him who failed to read distinctly and make the proper pauses. The Doctor roared at him, just as in a lesson from Euripides or Cicero. I remember I used to count the verses and the boys above me, to see which verse would fall to my lot, and carefully studied how to read it with due attention to the prescribed rules. Generally, I succeeded pretty well. Sometimes, however, a boy read so badly that the next to him had to read the verse again. This put my calculation out, and I learnt as a precaution to study one or two verses preceding that which would properly come to me. It was not a bad lesson in reading, but had not much of religion in it. . . .

'When I was about fifteen years of age, I was confirmed with others by Bishop Blomfield. His charge to us boys was most impressive. I remember well the effect it had on myself, and the earnestness with which I prayed for help, and the good resolutions I formed. Many of these impressions were blurred and destroyed in the course of ordinary school life, but some remained and exerted an influence over all my days. Charterhouse, indeed, at that time, in common with most other schools, was not a place to foster religious impressions or to bring out the best part of a boy's nature. I believe I passed through the ordeal with less scathe than many others. I am sure that my aspirations rose to a higher level than they attained at the wretched Yorkshire school, from which I passed to the great London school. Thank God, these things are better now. . . .

'In July or August, 1829, I left Charterhouse. Never did pilgrim departing from an inhospitable mansion shake the dust from off his feet with more hearty satisfaction than I did on quitting the noble foundation of old Thomas Sutton. It grieves me now, when I see how differently boys regard their old schools, to think how cordially I hated both my own places of education. I do not think it was *entirely* my own fault. What I have written above may in some degree justify my feelings.

But I was too happy at home to have loved any school.

'I left Charterhouse a fair grammar scholar, but with very little classical reading. Russell's teaching did not favour extensive acquirement. Four or five Greek plays, with Porson's notes, two or three books of the Iliad, a little Pindar, Cicero's Offices and some of his Orations, with some few additions, constituted the bulk of what we read in school. But we learnt by heart all the Odes and Epodes of Horace (as I have before said), and the Georgics of Virgil, for which I am, and have been, always grateful. We also read most of the Satires and Epistles. But Greek Prose was almost untrodden ground. Herodotus and Thucydides were known only by name. I do not recollect having read any Greek Prose, except Plato's Apology. On the other hand, I devoured a large quantity of English Literature; and having at that time a tolerably retentive memory, I amassed a good deal of general information.'

The few letters which help to illustrate this period of Liddell's life are mostly written to his father, his constant correspondent. He left Charterhouse a tall thin lad, having somewhat overgrown his strength. He had, as he describes, been well trained there in Greek and Latin, although within a narrow range of authors, and had read a good deal of general literature. Of Mathematics he was as ignorant as the average schoolboy; but the instruction of his father's Curate soon made up the deficiency, and when he began residence at Oxford he had already gained some acquaintance with Differential Calculus and Analytical Geometry.

It was delightful beyond measure to exchange smoky London for the country home in the north. That home was indeed no longer at Boldon, his father having recently accepted the living of Whickham, a village two miles from Ravensworth. It may seem strange that school life had no pleasing memories for him; but he was of a somewhat shy and reserved disposition, of studious habits and tastes, not ready to make many friends, and with his dearest thoughts and affections centred in his home. And a home so far distant from London had not been easily accessible. The journey by coach occupied a long while and cost several pounds. It was therefore usual for Liddell to spend the shorter holidays, at Christmas and Whitsuntide, with his aunts at Bath, or at Shotesham Rectory in Norfolk with his aunt, Mrs. J. Fellowes. No wonder then that home visits were exceptionally dear, and that the prospect of spending nearly a year with his family, in the interval between school and college, was eagerly welcomed.

# CHAPTER II

LIFE AT CHRIST CHURCH, 1830–1846

SHORTLY before leaving Charterhouse in the summer of 1829, Liddell went to Oxford, in order that he might be entered on the books of Christ Church. He was matriculated on May 9. The Dean at that time was Dr. Samuel Smith, who two years later exchanged the Deanery with Dr. Gaisford for the Golden stall at Durham. The Senior Censor was Thomas Vowler Short, afterwards Bishop of St. Asaph.

The matriculation completed, Liddell returned to Charterhouse, and when the summer holidays came, he travelled home, and waited there for a summons into residence at the University. This never came, and after Easter, 1830, it was thought expedient to send him up to Oxford. He was unable at first to secure rooms in college, and for a fortnight lived at the Mitre Hotel, attending Chapel, Lectures, and Hall dinner. He ultimately was assigned small rooms in the now demolished Chaplains' Quadrangle.

'So began my life at Christ Church. I felt very solitary. Not a single man in college did I know, except Andrew Dunlop, an old Carthusian. When there was a knock at the door, I looked longingly for the person entering, hoping that some one had taken compassion upon me. I was very shy, and it was a kind of penance to go into Chapel or Hall under the eyes of the old stagers . . . and I got into the habit of going in early that I might avoid the supposed inquisition of strange eyes. In Lecture I felt more at ease. My Tutor, Robert Biscoe, soon discovered that I took pains in preparing my work, and used to appeal to me to correct the errors or ignorances of some of the other men. . . . In Lecture I was now first introduced to the intricacies of Thucydides, and was fain to have recourse to Hobbes' translation, which however was nearly as difficult as the Greek. It was the first time in my life that I had ever used a "Crib," and I do not remember that I ever indulged in another such assistance till I had to grapple with the Rhetoric and Ethics of Aristotle.

'I returned to Christ Church, of course, after the Long Vacation. Soon after we met, my Tutor intimated to me that there was to be an Election to Bishop Fell's Exhibitions, and that I was to be a candidate. One of the conditions for election was one year's previous residence. Now I had only resided for the two short Summer Terms, and a few days of the Michaelmas Term. How this difficulty was got over, I know not. But I was admitted as a candidate, and was duly elected, to the great joy of myself and my parents. I remember I went down on my knees and thanked God that

I had been enabled to relieve my father of some portion of the expense of my education, though, as I remarked in my letter announcing the fact, "£40 a year is poor interest for all the money you have spent on me."

'On December 15 of the same year I wrote: "My dear father and mother: Never did I take up my pen with more pleasure than I do now to tell you that I have this day received intimation from the Dean that I am to be a Student. After Collections he called me up and said that Dr. Dowdeswell [a non-resident Canon] had most kindly allowed him to nominate a Student for him; and that he was most glad that he had an opportunity of showing his entire satisfaction with my conduct since I had become a member of Christ Church." To explain this, I may notice that in those days the Dean and Canons in rotation nominated young men to Studentships. In many cases these nominations were mere matters of favour, and were bestowed on the sons of Canons, or some other of their relations and friends, without regard to merit. But the Dean and some of the Canons had begun of late to nominate Commoners of the House on the recommendation of the Censors and Tutors, and to such a recommendation my appointment was due. Robert Scott, Fellow and then Master of Balliol, was one of the batch of Students appointed at the same time; and he also was recommended for merit: the rest all, I believe, owed their nomination to favour and interest. Mr. Gladstone had been appointed two years before, just before he took his degree—better late than never.

'After I became Student I had not to complain of

solitariness. Our Mess in Hall was a pleasant one, and I had to resist, rather than seek, invitations. . . . I was elected to the Union Debating Society, and heard Gladstone make his last speech there, against the Reform Bill. He struck me as equally fluent and able as a speaker as in future times. Of course his knowledge was more limited and his experience less; but in copiousness of language, ease in delivery, and lucidity of arrangement there was nothing to desire.

'In the summer of 1831, the old Dean, Samuel Smith, exchanged his Deanery for a Prebendal Stall at Durham, with Thomas Gaisford, Professor of Greek at Oxford; and on our return in October we found the new Dean in possession. The exchange was, I believe, effected by Bishop van Mildert of Durham, whose niece (Miss Douglas) Gaisford had married. I do not remember that the change of rulers was much felt, and I find no notice of the matter in my letters.

'In January 1832, I reached Oxford a day late, and was hauled up before old Gaisford on Monday morning, though in very good company, there being about forty others in the same scrape with myself. . . . When I began to apologize and excuse myself for not having been back in time, my set oration was cut short by Daniel Veysie, the Censor, who exclaimed: "Well, Mr. Dean, perhaps you will not notice Mr. Liddell's absence this time, as I believe it is the first time he has ever missed being back in time." Of course I was a man of too much politeness to contradict the reverend gentleman's assertion; but the real fact is, I never was back to the day from the time I became a resident

THE CHAPLAINS' QUADRANGLE, CHRIST CHURCH.

A—Entrance to Passage from Cloister to Meadow.   B—Dean Liddell's First Rooms were on this Staircase, Ground Floor Left.

member of Christ Church. This is a sad confession. I hope it will not come to the ears of Christ Church undergraduates.'

In 1832 Liddell became one of the original members of a club which, from its consisting of ten members, and meeting at the house of Tribe the tailor, opposite Tom gate, was called the 'Ten Tribes'; to which was added 'and little Benjamin their ruler,' Benjamin Harrison being the President. Of the ten original members, five were Bachelors of Arts and five undergraduates. The list, as given by Liddell, is worthy of record. The five Bachelors were Charles Wordsworth (afterwards Bishop of St. Andrews), Walter Kerr Hamilton (afterwards Bishop of Salisbury), and Benjamin Harrison (afterwards Archdeacon of Maidstone)—these three had taken first classes in Classics ; the remaining two were Henry Denison (afterwards Fellow of All Souls), who had taken a Double First, and Henry Anthony Jeffreys, a First-class man in Mathematics (afterwards Vicar of Hawkhurst). Jeffreys outlived all the rest, and died a few months after the Dean.

Of the undergraduate members, all were subsequently distinguished. They were Francis H. Doyle, afterwards Sir Francis (Fellow of All Souls and Professor of Poetry); Stephen Denison (Scholar of Balliol and Fellow of University College); Henry Halford Vaughan (Fellow of Oriel and Regius Professor of Modern History); James Ramsay (afterwards Marquess of Dalhousie and Governor-General of India); and Liddell himself. All were members of Christ Church, except Stephen Denison. The club met of an evening after Hall dinner, for wine and talk, but so moderate were their habits that the ten members consumed, in four nights, less than four bottles of wine.

The life of an undergraduate of studious tastes, busily engaged in reading for honours, was not likely to be full of incident. Liddell enjoyed the companionship of a few chosen friends, among whom were Canning, the future Governor-General, and Lord Lincoln, afterwards Duke of Newcastle, in addition to those already mentioned. Fifteen months before the time of examination he had read through all his prescribed books, and had every reason to look forward hopefully to the result.

'But,' he writes, 'I fear there will be a good deal to do yet. For though I have, it seems, gone through all the regular books, yet there remains behind a world of volumes explanatory and illustrative of them, which it would be highly advantageous, if not absolutely necessary, to know. However, it is satisfactory to know that the line of road is cut, and that now there is nothing to do but to lay down the stones and get them well beaten in.'

He determined to forgo the delights of a visit to his home in the Long Vacation, and was anxious to be allowed to remain at Oxford, if only the Dean would grant permission. He urged his father to state his case to the Bishop of Durham, and get him to intercede with the 'Old Bear,' as he called the Dean. But Gaisford was obdurate. The difficulty, however, was met by a kind invitation from Augustus Page Saunders, who up to that time had been Mathematical Tutor at Christ Church, and was now just elected to the Headmastership of Charterhouse. Saunders held the Curacy of Cuddesdon, a living then attached to the See of Oxford, and he invited Liddell to spend the summer months with him there, together with three other Christ Church men, Bruce (afterwards Lord Elgin), Lincoln, and Canning. On the departure of Saunders for his school work in September, George Anthony Denison took his place as Curate, and the invitation was extended to the close of the Long Vacation. It was a happy and profitable time.

'We keep very steady to our reading, average nine hours per diem, cricket and bathing in the intervals. I am improving immensely in water transactions, take running headers, jump over vast bushes into the water, &c.; and at cricket dare look at the ball without shutting mine eyes. We had a match with the "clods" the other day, in which I played, and to my own and other people's astonishment smote the ball with most wonderful "vis," and added some dozen to the score.'

Denison was a delightful host. Many years afterwards Liddell writes of him:

'In those days he was, I might say, a radical reformer, and took in the *Westminster Review*. I remember the glee with which he sketched a picture of himself being sent down as a Commissioner to inquire into the state of the University of Oxford, summoning Dean Gaisford to appear before him. "Take a seat, Sir," he would affably say, "and attend to the questions I am about to ask." Quantum mutatus!'

At Christmas, 1832, Liddell allowed himself a short holiday at home, partly perhaps that he might see his father's new abode at Easington, a parish situated about two miles from the sea, on the high road between Sunderland and Stockton, in a bleak position, its church serving as a landmark to seamen. This was his father's home till he gave up clerical work.

With the year 1833 the Final Examination was drawing perilously near. The beginning of June was the fatal time. In January of that year he writes:

'Reading is not going on as well as I could wish. Thank God I am perfectly well, and shall have no excuse to offer on the ground of health. Canning is going on pretty well too. He comes to breakfast with me every morning before Chapel, which is a wonderful effort of voluntary exertion on the part of two men who, I believe, love their beds as sincerely as any of God's creatures, except perhaps that absolute dormouse, my brother Charlie.'

It is interesting to note that, as a recreation in the intervals of hard work, Canning, Vaughan, and Liddell used to read together the early poems of Tennyson. In a letter addressed to the present Lord Tennyson in October, 1897, Liddell writes:

'I have been reading, as many more are doing,

your memoir of your father with intense interest. Will you allow me a word or two? In vol. i. p. 206 Dean Bradley seems to claim the merit of being the first to introduce your father's poems into Oxford. This claim appears to refer to 1842. I must, for the honour of a few Oxford men, be allowed to put in an earlier claim. In June 1833, three Christ Church men took their degree. They were reading hard, and met every evening for an hour for tea and recreation. The recreation consisted in reading aloud the poems published in 1830 and 1833. I have the two thin volumes before me, and looking them over remember our especial delight in *Mariana, The Arabian Nights, Oriana, The Lady of Shalott, The May Queen*, &c., but especially in *The Lotos Eaters*.' [The three young men's names are then given.] 'Nor were we the only Oxford men who were thus early devoted to your father's works. I may mention Doyle, afterwards Sir Francis, who said to me after the appearance of the *Idylls*, "If Milton could read *Guinevere* it would make him pale with jealousy".'

The result of the examination satisfied Liddell's most sanguine hopes. He gained a Double First Class. On June 15 he wrote to his father:

'I have to announce my final success, for which most devoutly do I thank Heaven, and under that your kindness and care of me in so providing for my well-being now and of old.'

It was a brilliant Class List, containing, besides Liddell, four other Christ Church men, Canning, W. E. Jelf, R. Scott, and H. H. Vaughan; Jackson of Pembroke, afterwards Bishop of London, and R. Lowe of University, afterwards Viscount Sherbrooke. Liddell was the only Christ Church man who achieved the distinction of a Double First Class, his great friend Canning being in the Second Class in Mathematics.

'I was anxious to start at once for Easington, knowing well the real pleasure I should communicate to my parents and the delight I should myself enjoy. But Saunders was very anxious to parade a Double First Charterhouse man to his boys, in hopes of exciting them to do likewise. I at once consented, being, as I said, "bound to do all in my power" to assist him, after all that he had done for me. Accordingly I went, asked for a holiday for the school, and dined with the masters in Brook Hall. My health was proposed, and I had to return thanks. It was the first speech I ever made, and I should not have been sorry if it had been the last. Oratory was not, is not, my forte.'

Then came the well-earned rest of the Long Vacation; a time spent partly at Easington, and partly in Scotland in company with his cousin, the Hon. Henry T. Liddell, afterwards first Earl of Ravensworth. Edinburgh, a city which he had not seen since he was twelve years old, won his unstinted admiration.

'I am now,' he writes, 'in the queen of cities, the modern Athens, the most beauteous of the beautiful; the — but words fail me when I attempt to express the extreme admiration I feel for all around me.

It is in sooth a glorious place. I could spend hours in gazing on the magnificent views which present themselves at every turn.... Whether I go to Rome or Naples or Athens or Constantinople, never shall I see a city so noble as is this.'

From Edinburgh they went to Invercauld, and thence to Blair Athol, where they were hospitably received by Lady Glenlyon, mother of the young Duke of Athol. Here Liddell killed his first stag.

'One incident I must record,' he writes to his father, 'inasmuch as therein is contained a triumph little inferior to those which I once had the pleasure of conveying to you by letter from Oxford. With my own hand, and the gun of the Hon. H. T. Liddell, of Eslington House, did I slaughter a noble hart. His horns are not remarkable, but I am resolved to perpetuate the memory of so great a triumph by carrying off his head, the which I shall hope to show you. The deer shooting here is much harder work than at Invercauld; for the deer are so numerous, and congregate in herds so large, that it is impossible to stalk them quietly and calmly; they are generally found below you, under the summit of a very steep hill; then you run full tilt down upon them, among stones huge and rough and loose, till you arrive at a ledge over which you look, and behold the most magnificent sight in the world, a hugeous herd of red-deer, who, the moment you come in sight, look up, give a snuff, and off they gallop. It is not much in favour of shooting that you have had this run, for it cannot be expected that your head and eye can be very steady after such a feat, for the run is sometimes, in the case of novices, about a mile.

The old hands run nearly all day. My deer was achieved after a run of about a quarter of a mile, and I fired off my arm without a rest. . . . The sport is grand. Nothing I ever saw equal to it[1].'

In October 1833, Liddell returned to Oxford. His future was now assured. More than three years before his tutor, Robert Biscoe, had sounded him as to his intentions of staying up and becoming a tutor, and he had answered that, though he had not even dared to hope for a studentship, and had never considered any consequences of such an event, he had not the slightest objection to embracing such a career. Now, after his brilliant success in the Schools, a tutorship would as a matter of course be offered him in due time; in the meanwhile there was a delightful interval, to be spent in equipping himself more completely for his future work. The Dean gave him kind counsel.

'He recommends me to recover all my French and proceed with German, accompanying this advice with a recommendation to pursue my classical studies, to verse myself in Divinity, and not neglect my scientific pursuits. He added that what leisure time I had would be fully occupied by keeping pace with the reading of the day, without which no gentleman can go into society.'

Some time later the Dean took advantage of Liddell's German knowledge by asking him to trans-

---

[1] It should be mentioned that this method of stalking in Athol Forest, now obsolete, is described in Scrope's *Deerstalking*, published in 1839.

late for his use Godfrey Hermann's Review of Göttling's *Hesiod*. Gaisford himself had never learnt German. He is said indeed to have visited the continent only once, when he made an expedition to Leyden to consult some MSS. Here he became acquainted with sundry Professors; and it happened on one occasion that one of these learned men made a slip in some metrical rule. Gaisford interposed, and poured forth (in Latin) a flood of learning from *Hephaestion* and other Greek authors on metres. The Dutch Professor held up his hands and exclaimed: '*O vir magnae profecto sapientiae, si tam in rebus quam in verbis incaluisses!*'

There is no period of academic life more profitable and agreeable than the time immediately succeeding the struggle of the Honour Schools. The drudgery of work is over; one's own tastes may be pursued without misgivings; the methods of study acquired by the discipline of the Schools may now be applied on an extended scale; the mind has been enriched, and strengthened for further efforts. Moreover, Liddell had good friends among his brother students to foster his intellectual growth: among them H. A. Jeffreys, a brilliant mathematician and a man of singular beauty of character, '*τῶν ἡμεῖς ἴδμεν* longe optimus,' as Liddell described him some years afterwards, and Robert Scott, one of the most fastidious scholars of his time. Scott and Liddell had been appointed by the Dean to the post of Sub-Librarian, and had thus constant access to the splendid collection of books, pictures, and engravings contained in the College Library. In making the appointment Gaisford advised Liddell to make himself well acquainted with the contents of the Library, referring with much gusto to the motto he had seen over Bishop Cosin's Library at Durham : *Nosse bonos libros non minima pars est bonae eruditionis.* This phrase Liddell used in after-days to quote when himself appointing young students to the same honourable post. He also spent some time with private pupils; among them was Viscount Leveson, afterwards Earl Granville. He describes him as

'A very nice fellow, a great friend of Canning's, though, I fear, inexorably idle. But he has to work for his bread, and I hope he may reform. He is to be, if possible, a Diplomatist. When he came up to Christ Church, Canning said to him, " Leveson, your mind is like a garden that has been left without cultivation, and the only wonder is there are so few weeds in it." At that time he had such an objection to work that I used (with his consent) to lock him into my study, so that he could not get out without my leave, nor could any idle friends come in to disturb him. I carried him successfully through his examinations, and he remained my kind friend to the end of his life.'

His letters show him hard at work at classics, French, and German; and having now made up his mind to enter Holy Orders, he was studying Divinity, and attending the lectures of the Regius Professor, Dr. Burton. The works of Bull and

Waterland, the gift of Lord Ravensworth in commemoration of his Double First, served as the first instalment of his Theological library. At the Gaudy of 1834 he delivered the Commemoration Speech, celebrating Archbishop Dolben. He wrote for the Latin Essay on 'The Administration of the Roman Provinces,' but was beaten by Scott. There was a question of his standing for a Fellowship at Merton and at Balliol, where the emoluments were higher than at Christ Church, and the position in some important respects more dignified. He was also tempted by an offer to pursue researches in Asia Minor, in succession to Mr. Pashley, who had accompanied one of H.M.'s frigates which was exploring those coasts. This offer he was strongly inclined to accept, but he was dissuaded by the Dean and Dr. Pusey; and in the end remained quietly at Christ Church, till the time should come when a Tutorship would fall to him. His vacations were spent in various places. At Easter, 1835, he visited Cambridge with his friend Charles Wordsworth, stayed at the Lodge at Trinity, and saw 'the celebrated Fellows of Trinity, Sedgwick, Whewell, Peacock, and Thirlwall.' In the Long Vacation of that year he spent some weeks at Heidelberg, in company with H. Halford Vaughan, and worked hard at German; visiting on his way home the chief beauties of the Rhine.

In January 1836, he became Tutor. Thirteen pupils were assigned to him, among whom were the future Bishop Ryle, Charles T. Newton, and

Henry W. Acland. The Earl of Wemyss (then Mr. Charteris) was soon afterwards added to the number.

'I would gladly have waited a little,' he writes, 'for I had only just taken my M.A. degree, and should have been glad of a space of time for preparation. I wrote to my mother that I was meditating over the air, tone, and gesture to be assumed when my first Lecture enters the room, all properly attired in academical costume, and some of them perhaps more fit to lecture their Tutor than to receive instruction from him.'

In April of the same year he again writes:

'I have again assumed the tutorial chair, and circles of reverential youths look to my nod, as that of great wisdom. Moreover, I know not whether they have been awed by my sternness at Collections, or if dignity has insensibly accrued to my person, but I find that these youths respectfully lift their caps from their heads when they cross my path in the Quadrangle.'

He speaks of his own pupils as 'a *very good* set who will keep all my wits at work.' And it should be remembered that the duties of a College Tutor in those days—and indeed till much later—were not quite what they are in modern Oxford. There was none of the sub-division of subjects which is now (to the clear advantage of teacher and learner) universally adopted. The College Tutor was expected to guide and supervise the whole of his pupils' work, and more or less to

read with them the chief ancient authors which they were taking up, whether poets, philosophers, historians, or orators. There were indeed on the staff of Christ Church certain college officers, who delivered formal courses of Lectures to the men of each year—the Catechist, the Rhetoric Reader, and the Greek Reader:—but these officers were Tutors also; and for the bulk of the instruction each Tutor was almost solely responsible, so far as his own pupils were concerned; and if he was anxious to do his best for them, his labours were very heavy and covered a vast field. And the Tutor's relation to his pupils was also, in theory at least, of a more directly pastoral character than is now the case. As a rule, the College Tutor of those days was in Holy Orders; for indeed all but a few Fellowships or Studentships were tenable for any lengthened time only under this condition. At Christ Church the first twenty of the hundred and one Students were called 'Theologi,' and were bound to be in Priest's Orders. This restriction placed the tuition of a college in the hands of clergymen, and a conscientious Tutor would regard his position as involving the discharge of sacred duties in safeguarding, as far as possible, his pupils' career, and giving them help in their religious life.

Liddell devoted himself heart and soul to his new work; and many of his early pupils, separated from him by only a short interval in age, became his close personal friends. His admirable scholarship, his wide literary culture, and his refined artistic tastes, all combined to interest and even to fascinate them. It is now for the first time that his letters speak much of art; but he had the hand and eye, as well as the enthusiasm, of an artist, and his life-long friendship with Newton, Acland, and Ruskin was founded in a large measure upon the profound artistic sympathy which then united them. Mr. Ruskin was not indeed, strictly speaking, a pupil of Liddell's; his college Tutor was the Rev. W. L. Brown. But they were drawn together, even in those early days, by common artistic tastes and sympathies; and in his 'Praeterita' Mr. Ruskin refers to Liddell in words which deserve to be quoted:

'There was one Tutor however, out of my sphere, who reached my ideal, but disappointed my hope then — as perhaps his own, since:—a man sorrowfully under the dominion of the Greek ἀνάγκη—the present Dean. He was, and is, one of the rarest types of nobly-presenced Englishmen, but I fancy it was his adverse star that made him an Englishman at all—the prosaic and practical element in him having prevailed over the sensitive one. He was the only man in Oxford among the masters of my day who knew anything of art; and his keen saying of Turner that "he had got hold of a false ideal" would have been infinitely helpful to me at that time, had he explained and enforced it. But I suppose he did not see enough in me to make him take trouble with me,—and, what was much more serious, he saw not enough in himself to take trouble, in that field, with himself.'

So anxious was Liddell to spare no pains to make himself fit for his new duties that, when the Long Vacation of 1836 came, he resolved to spend almost the whole of it at Oxford.

'I cannot say for certain,' he writes to his mother, 'whether I shall visit you or not this summer. Believe me, I should only be obeying my *inclination*, if I were to stay the greater part of the Long Vacation at home. But I must fairly tell you, it appears to me incompatible with my office in this place so to do. I have much, very much, to learn to qualify myself for the fit discharge of my Tutorial duties; and the only opportunity I have to make up deficiencies is during the vacations. I am sorry to say that at home I cannot read with effect: I have tried and it has failed. My duty therefore is to stay in such places as will enable me to do so; and the most congenial place is Oxford.'

As a matter of fact he did go home for a short time; but most of the Vacation was spent at Oxford, and, from his account of his way of life, well spent.

'I have adopted a new style of life on the advice, and backed by the example, of Talbot, a student of Christ Church, and nephew of Lord Fitzroy Somerset. I get up at six or a little after and take a walk, sometimes diversified by a bathe, before breakfast. The effect is excellent. I find myself able to sit at my books from 9.30 to 5 without inconvenience, and I never was better. Indeed, so pleasing is the quiet and peace which reign here, that I look forward with great regret to the approach of Term, when turbulent youths will once again break the stillness of the academic groves.'

That stillness had indeed been rudely broken in the preceding six months, by the din and violence of the controversy connected with the appointment of Dr. Hampden to the Regius Professorship of Divinity. It is interesting to read Liddell's account of the affair, and his judgment on its merits. Dr. Burton's unexpected death had caused the vacancy.

'I had attended Dr. Burton's lectures in preparation for my Ordination, and, in common with others, felt the highest admiration and love for him. Great interest was felt in his successor; for the appointment rested with Lord Melbourne, who did not possess the confidence of Churchmen. On Feb. 8, 1836, came a letter from his Lordship, offering the chair to Dr. Hampden. The Doctor was an Oriel man, who had become Principal of St. Mary Hall. In a letter to my father, I speak of him as a person well known for the amiableness of his manner, and the uprightness of his life (I might have added, for his learning in Aristotelic philosophy), but who was unhappily distinguished for very strange, undefined, and almost unintelligible notions on Theological subjects. Such were the self-confident opinions of a young man of twenty-five years. I continued:—" On Tuesday, Pusey, Newman, and others of that party assembled and prepared a memorial to His Majesty, setting forth that they apprehended danger to the Church by the appointment of a Professor holding such opinions as appeared in Dr. Hampden's theological works, more particularly in the Bampton Lectures for 1832. This was signed by upwards of seventy M.A.s, chiefly Tutors, and dispatched to the Archbishop on the following night. On Wednesday the Heads of Houses, roused by the energy of the Movement party, called a meeting. To the horror and surprise of the Doctors, the Principal of St. Mary Hall himself appeared. 'Strange,' said the Dean of Christ Church, 'very strange, that *you* should be here, Mr. Principal: we have met to talk of you. Do you mean to stay?' 'I do,' was the reply. 'And to vote?' interposed Shuttleworth (Warden of New College). 'I have not made up my mind,' said Hampden.

'" A very angry discussion followed, after which certain propositions (I know not what) were put to the vote. On the first two, Hampden was left in a minority, himself taking no part. On the third, the division was equal, whereupon Dr. Hampden interposed, and by his vote turned the decision of the august body in his own favour. They separated in no good humour: and the minority dispatched a private remonstrance to Lord Melbourne, which his Lordship diplomatically promised to give his attention to. After this strong display of opinion, Hampden wrote to Ministers offering to resign, if he inconvenienced them at all. This was on Thursday. On

Saturday, Newman put out a pamphlet entitled, *Elucidations of Dr. Hampden's Theological Statements*, being a summary of his opinions on various heads arranged in numbers, as I. Rule of Faith. II. The Holy Trinity. III. The Incarnation, &c., and each head copiously proved by extracts from the Professor-elect's Bampton Lectures, &c. As I said before, the statements are very obscure; in the hands of a Socinian they might be stated as Socinian principles; in Dr. Hampden's probably they may all be shown to be Church of England. But even this *most favourable* statement of them will show how improper a person he is to be Divinity Professor. He would do no good, nor, I apprehend, much harm; for he is a man without eloquence, or any moral power over men's minds, so far as appears: so that the chief harm would be that the Professorship would be entirely nugatory; all solid meat would be taken out of men's mouths, and dust blown into their eyes. Here the matter rests. I did not sign the Masters' memorial, because I conceived this proceeding to be unconstitutional and irregular; and the delay, if not refusal, of the Archbishop to present it (for it has not been presented), makes me think he takes the same view. I see by to-day's paper that Lord Melbourne has had an interview with the King at Brighton; and I am told that in a Ministerial paper has appeared a letter detailing the proceedings in 'Golgotha.' As Shuttleworth is very indignant at this letter, it is presumed the statement is accurate, and therefore proceeds from an eye-witness."'

In May following he adds the sequel:

'You want to hear more about Hampden, and the statute which has been passed concerning him... The University has withdrawn from him all she had before entrusted, *on her part*, to the Professor, viz. the appointment of Select Preachers, and the judging on heresy, &c., in sermons preached by others; which, though in itself almost nugatory, yet amounts to a strong vote of censure. I was very glad not to have a vote, as I know not how I should have exercised it. But pray most flatly contradict the notion that the leaders of the business had any *political* bias. I really and truly believe that if they were asked to-morrow whether Lord Melbourne or Sir Robert Peel was to hold office, they would (supposing the thing depended on their word) decline giving judgment. They were actuated simply by what they judged a high duty, and believed they would be betraying their trust if they did not use it. Of course this is no defence of what they *have done*; that must stand or fall on its own merits; but it *is* a defence of their *motives* and *wishes* against such shocking and unchristian attacks as that which has appeared in the *Edinburgh Review*, and which (I am shocked to say) is the production of a man for whom I had a high respect and great admiration—even Dr. Arnold of Rugby[1]. Alas, poor human nature! What a miserable thing art thou, breaking forth and

---

[1] In a letter to Vaughan he describes the famous scene in the Theatre: 'Arnold came, saw, and of course did not conquer. I am sorry to say that his physiognomy by no means counteracts the extremely unpleasant notion I had been led to form of him from the "Malignants" article. A more savage, truculent expression than that day sate upon his brow, I think I never saw. He did not speak, sate upon a bench retired, and withdrew early.'

deforming and blotting over qualities and characters that might adorn a higher race of beings. I hope that, for the present at least, we are quiet again. Dr. Hampden has issued notice of lectures without as heretofore requiring a certificate from the Head or Tutor of the respective colleges to which his hearers may belong. The Bishops have taken diverse lines. The Bishop of Exeter wrote long ago to Exeter College (whence come most of his candidates for Orders) saying that he would not require attendance on either Professor's Lectures (Regius or Margaret); college testimonials would suffice. The Bishop of London told a Christ Church man, who asked him whether of the twain he should hear, that he would abide by the recommendation of his college; whereon the Dean refused to give any such recommendation. So anomalous is our present condition.'

To those who knew Liddell in later days, and appreciated his attitude towards all religious controversy, especially when introduced into academical questions, the tone of these letters will appear somewhat surprising: but it is interesting to read his own comment on them, when he perused them in his old age.

'Notwithstanding,' he writes, 'that the opinions expressed in these letters savour something of presumption, considering that they were written by a young M.A., who had not yet the right to vote in Convocation, I must say that on the whole they are moderate and impartial. I see nothing for a man of eighty-two to be ashamed of in them.' 'The word "moderate,"' he adds, 'recalls to my mind a little incident that must have occurred about this time. My friend Vaughan, who had been elected to a Fellowship at Oriel, was having tea with Newman, who was anxious to enlist all the younger Fellows in his cause. "Do you like your tea strong?" asked Newman. "No thank you," said Vaughan, "rather weak than otherwise." "Ah, I see," retorted Newman, "*moderation* in all things."'

Liddell's attitude towards Dissenters was then strangely different from what it afterwards became.

'I hope,' he writes to Vaughan in 1834, 'you have already signed a petition against admitting Dissenters to the Universities. If not, you will find one either at Rivington's or Hatchard's, whither instantly repair, and enrol your name among all the good and wise of the land.'

One more reference to Dr. Hampden's case may be noted. About the middle of the ensuing Michaelmas Term the new Professor took up his residence in Christ Church.

'He appeared in chapel this morning (November 5) for the first time, and, strange enough, the chapter read for the second lesson was Acts xxiii—the very passage which had been applied by Arnold in the *Edinburgh Review* to his " Persecutors."'

Some years afterwards—in 1843—Liddell was again concerned with Dr. Hampden, in the then famous but now forgotten suit of Macmullen *v.* Hampden. A letter to his mother, dated Nov. 30, 1843, tells the tale as far as it relates to his own share in it.

'Yesterday I had an occupation which I hope will be the last of the kind that I shall ever have,—viz., to sit in judgment for nine mortal hours. Dr. Hampden, the Regius Professor of Divinity, has refused to take such steps as will enable a Mr. Macmullen to take his degree of B.D., because he thinks that Mr. Macmullen has (on his part) taken a wrong course. Mr. Macmullen, not being able to take his degree, is debarred from certain advantages which would otherwise accrue to him in his college (Corpus). And therefore he brings an action for damages against Dr. Hampden. The cause having been decided against Dr. Hampden in the Vice-Chancellor's Court, an appeal was made to the court above (called the Delegates of Appeals in Congregation) to reverse the decision. Of these Delegates—seven in number—I unluckily am one. And yesterday we took our seats at *ten*, and sat listening to legal arguments from Mr. Erle, one of the first Barristers in Westminster Hall, on Hampden's side, and Hope, a contemporary of my own, against him, till seven o'clock in the evening, with one quarter of an hour's interruption. A pleasing variety to a studious life this, is it not? And now we have to plod through all these long-winded arguments, looking up authorities, cases, &c., &c., and hold conferences in order to make up our minds how to give judgment. I hope we shall do it right. But I fear we are quite as likely to be wrong as right. However, we must do the best we can. When any cases of appeal came before the Duke of Manchester, when Governor of Jamaica, he used to say, the moment the Counsel began, "Stop sir, stop! I affirm the judgment of the

Court below." "But, your Grace," began the horrified Counsel.... "I affirm it, with costs," interrupted his Grace. I fear it will hardly do to follow this summary and convenient course here.'

Among his pupils in this early stage of his tutorial life was one who has lately passed away, and whose memory will long be affectionately cherished by very many Christ Church men, the saintly George Marshall, afterwards Censor of Christ Church, and in later life Rector of Milton. Marshall had just come up from Charterhouse, and to Liddell's high delight had won a college exhibition, the prelude, in his case, to a distinguished academical career. He was among the first fruits of Saunders' work at Charterhouse.

'I hope and trust he will not fall off under my care. He is a well-disposed, modest, clever lad, and it would grieve me, I am sure, quite as much as it could his nearest and dearest friends, to see him go wrong. However, I hope that, humanly speaking, there is very little chance of it. But I cannot help feeling, more and more, how heavy a responsibility rests upon me; while, from the nature of the place, one has much less power of interfering with a man's acts and habits, than at school and elsewhere.'

These words will serve to illustrate the feelings with which Liddell regarded his position as Tutor, and with which he entered Holy Orders at Christmas, 1836. His letters at this time dwell upon the necessity of a season for thought and preparation for 'so important, and—for me—so awful a change of life.' A few weeks before the Ordination he writes in answer to his father:

'Your letter was doubly welcome, both as coming from those I love so dearly, and yet so much less than in duty and gratitude I ought, as also by reason of the principal topic it dwelt upon. Yes, indeed, my dear father, I do want your prayers, yours and my mother's, and of all that feel any interest in me. The step I am going to take is one of awful responsibility. Would I could feel as deeply as it deserves the depth and breadth of its importance! But I am sorry to say that my mode of life has a strong tendency to attach my first thoughts to other subjects of a too worldly kind; and it often requires an effort to fix my mind on that which ought to be—if it could be—the *only* subject on which it delighted to dwell. However, this cannot be. I am obliged to spend most of my time in preparing lectures on alien subjects, and the very week before I present myself for Ordination will be spent amid the bustle and excitement of a college examination. But I am sensible that I cannot complain of this: all kinds of life must have their peculiar temptations, and I doubt not but that this of mine has its advantages, which, transplanted to another soil, I might miss just as much as I do now the quiet and leisure which I should desire for a season, to devote myself to the studies and meditations immediately suited for my approaching change of life. But still these temptations are many and great, and therefore much need have I, as I said before, that you and all of you should earnestly intreat the Giver of all good gifts to support me by His Grace, that I may not greatly fall. Mysterious dispensation, that the prayers of men, who cannot save their own souls, should stand in stead others besides themselves! Yet, thank God, I feel and believe that it is a very truth. In my prayers it is that I can best know what a son's affection for his parents, a brother's for his brothers and sisters, is and ought to be. And you think of me then with a more thorough love than otherwise; you have assured me that you do so. Thank you for that assurance; it has done me good. And so partly while we feel that each perhaps at the same moment is sending up prayers for the other, and so are kindled to a higher and holier frame of mind—partly by recollecting that the Spirit hath said how effectual shall be the fervent prayer of a righteous man (O Lord, grant that I too may be righteous!), we know that in some measure our salvation depends on our mutual efforts, and so our affections are not confined to this side the grave, but stretch forward into the boundless realms of Eternity.'

It is interesting to remember that this simple and pathetic letter was written at a time when Newman and Pusey were already exercising a mighty influence over the religious thought of Oxford, and three years and a half after Keble's Sermon on *National Apostasy*. It may be inferred that Liddell was quite untouched by that movement; and indeed in the letters preserved in his family scarcely a reference to it can be traced. Newman was just ten years his senior; and ten years make a vast interval in college life. Liddell's tastes were at no time ecclesiastical. He was now busily occupied with his pupils and his own studies; and his leisure hours were devoted to the improvement of his artistic knowledge and skill. He always disliked controversy; and for the present was thoroughly contented with the Church position as defined by the more moderate school of English Divines. Yet he did not wholly elude the magic of the great teacher. In later years he would sometimes call up the memories of those early days, and tell of his being persuaded by Newman to undertake the translation of some passages from the Fathers for publication. 'I can show you what I did,' he said one day, and took down some volumes from his library shelves. Then, after a long and fruitless search, he shut the books: 'Pshaw! I cannot. I have entirely forgotten which were the passages that I translated!' It would, however, be a mistake to infer that Liddell was untouched at the time by the influence of a movement which swayed the whole religious life of Oxford. He was an occasional attendant at the meetings of Dr. Pusey's Theological Society: and in a sermon preached at Christ Church in 1890 he recalled some memories of Newman as he had known him.

'Comparatively few persons now living,' he said, 'can remember the days when Newman began to influence academic life, and to be a power among us. I am of that number. I was admitted to what I considered a high honour, to some degree of intercourse with the great theologian of Oriel, and I undertook (at his request) to make one or two of the translations from ancient ecclesiastical documents which appeared in the early numbers of the *Library of the Fathers*[1].

'He exercised a sort of spell over the younger men with whom he came in contact. This was some half-century ago. What a vista to look back through! What changes have taken place in thought and feeling, ecclesiastical, theological, philosophical, scientific, political, social, in that half-century! It seems like a dream, a dream indeed full of vivid recollections. It makes me look back on the time when, with many others since departed, I hung upon the sermons which he preached from St. Mary's pulpit, or listened to those penetrating discourses which he used to deliver on (I think) Wednesday evenings in Adam de Brome's chapel. Some of those hearers followed him without flinching, however far he advanced from the teaching of that Church in which he had been reared; some, alarmed by the manifest direction of his steps, drew back and refused to listen any longer to his persuasive accents. I need not attempt to enlarge on the character of his intellect, the subtle charm of his language, his lofty and self-denying purpose. . . . But one thing I cannot but notice,—that, whereas most of those who leave the Church of their fathers, be it the Church of this realm or another, prove to be the bitterest enemies and the most active opponents of that Church, Cardinal Newman never followed that unworthy course. He had convinced himself that there were things in our

---

[1] They were really some passages from Ignatius, and form Nos. 1–12 of the 'Records of the Church,' to be found among the *Tracts for the Times*.

Church that he could not away with, and that he should find in the Roman Church a satisfaction and a cure. But he did not therefore, as the manner of many is, assail us with acrimonious criticism or contemptuous reproach; and if at times he replied to attacks somewhat sharply, he seemed to do so in obedience to the imperious and inflexible principles of his new mistress.'

In the same sermon he contrasts the style of preaching of Cardinal Newman and Dr. Liddon, whose death had just occurred.

'Let me pause for a moment in order to say a few words as to the preaching of the Cardinal and Canon. My reminiscences may seem trivial or superficial, but they are, I think, somewhat characteristic. It has been my fortune to hear both these great preachers, one in my earlier years, one at a mature age. It is difficult to say which was the more impressive; but it is certain that the impressions were produced by means so different as to be almost contrary. I seem to see John Henry Newman, standing (to use a familiar phrase) bolt upright in the pulpit, with spectacles on nose, with arms as it were pinned to his side, never using the slightest action except to turn over the leaves of his sermon, trusting entirely for effect to the modulation of a voice most melodious, but ranging, I believe, through a very limited scale, yet riveting the attention of his hearers as if they were spell-bound. One sermon still dwells in my memory with vivid force—it was that on the character of Saul the King. We marvelled how so little apparent effort was followed by effects so great and permanent. Many who now hear me must have seen our lost friend, Dr. Liddon, with no less sweetness but much greater vehemence of voice and tone, exerting himself to the utmost, with head thrown back, with flashing eye, and such intense energy of declamation, as left him at the close of his discourse in a state of great exhaustion. The earnestness of both these great teachers was the same; the thoughtfulness inspired by them was equal. We may be proud that both were sons of Oxford.'

The beauty of this extract will justify its insertion:—and it shows Liddell's appreciative estimate of Newman's influence, an influence by which he was never for a moment dominated.

But if there is little trace of his sympathy with the Oxford movement, he gave but cold support to the Evangelical protest against it.

'There is a project here,' he writes in 1838, 'to put up a monument to the martyred Bishops, Cranmer, Ridley, and Latimer. There are and will be many difficulties about it, arising from the disturbed state of the theological opinion both generally in the country and particularly at Oxford. However, I hope the thing may be got successfully forward. If so, when the architectural question of what is to be comes to be discussed, I shall take a very lively interest in the business.'

Then, and apparently not till then!

In the years 1837-8, his pupil Acland was travelling in the Mediterranean for his health. In a letter written to him at Athens, after giving a budget of home news, Liddell adds:

'But what can these Western turmoils have of interest for you, who are now, I hope, enjoying the pure air of Attica, and warming all your classical associations by treading the ground which gave them birth? What would I give to be with you, while you trace the long walls, and seek the olives of Academus, and the white hill of Colonus, and all those other places whose names are to us as household words! Now do, my dear Acland, take pains, and make *many* (I need not add *faithful*) sketches of that fair land, and gladden my eyes with more representations of these spots which I have sometimes fondly dreamed to look on, but now can scarce expect to do so. Especially will you make me a correct drawing of the Temple of Niké Apteros which they have lately restored? Also, will you find out what the rock of the Acropolis is, and generally what is the nature of the soil? Lastly, the *precise* distances of well-known points would be a very useful thing to know. But it were endless to suggest points on which you might give me information. I should like to hear all and everything that you observe.'

This extract serves as an instance of his relations to his favourite pupils, and his enthusiasm for ancient art. Lord Wemyss, in a letter to Mrs. Liddell, adds a characteristic touch to the picture.

'I regarded myself as the most fortunate of undergraduates at Christ Church in being assigned to him as one of his pupils, and from the first we became fast friends—a friendship that, as you know, lasted through life. Art was a great bond of sympathy between us; and I well recollect his handing to me, to look at, an engraving of a Raphael picture. This, when he handed it to me, I took hold of with *one hand*, to his great consternation. He quickly took it from me and said, "Never hold an engraving with one hand, for then you mark and crumple it. Always use two hands and hold it thus:—one hand near the top, on one side, the other near the bottom on the opposite side." Need I say that *this* lesson I have never forgotten, though I fear the Classics he so well taught me are things of the forgotten past!'

But Lord Wemyss ought not to have forgotten them, for Liddell was an excellent Tutor.

'I admired and loved him from my heart,' writes another old pupil, the Rev. H. A. Harvey. 'His mode of giving advice and instruction endeared him to me. They were given in few, but telling words. You felt that your sense and your honour and your character as a Christian were appealed to; you were not coaxed or preached to. Some thought him rude and haughty; he appeared to me to be a good specimen of the μεγαλόψυχος, the character in Aristotle which he evidently admired. He used to instance it in Dr. Johnson. I owe an immense deal to Liddell. He fired my ambition, and he taught me to read the Greek Testament regularly and "like a Christian," for he had no idea of cramming for an examination. . . . He was a great man for the *text* of books. At that time it was not customary for the Tutors to see their pupils of an evening; but Liddell did it, at least with me, and would give me special help then in any books in which he thought me behindhand. The example which he himself set of industry was evidenced by the way in which we used to find him working at his Lexicon. In the interval between one Lecture and another he would be found standing at his desk over his interleaved copy of the first edition, correcting and amending it. And that standing desk recalls his advice which I have ever since treasured both in reading and in writing: "Keep your books open, ready to be returned to when you come back to work."'

In the year 1838 he experienced a very heavy sorrow, the first great bereavement of his life, in the unexpected death of his sister Harriett, at the age of eighteen. She was a singularly beautiful girl, and had already attracted the love of one of Liddell's most intimate friends, Stephen Denison, who has been before mentioned as a member of the 'Tribes' club, and had, like his brother, attained high distinction at Oxford. Harriett Liddell had shown symptoms of delicacy in the winter of 1837–8, but nothing serious was apprehended; and though, during the early spring, she had been ailing and weak, plans were being formed and discussed for a happy summer tour on the continent. However, in the end of April, a visit to London, and consultation with Sir James Clarke, revealed the existence of very grave lung mischief, and she grew worse so rapidly that she sank to her rest before the end of the second week of May. The blow, so sudden and so heavy, brought out all that was deepest and tenderest in Liddell's character. His letters show the poignancy of his grief, the warmth of his affection, and his anxious desire to comfort the mourners and the almost broken-hearted Stephen Denison. He would not have wished his words to be quoted. After the funeral at Wimbledon he was obliged to return to his Oxford duties, but

'though I can get on pretty well when I have a lecture, yet alone I find it impossible to collect my thoughts and prevent them from straying to other scenes and other times.... I have resumed my original intention of being ordained Priest on next (Trinity) Sunday. Reading the Bible, I find, is the only thing in which I can find lasting relief just now, and I do not know any reason to put it off.'

And on the day of his Ordination he writes:

'I have read your memoir of our beloved, not with dry eyes—not with dry eyes. I would set my seal to the truth of every word of it. No parent's fondness could exalt or magnify the gentle unassuming virtues of that bright and lovely creature. It is a trite saying, but the more I think of it, the more true I think it in her case, that she was too good and pure to remain among us. And earnestly did I raise my mind in prayer, while I knelt this day before the Bishop, that I might by God's Holy Spirit be enabled so to purify myself here on earth, and so exalt my being while I am left here, that I may be able of a truth "to put on Christ," and be made meet to see her once more face to face, and to dwell with her never more to part.'

The wound healed gradually; and work at Oxford went on quietly, strenuously, and successfully. The great labour of his life, the Lexicon, had now made considerable progress, and was the constant companion of his spare hours. His duties as a Tutor grew in interest and importance, as the number of his pupils increased, and they requited the pains bestowed upon them by acquitting themselves brilliantly in the Schools. The excellence of his College lectures is still remembered; and Sir Henry Acland tells of a petition made by those who were attending his weekly lectures on the Acts of the Apostles that he would break through the customary rule, and give them every week some additional lectures on the subject. After full consideration he felt obliged to decline the request, on the ground that his consent might seem to cast a slur upon his brother Tutors.

His taste on all matters of Art, carefully trained by congenial study, had by now gained a wider appreciation; he was recognized as an authority on the subject in Oxford.

'I have lately,' he writes in Nov. 1839, 'had an office conferred on me which pleased me, though it is rather honourable than profitable. Mr. Taylor (father of little Michael Angelo Taylor), some time an Oxford Tutor and dignitary, left a sum of money for building and endowing a College for the promotion of modern languages and literature. This sum was paid on Michael Angelo's death. Also a Dr. Randolph left some money to build a Picture and Statue Gallery. The two are to be combined, and one building erected for the two purposes—one building that is, as to outward appearance, though within the two will be kept separate. Now the University have desired a number of architects to send in plans for competition, and have appointed a Delegacy to decide on the best. I am one of the said Delegacy. So you see the Liddell name becomes connected with the Fine Arts on all sides. Tell my father that Mr. Cockerell (an old schoolfellow of his) and Salvin, whom you know, I think, have sent in far the best plans, *architecturally*, and I do not doubt one of them will get the prize. But Cockerell's will be far too expensive to *execute*. I hope Salvin's may be managed. But do not say anything about this. I ought not to talk of it.'

Professor Cockerell's design was, as is well known, ultimately accepted.

As time went on, additional honours and duties fell to his lot. In 1838, Gaisford had appointed him Greek Reader in Christ Church, in the place of Kynaston, who had been elected High Master of St. Paul's. This involved the preparation of lectures to be delivered to the whole of the first year men. He was appointed, he writes,

'above the head of one of my seniors, which, though gratifying to me, will be more so to you probably. For indeed, I had rather he had been appointed, partly because I have quite enough to do, partly because some little heart-burning may arise in consequence of the old boy's marked preference for me, on this as well as on some other occasions.'

In 1842 he became Select Preacher for the first time[1], and during his tenure of that office he wrote to his sister:

'I have now preached both my sermons for the Term before the University, not without applause. I must tell you that the Dean told me he was very much pleased with my second sermon: "Very much, I liked it very much. I thought it a very excellent composition." This is much from him, and I did not in the least expect it. He did not hear my first, he said. "He debarred himself from the pleasure of hearing me, because of the badness of the day." I suppose this will give you pleasure to hear, and therefore I record it.'

A little later, in June 1844, he writes to his mother:

'I preached my last University sermon yesterday. I had great compliments. Gaisford and Dr. Hampden, wonderful to relate, concur in their praises. The subject was *Unity*, not *Uniformity*; an attempt to persuade people to *agree* to *differ*, a rather delicate subject; but I am assured I handled the matter so as not to appear a partisan, or to attack any persons specially—so the Dean says.'

He was naturally called upon to act as Public Examiner; and in 1845 was elected White's Professor of Moral Philosophy. In the same year

---

[1] Canon Ellacombe, who was examined by him for his B.A. degree, heard his first University sermon. 'As he stood up he looked the picture of firmness and almost defiance; but I can remember the astonishment of the undergraduates when they saw the evident nervousness of the man whom they so dreaded.'

he became Censor; and was also appointed by Bishop Blomfield to the office of Whitehall Preacher. In the following year he became Proctor. In January 1846 he writes:

'The Tutor next to me has a brother who has turned Roman Catholic, and *he* is not quite clear of suspicion; so he has resigned his place, though he declares that he has no intention of leaving the Church. This throws all our arrangements into confusion, and puts four new pupils into my hands, so that in all I have no less than thirty-six. What with the Professorship, and my Whitehall Sermons, and lecturing these thirty-six, I shall have no easy berth. And I fear with my Proctorship, an office soon to come to me, it will be still worse.'

Of his work as Professor, Osborne Gordon, who succeeded Liddell as Proctor, spoke with great admiration in his *Oratio Procuratoria*. He mentioned the crowd of students who attended, and the clearness with which the opinions of ancient Philosophers were illustrated and explained in their bearings on questions of modern days. Liddell used to illustrate the Ethics by quotations from Jane Austen's novels and other modern writings.

One more distinction must be recorded; his appointment in January 1846 as domestic Chaplain to H.R.H. Prince Albert. On January 14 he wrote to his sister:

'You will be glad to hear that, on my return to Oxford yesterday, I found a letter from Mr. G. Anson, Secretary to Prince Albert, offering me the

Prince's Chaplaincy vacated by the elevation of Wilberforce to the Episcopal Bench. It is only an *Honorary* appointment, i.e. there is no pay. Still it is an honour, and the offer is conveyed in very handsome terms, for it speaks of my " eminent Academical and professional career"; and says the Prince is anxious to attach to his person "one who has kept the even tenour of his way amid the perils by which his path at Oxford was beset." So that I suppose I may consider it as a sign that my name is not unknown or unnoticed in high quarters. Also, Mr. Anson was pleased to say that the Prince was anxious that the appointment should not be merely nominal, but that he wished sometimes to have personal communication with his Chaplains, yet that the duties would not be of such a kind as to infringe upon my time.'

This appointment was the beginning of a gracious friendship which ripened from year to year, as the Prince learnt to appreciate more and more the sound judgment and generous theological opinions of his new Chaplain. He always showed cordial and helpful sympathy with his subsequent work at Westminster, paid frequent visits to the school, and took a keen interest in the proposal for its removal into the country, even visiting, in company with the Headmaster, several sites which had been suggested for its new home. The Queen, it is not improper to state, shared her Consort's feelings: their confidence in him was shown by placing the Prince of Wales under his charge at Oxford in 1859, as well as by many other marks of Royal favour. In April 1846 he was for the first time summoned to Windsor to preach before the Court.

His sermons before the University and in the Chapel Royal, Whitehall, attracted considerable notice, from the grace of their diction, the dignity of their delivery, and the calm and deliberate judgment with which the fundamental truths of Theology were brought into relation with the questions and needs of the day. Liddell was never a popular preacher, in the usual sense of the expression. He never aimed at mere effect, he never studied to please his audience, or engage their attention by rhetorical arts. His language was always severely simple, but never lacking stateliness and beauty. He was rarely, if ever, controversial; he desired to go beyond controversy, and exhibit Divine Truth in a more exalted relation. And at Whitehall, in those days, an opportunity was afforded of speaking on weighty topics to a congregation singularly well adapted to encourage the preacher to put forth his very best. It was customary for the Bishop of London, as Dean of the Chapels Royal, to nominate two persons, one from each of the old Universities, who held office for a period of two years, and were responsible for the bulk of the Sunday sermons. The Chapel was the Banqueting Hall of the ancient Palace—now the United Services Museum—fitted up, somewhat incongruously, for Divine worship. A huge Royal Pew faced the Pulpit, which was placed midway along the Eastern side of the building, with reading desk and clerk's pew in front of it. There were special sittings assigned to members of the two Houses of Parliament, to Cabinet Ministers, and the various Heads of Departments who occupied official residences in Whitehall. Many distinguished families also were then resident in that neighbourhood—a district not as yet abandoned to clubs and offices—and had the privilege of seats in the Chapel; and the general public were not excluded. The congregations, especially during the sessions of Parliament, were very large, and comprised many of the foremost and ablest men of the day. Liddell was fully equal to the task of preaching before so critical an audience, and attracted great numbers to hear him. He speaks more than once in his letters of the large congregations—many people standing, some even sent away; of Peel and Canning among his hearers; and of requests by strangers to be allowed to read the sermon just delivered.

Dean Boyle, in his *Recollections*, writes:

'It was interesting to see Peel and some members of his Government on Sundays at Whitehall Chapel, listening attentively to the Oxford and Cambridge preachers. H. G. Liddell, afterwards Dean of Christ Church, preached once on the text "Stretch forth thy hand." "One of the most remarkable sermons I have ever heard," said Peel to a friend as he left the Chapel; and on my telling this to Mr. Packe, then M.P. for Leicestershire (I think), he said, "I daresay Sir Robert will put Liddell's name on his Bishop's list".'

A comment in Liddell's handwriting adds:

'I am heartily glad Mr. Packe's prophecy was not fulfilled. I hope I should have had resolution enough to decline such an offer. I was quite unfit to be a Bishop.'

Up to this time Liddell's career had been one of uninterrupted progress and well-deserved success. He was among the foremost of the Oxford Tutors: he had gained a Professorship, and was discharging its duties admirably, attracting many graduates and undergraduates to his official lectures: he was becoming very favourably known as a preacher: and the publication of the Lexicon in the summer of 1843 had won for him the grateful approbation of every Greek scholar, and had already made "Liddell and Scott" a name full of awful meaning to every schoolboy.

It is interesting to read the estimate formed of him at this time by his very intimate friend Stephen Denison, who writes to Mr. Thomas Lyon Fellowes in May 1845:

'As I know that Henry Liddell has confided to you a secret (which I need not further particularize) I cannot resist taking the opportunity of half an hour's leisure to say how very great an interest I take in his success, and how extremely anxious I am that his hopes should be realized; and as you are so closely connected with the object of his attachment, I believe you will not think me impertinent in saying a few words about one of the dearest friends I have in the world. I have known him so long, and been so very intimate with him, and under such very peculiar circumstances, that I believe no man is better authorized to speak of him than myself. ... I have now known him about fifteen years as intimately as possible; and I have always noted him down in my mind as the most nearly "blameless" man I ever knew; the most generous, kind-hearted, amiable fellow, with a delicacy of feeling and taste almost too refined for the rough work of everyday life. I need not speak to you or to any one of his intellectual powers: they are known to all the literary world. But I may say that I know no one with such abilities and learning who is at the same time so modest and unpretending. If an amiable, excellent, very clever and accomplished man, highly connected, belonging to a delightful family, having innumerable friends, enjoying a reputation both for talent and excellence rarely attained so early in life, and whose prospects of advancement and honours are the fairest that can be:—if such a man can make a woman happy, Henry Liddell is the man.'

This letter refers to an event which took place early in 1845, and which soon changed the course of his life and formed the prelude to more than fifty years of domestic happiness, his engagement to be married to Miss Lorina Reeve. It would be unbecoming to dwell at length upon this occurrence, and all that it involved. It is enough to insist, in passing, upon the fact that no estimate of Liddell's character would be complete which did not take into account the brightness and helpfulness of his domestic life in all its relations; his devotion to his wife and children; the close bond of deep mutual affection; the prominent place they occupied in all his thoughts and plans of usefulness. The love which hitherto had been centred in his parents and brothers and sisters, now — without losing its old objects—gathered new ones for its exercise, and received in turn strength and steadfastness from them; and, in the joys of an almost ideally refined and charming home, was found a consecration of all labour, and a resting-place of all ambition.

'Be not ambitious,' he writes just after receiving the appointment to the Royal Chaplaincy, 'desire not high place for me. We shall be far happier in a private station with a competency than with dignity and wealth. I feel it to be so from the bottom of my heart. Cares, occupation, troubles, business, all sorts of things will interfere with the placid and happy enjoyments of life. . . . Freedom, contentment, sufficiency — that is what we want. More than this is "vanity and vexation of spirit".'

The immediate effect of his engagement was a resolution to leave the work at Christ Church, and to seek some sphere of activity which a wife could share. The College would miss him much. Gaisford, in his quaint way, told Dr. Bull that 'he was going to sustain a great loss; that he found that love and lexicography were not incompatible.' Liddell had determined to resign his various offices at Oxford in the summer of 1846, at the end of the academical year, and was discussing future plans, when the offer by Dean Gaisford of the Headmastership of Westminster brought a happy solution of the question.

The offer was not wholly unexpected. Dr. Williamson's resignation of the Headmastership, after eighteen years' service, was rumoured in the spring of 1846, and the nomination of his successor rested absolutely with the Dean of Christ Church. It was not likely that, when the choice had to be made, Gaisford would prefer any one to Liddell, whose claims were conspicuous, and for whom the Dean had already on many occasions shown his high regard. He was known to be engaged to be married, and to be seeking fresh work. The offer came on May 5.

'This morning, after Chapel, the Dean called me to follow him to his house, and without many words told me that he had determined to propose to me to become Headmaster of Westminster. He said he did not wish for an immediate answer, for there would probably be several questions I would wish to ask before I determined.'

The matter had indeed been already privately discussed between Liddell and his friend Saunders of Charterhouse, and inquiries about the condition of the school and the chief difficulties to be faced had been made of the Rev. T. W. Weare, a brother student, then Under-master at Westminster, who was most anxious to secure Liddell for his new chief. There were many questions to be considered. The numbers of the school had fallen of late to between seventy and eighty, and its ancient prestige had greatly declined. The neighbourhood of the school was bad; parents preferred country schools; and for these and other reasons it had come to pass that the College and the boarding-houses were only partly filled. The school, moreover, had no property of its own, but was dependent on the Dean and Chapter for all its funds beyond a few small statutory allowances; and all money spent upon improvements diminished their income. There were three boarding-houses, Grant's, Benthall's, and Scott's; but these were not Chapter or school property. They belonged to private owners who had bought them on speculation when the school was flourishing, and could only be re-purchased at a considerable price. In two of them, no master lived, and the discipline was under very imperfect control. The forty Queen's Scholars were lodged in the College, and were more or less under the supervision of the Under-master, who occupied the adjoining house: but, as the Queen's Scholars were always elected from the town boys, who, with the exception of a very few day boys, were the occupants of the boarding-houses, it was clear that if the College was to be in a satisfactory state, the condition of the boarding-houses must be first looked to.

The teaching staff, moreover, was very small and ineffective. The Headmaster took the highest

Forms, the VIIth and VIth. The whole of the Lower School was taught by the Under-master. The intermediate Forms were in the hands of three Ushers, two of whom were 'old stagers.'

'The Shell Usher' (writes Canon Rich, who was Captain in Williamson's last days) 'was rather a jolly old fellow, but he got very little out of his Form; and sham exercises were often given up on the chance of their not being looked at. The Usher of the Vth was certainly a clever man, but I am not sure that he was a good teacher.'

There were no Class-rooms, except the Library, where the Headmaster taught his boys. The rest of the work was all done amid the publicity and noise of the big schoolroom. In College there was but one spacious chamber, the long Dormitory, used day and night, for study and sleep, by the forty Queen's Scholars.

It was clear that the new Headmaster would have to make many changes, and offend many prejudices, if he were to bring the school up to a decent level. Liddell had a high conception of efficiency, and a brilliant reputation to sustain, and he was determined not to accept the Mastership unless he came to some clear understanding with the Dean and Chapter, and knew exactly what to expect from them. Fortunately Dr. Buckland, who had lately succeeded Samuel Wilberforce as Dean of Westminster, was equally anxious to effect improvements; and as he was at this time still a Canon of Christ Church, Liddell was able to consult him at once, on the very day on which the Dean's offer was made.

'I met Buckland by appointment, and walked three times round the meadow with him, discussing the whole subject. He told me freely all that it was intended to do, and all that I might expect from the Chapter. He said they were going to make a thorough reform of the whole management of the institution; that means might be devised for getting rid of two Ushers who at present interfere with all prospects of improvement; that all Old Westminsters with whom he had spoken—the Archbishop of York, Lord Granville Somerset, &c.—had expressed their hopes that I should be appointed; that Sir Robert Peel and Sir James Graham both desired it; and that all Westminsters confessed that they had no man of their own who could hope to restore the College to its ancient glories. The present emoluments are £600 or £700 a year. The house is very good, he says, but no one can live in it under £1,000 a year; and as the Dean himself cannot keep a carriage, of course a Prebendary cannot, nor the Master, unless he has a private fortune.'

Liddell was naturally not without perplexity; if he took the post, it would be necessary to have a clear promise from the Chapter, as to ways and means; he would be obliged to supersede some of the Ushers, a painful task; and to get effective control over the boarding-houses. But all this was so far satisfactorily settled, or in the way of settlement, that before the end of May he felt himself able to write to his future wife:

'I have seen Dean Buckland, and have accepted the terms offered. It is now publicly known that I am *Archididascalus Westmonasteriensis* elect. I have been already congratulated by several Old Westminsters with warm wishes for my success. . . . And so, now, it is all settled, and a heavy weight is off my mind, though I have taken a heavy yoke upon my neck. At least, there will be some very disagreeable work to *begin* with. But I have made up my mind to begin in earnest, and go through with it.'

At the close of the Summer Term he left Christ Church. His marriage took place at the end of July, and, after a short holiday in North Wales, he settled down to his new and arduous task.

# CHAPTER III

### THE LEXICON

THE Lexicon was the great work of Liddell's life. It was begun while he and Robert Scott were still Bachelors of Arts, perhaps as early as 1834. After many years of arduous labour, it was published in the summer of 1843. But that date marks the completion of only the first stage in an undertaking which was continued almost to the close of his life; the eighth edition being published, after careful revision, in 1897. The Lexicon was his constant companion in Term and in Vacation. His spare moments were regularly devoted to the task of revising, correcting, and enlarging its pages, and bringing it up to the level of advancing scholarship. For many years with Scott as his coadjutor, and then for many years unaided, he continually endeavoured to make the bulky volume as perfect as possible: and to this unremitting care is due the permanent success of the work. There has been no room for a rival: it has never become out of date.

It cannot now be ascertained to what cause the

book owed its origination. The simplest account is that it was due to a request from Talboys, the well-known Oxford publisher, for whose firm it was undoubtedly at first undertaken. It is said that Talboys first sounded Scott, who, after taking time to consider the proposal, said that he would accept it if Liddell would join with him. Talboys' death led to its ultimate publication by the University Press. There is, however, a tradition that the authors were first encouraged to their task by the suggestion of William Sewell, then Fellow of Exeter and a leading Oxford Tutor, known afterwards as Founder and third Warden of Radley College. Sewell is reported to have met Liddell at a gathering of some Essay Club in Oxford, at which the subject of Greek Lexicography was discussed, and to have urged him to undertake the task of compiling a Greek-English Lexicon. Undoubtedly Sewell was well able to judge of the ability of Liddell and Scott to perform such a work, for he had but lately examined them both for their Degree: and the need of a new Lexicon was universally acknowledged. It is certain that Gaisford gave the writers constant encouragement: and his own example would have been a powerful incentive to the two young Students of Christ Church. In a letter to Vaughan Liddell writes:

'Sewell thinks the Oxford mind is running too much to pure Theology: if you think so too, and also like him regret it, you will be glad to hear that some of us are—in all likelihood—about to close an engagement with Talboys for a Lexicon founded chiefly on Passow; indeed I dare say it will be nearly a translation. This sentence is rather arrogant, for the "some of us," after all, is only Scott and myself. At present you need say nothing about it. The Dean encourages the project very much, and has given us a number of valuable hints.'

It is indeed a matter of surprise that such a work had not already been done. We can scarcely understand how—without some such help—the average student in those days was able to fight his way through Greek authors. Till a very few years previously, there had been no such book as a Greek-English Lexicon; Greek was interpreted to the English reader only through the medium of the Latin tongue. One can still remember Schrevelius, Hederic, and Scapula as the ultimate authorities at school; and formidable volumes they were. Some poor attempts had been recently made to provide a Greek-English Lexicon by Donnegan, Dunbar, and Giles; but none of these books was at all adequate to the requirements of scholars: they were unscientific in the treatment of words, and suffered from lack of methodical arrangement, and redundancy of English equivalents; or else from over-brevity. In Germany, however, a better type of Lexicon had been published by F. Passow, based upon the profound work of his elder colleague Schneider. Schneider, who was Professor and Chief Librarian at Breslau, had, at the beginning of the century, issued a Greek-German Lexicon, which he subsequently enlarged and improved. This became the standard work in Germany. It was a monument of industry and learning; but it suffered from lack of methodical arrangement. It was reserved for Passow, a pupil of Jacobs and Hermann, and himself a Professor at Breslau, to make use of the materials provided by Schneider, and to exhibit them in orderly and instructive arrangement.

' His leading principle was to draw out, wherever it was possible, a kind of biographical history of each word, to give its different meanings in an almost chronological order, to cite always the earliest author in which a word is found—thus ascertaining, as nearly as may be, its original signification—and then to trace it downwards, according as it might vary in sense and construction, through subsequent writers [1].'

In order to carry out this plan, Passow spent his first efforts upon Homer and Hesiod, and in subsequent editions added an examination of the Ionic prose of Herodotus; but his early death in 1833, at the age of forty-six, prevented the completion of a wider undertaking.

It was upon this work of Passow that the new Oxford Lexicon was avowedly based: and in the first three editions his name appeared on the title-

---

[1] *Quarterly Review*, March 1835. From this article, and another in March 1845, both, it is believed, from the pen of Mr. Fishlake, much may be learnt about Greek lexicography.

page. But from the outset a vast amount of additional work was found necessary. The Preface to the first edition is now so little known that it may be well to quote from it the authors' description of the task which they undertook:

'We at first thought of a *translation* of Passow's work, with additions. But a little experience showed us that this would not be sufficient. Passow indeed had done all that was necessary for Homer and Hesiod, so that his work has become a regular authority in Germany for the old Epic Greek. But he had done nothing further *completely*. For though in the fourth edition he professes to have done for Herodotus the same as for Homer, this is not quite the case. He had done little more than use Schweighäuser's Lexicon—which is an excellent book, and leaves little of the *peculiar* phraseology of Herodotus unnoticed, but is very far indeed from being a complete vocabulary of the author. One of us, accordingly, undertook to read Herodotus carefully through, adding what was lacking to the margin of his Schweighäuser. The other did much the same for Thucydides. And between us we have gone through the Fragments of the early Poets, Lyric, Elegiac, &c., which were not in the Poetae Minores of Gaisford; as well as those of the early Historic and Philosophic writers; and those of the Attic, Tragic, and Comic Poets, which were dispersed through Athenaeus, Stobaeus, &c. . . . But besides all our own reading and collections, we have made unfailing use of the best Lexicons and Indexes of the great Attic writers—Wellauer's of Aeschylus, Ellendt's of Sophocles, Beck's of

Euripides, Caravella's of Aristophanes, Ast's of Plato, Sturz's of Xenophon, with Reiske's and Mitchell's of the Attic Orators. The reader will see by this that we have thrown our chief strength on the phraseology of the *Attic* writers. We have also sedulously consulted Böckh's Index to Pindar; and for Hippocrates, who ought to be closely joined with Herodotus, we have used Foësius' *Œconomia*, with the references in the Index of the Oxford *Scapula*. After the Attic writers, Greek undergoes a great change; which begins to appear strongly about the time of Alexander. Aristotle's language strikes us at once as something quite different from that of his master Plato, though the change of styles cannot be measured quite chronologically: as, for instance, Demosthenes was contemporary with Aristotle; yet his style is the purest Attic. Here, as in painting, architecture, &c., there are transition periods—the old partly surviving, the new just appearing. But the change is complete in Polybius, with the later Historic writers, and Plutarch. We have therefore not been anxious to amass *authorities* from these authors, though we have endeavoured to collect their *peculiar* words and phrases. For Aristotle, we have used Sylburg's Indexes, and those in the Oxford editions of the Rhetoric and Ethics; for Theophrastus, Schneider's Index; for Polybius (of course) Schweighäuser's Lexicon; for Plutarch, Wittenbach's Index. Attic phraseology revives more or less in Lucian; but for that reason most of his phrases have earlier examples, though in some of his works (as the Verae Historiae, Tragopodagra, Lexiphanes, &c.), many new or rare words occur. We have taken them from Geel's Index to the edition of Hemsterhuis and Reiz. But in these, and writers of a like stamp, we have seldom been careful to add the *special* reference, being usually content with giving the *name* of the author. Another class of writers belongs to Alexandria. We have not neglected these. The reader will find the Greek of Theocritus pretty fully handled; and he will not turn in vain to seek the unusual words introduced by the learned Epic school of that city, Callimachus, Apollonius, &c., or by that wholesale coiner Lycophron. We have also been careful to notice such words as occur first, or in any unusual sense, in the Alexandrian version of the Old Testament, and in the New Testament. We must not omit to mention, that in the first part, viz., from B to K inclusive, we have been saved much labour, and have very much enriched our Lexicon, by consulting Hase and Dindorf's new edition of Stephani Thesaurus. We only wish we could have had their assistance for the whole.'

Such was the task undertaken by two young men, who, though at the outset fairly at leisure, soon found that they were able to devote to it only those few hours of each day which could be spared from other duties. Liddell, as we have seen, became a College Tutor at the beginning of 1836, and Scott won a Fellowship at Balliol College in 1835, and after five years of residence there accepted the College living of Duloe in Cornwall, and settled down, as a married man, to parochial work in that distant part of England. He did not give up his share in the labour which they had jointly undertaken; but the separation rendered the work far less easy, and a heavier portion of the burden was necessarily thrown upon the partner resident in Oxford, within reach of Oxford libraries and the Clarendon Press.

Passow had not only provided a solid foundation for future workers, but he had also indicated the true system on which a Lexicon should be constructed; and among the many excellences of the new Lexicon none was more remarkable than its admirable and instructive arrangement. Instead of the old and bewildering fashion of grouping words, including compounds, under their primitive forms (or forms supposed to be primitive), a uniform alphabetical arrangement was adopted. The uses of each word were traced from its simplest and most rudimentary meaning to its various derivative and metaphorical applications; the steps which connected these different shades of meaning were clearly marked; and each gradation was illustrated as far as possible *historically*, by apt quotations from authors of successive dates [1]. For such a treat-

---

[1] In a very interesting article in the *Fortnightly Review* of January 1899, Professor Max Müller writes:

'The value of Liddell's Greek Dictionary consists in the consummate sobriety of its author. There is never too much, and yet there is hardly ever any essential meaning or any classical passage left out. The various meanings assigned to each word seem to spring up in regular succession, and we seldom find a Hysteron Proteron even from a merely chronological point of view. Yet chronology is not the only measure by which the stages or the growth of a word should be determined, and the Dean's good sense has generally kept him on the *via media* between a purely chronological and purely logical arrangement of meanings.'

ment of the language there were requisite not only the guidance of a methodical and logical mind, and a thorough knowledge of the principal Greek writers, but also a perfect mastery of the English tongue, so as to select with readiness the appropriate renderings, and to distinguish with nicety between the various so-called synonyms. The illustrations chosen should be sufficient, but not too numerous; and so chosen as to display the delicate transitions of signification. To achieve this successfully, scholarship in the fullest sense of the word was absolutely necessary, together with a keen appreciation of idioms, of the force of particles, and of those subtle distinctions of phraseology with which Greek pre-eminently abounds. To these high qualifications some measure of philological and antiquarian knowledge must be added; and to accomplish the task, a dogged perseverance, undaunted by delays and weariness. Liddell, in one of his letters, expresses a longing for the χαλκεντερία of the grammarian Didymus, untired by the drudgery of his monotonous toil.

The progress of the Lexicon is not often mentioned in Liddell's correspondence; but occasional references are found. He describes how Scott and he used to meet in his rooms at the south-west corner of the Great Quadrangle (Staircase III. 4) and work away from seven till eleven each night, one holding the pen, the other searching for authorities in books and indexes which lay open on the table. On one of these nights, in November 1838, Scott was late in arriving, and excused himself on the plea that he had been engaged in the Fellowship election at Balliol, and he added in a tone of satisfaction, 'We have elected an undergraduate, by name Jowett.' On another occasion Liddell writes:

'The Lexicon has been in abeyance during Collections, otherwise it has been going on reasonably well; but I rather shudder at the length of time it imposes on us, more, certainly, than I had calculated on. However, if we get through it, it will be satisfactory to think (as I believe we shall have good right to think) that we shall have performed a very useful and much wanted work. But if any one would appear who would undertake it, being also competent thereto, I would not be loth to resign my share, and make him a present of all I have done hitherto.'

He resolutely gave up to the work all his Long Vacations, with the exception of that which followed his sister's death, and postponed his first visit to Switzerland till after the publication of the book in 1843. As the printing advanced, the tie was closer; every page had to be carefully looked through and every reference verified. In spite of the devoted help of George Marshall, generously acknowledged in the Preface, the labour was very severe. In July 1842 he writes to Scott:

'You will be glad to hear that I have all but finished Π, that two-legged monster, who must in

ancient times have worn his legs a-straddle,

else he could never have strode over so enormous

a space as he has occupied and will occupy in Lexicons.'

He then draws a picture of the creature in human form, and adds:

'Behold the monster, as he has been mocking my waking and sleeping visions for the last many months.'

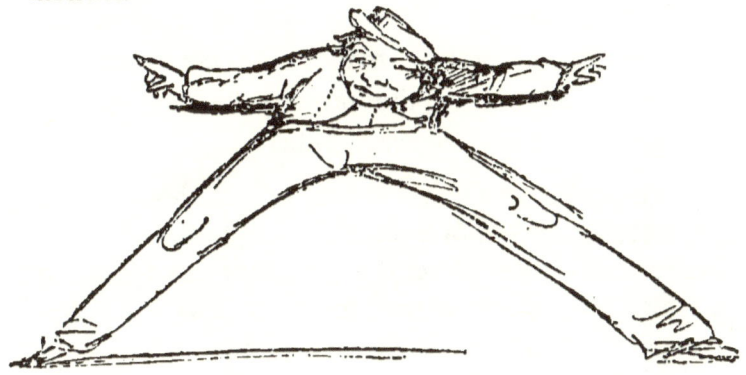

Later in the same Long Vacation he describes in a letter to his sister his mode of life:

'I get up at 5 every morning, work hard till about 6.30 or 7, have a cup of coffee and bit of bread, work hard till about 11, have breakfast, work hard till 2, go out with Vaughan or alone, walking or skiffing, dine at 5, work a little at night, and have tea (if any) with Vaughan, and go to bed at 9.30. I have got through a good deal of work, and hope that, as far as the Lexicon goes, I have broken the neck of it. We are going merrily along, and the printers, as well as myself, seem not a little glad that we are nearer the end than the beginning.'

So the work gradually grew to its completion; and by the side of the larger Lexicon was being prepared an abridgement for the use of schools, which the Press for convenience sake desired to print at the same time. This smaller volume was entrusted wholly to the care of George Marshall, who also took a heavy share of the laborious task of verifying all passages quoted in the larger book. Of the abridgement it is enough to quote the emphatic testimony of the *Quarterly Review* that it is 'by much the best manual for beginners that has ever come from the press.' In the summer of 1843 the Lexicon was published.

'We send it forth,' wrote the authors in the Preface, 'in the hope that it may in some wise foster and keep alive the accurate study of the Greek tongue; that tongue which has been held one of the best instruments for training the young mind; that tongue which, as the organ of Poetry and Oratory, is full of living force and fire, abounding in grace and sweetness, rich to overflowing; while for the uses of Philosophy it is a very model of clearness and precision; that tongue in which some of the noblest works of man's genius lie enshrined,—works which may be seen reflected faintly in imitations and translations, but of which none can know the perfect beauty, but he who can read the words themselves, as well as their interpretation.'

'We now dismiss our book,' they add at the close of the Preface, 'with feelings of thankfulness that we have had health and strength to bring it to a close. We know well how far it is from what it might be, from what we ourselves could imagine it to be. But we hope that, by pains and accuracy, we have at least laid a good foundation; and we shall be ready to profit by any criticisms that may be made upon it, whether public or private. For the present we shall be content if it shall in any sort serve that end of which we spoke in the outset; if, that is, it shall tend to cherish or improve the accurate study of the classical writers of Greece. We cannot look for much more. For the writer of Dictionaries, says Johnson in *his* Preface, has been "considered not the pupil, but the slave of science, the pioneer of literature, doomed only to remove rubbish, and clear obstructions from the path through which learning and genius press forward to conquest and glory, without bestowing a smile on the humble drudge that facilitates their progress." His labours have been compared to "those of the anvil and the mine"; or even worse,—

> Condendaque Lexica mandat
> Damnatis, poenam pro poenis omnibus unam.

'But our own great English Lexicographer, who with his gloomy mind delighted to heap reproaches upon himself, has himself also removed much of that reproach by the noble work which will carry his name wherever the English tongue is spoken. And we at least are well pleased to think that, if our book prove useful, it has been our lot to follow, however humbly, in the same career of usefulness that he chose for his own.'

The Lexicon was received with the utmost favour, and the demand for it exceeded the authors' expectation. In 1845 Liddell reports that:

'Dindorf, a *great* German scholar, has written a most complimentary letter to the chief printer, saying that he now relinquishes all intentions of undertaking a Greek-English Lexicon which he had projected.'

But though so warmly and deservedly welcomed, the work needed constant attention and unremitting care in supervision, so that each successive edition might mark a clear advance on the previous one. Within nine months of the publication a second edition was called for. This was issued in 1845, a third in 1849; the fourth edition, in which the name of Passow was omitted from the title-page, was published in 1855; the two next editions were in 1861 and 1869. The seventh, embodying perhaps the most important improvements of any, came in January 1883; and in 1897, ten years after Scott's death, and only a few months before Liddell himself was called to his rest, the eighth edition was issued, of the same bulk, and from the same plates, as the previous edition, but containing many corrections, and four pages of *addenda* and *corrigenda*[1]. Many

---

[1] By the courtesy of the Delegates of the Clarendon Press, the following information has been furnished as to the editions of the book.

The first edition was put to the press in March 1841, and was published (3,000 copies) in 1843 at 42*s*.

The second edition (6,000 copies) in 1845, at the same price.

The third edition (6,000 copies) in 1849, at the same price.

The fourth edition (8,000 copies) in 1855, at 30*s*.

The fifth edition (10,000 copies) in 1861, at 31*s*. 6*d*.

The sixth edition (15,000 copies) in 1869, at 36*s*. This was at the time intended to be the final revision, and the number then printed was calculated to last eleven years.

The seventh edition was revised by Liddell alone, and came out

words were re-written, and many new words inserted in the body of the work. And though he was then in his 87th year, his handwriting was as clear as in his younger days, and he took the same care with the accentuation.

Throughout this long period of fifty-four years the labour of improving the Lexicon was never intermitted. Author after author was read through, and careful references were made to every noteworthy use of word or phrase; the help of Indexes thus gradually giving way to the actual perusal of the whole text of the writers themselves. Even Passow's laborious treatment of Homer was found to be quite unsatisfactory.

'I regret,' wrote Liddell in 1853, 'to find how much better the Lexicon might be! I have been going over the Homeric part, and find, alas! many, many errors both of sense and taste. I wish we had at once seen that the best way was only to use Passow *as a convenience*, and that all real work should have been done by ourselves. It would have been less labour in the end.'

And not only the Greek authors themselves, but all the chief modern works dealing with the Greek language had to be carefully examined. The new

in 1883, and electrotype plates were then taken. From these plates additional copies were struck off in 1885, 1886, and 1890.

The eighth edition was ordered in 1895 and appeared in 1897. The corrections are such only as could be introduced into the existing electrotype plates.

Sir Henry Acland calculates that there are more than 20 million letters, stops, and accents in the volume; and this is confirmed by the Controller of the Press.

Paris edition of *Stephani Thesaurus* was, as it came out, in constant use. Much help was afforded by Rost and Palm's *Greek-German Lexicon*, and Dr. Veitch's *Greek Verbs, Irregular and Defective*. The etymological portion of the work was entirely recast, with the help particularly of the writings of Georg Curtius; and in the later editions, as the book was now widely circulated in America, Professors Drisler of New York, Goodwin of Cambridge, Massachusetts, and Gildersleeve of Baltimore, contributed very valuable assistance throughout the volume: Professor Drisler's name appearing on the title-page of the American edition [1].

So the life's work, or bye-work, went on; an engrossing occupation for spare moments in the busy career at Westminster and Oxford, and a recreation in the retirement of Ascot.

'I remember one day,' writes the Dean of Durham, 'having to call on Liddell on College business, and was told that he was in the Library. Thither I went to seek him, and found him seated in one of the small rooms to the south. As I came in, he looked up, with that kind look of his, and said, "You have found me at the very end of a life's

---

[1] 'Some of the old objectionable etymologies,' writes Professor Max Müller, 'have now been removed and replaced by others which are supported by Curtius in his *Grundzüge der Griechischen Etymologie*. But such has been the progress of Comparative Philology since the days of Curtius, such, more particularly, the improvement in the more delicate handling of phonetic rules, that a careful revision by a young scholar such as I was in the fifties and sixties would be very useful even now, and would be highly appreciated by classical scholars, who rightly recognize in every true etymology the pre-historic development of Greek words and Greek ideas.' (*Fortnightly Review*, Jan. 1899.)

task; for I am writing the last sheet of the last edition of the Lexicon which I shall undertake. I shall henceforth leave it to others to correct, or future editions may come out as I have left this one." I said, he would miss it very much, such an old friend; and after my bit of business, I left him. In the following October Term, I had again to trouble him; and hearing again that he was in the Library, I found him busy on one of the sheets of the lately issued edition, preparing already for the next. I reminded him of what he had said, and with a laugh he confessed that he could not keep his hands off it; that so many people had sent him corrections and suggestions for the new edition, that he felt he could not lay down the task. And so he continued working steadily at it, I believe, down to the very end.'

Sometimes Liddell's older friends, who had known the range of his artistic tastes, and remembered the rare promise of his younger days, were inclined to regret that he had devoted so much of his life to the drudgery of Lexicography. This regret is implied in Mr. Ruskin's words already quoted, when he speaks of 'the prosaic and practical element in him having prevailed over the sensitive one,' and describes him as 'a man sorrowfully under the dominion of the Greek ἀνάγκη.' When Liddell read those words, in 1886, he wrote to Mr. Ruskin as follows:

'Your *Christ Church Choir* I have read with much interest. It calls back old times and revives the memory of many things.... As for myself, I have to thank you for your kindly expressions. Kindly

I call them, though I am sensible that, under the kindliness, lies severe censure. But I think this censure is based upon an over-estimate of my umquhile capacities. To alter your phrase, I conceive you to say that by bowing my neck under some kind of ἀνάγκη, I have become a Philistine instead of becoming, as was possible, a true Israelite. Well, I hope I am not an absolute Philistine. But I am sure that I never could, with any success, have attempted a way

> —qua me quoque possim
> Tollere humo, victorque virum volitare per ora.

This, I suppose, is what you mean.

'None of us, in looking back, but must say with old Samuel Johnson, "I have lived a life of which I do not like the review." But this is different from imagining that one might have done great things instead of little. Enough of myself.'

To this Mr. Ruskin replied:

'I am very grateful for your letter. What was held back in my reference to you was chiefly my own mortified vanity, at your praising other people's lectures, and never mine! and sorrow that you kept dictionary making, instead of drawing trees at Madeira in *colour*.

'I hope what further words may come, in after times, as I go on, will not pain you; though I was very furious about the iron railing through Christ Church meadow.

> 'Ever your affectionate pupil,
> 'JOHN RUSKIN.'

The publication of the Lexicon gave a respite from incessant occupation; and in the Long Vacation of 1843 Liddell paid his first visit to Switzerland. His impressions of Swiss scenery are recorded in two letters. To his sister Charlotte he writes from Thun:

'Here I am, rather unexpectedly, in the midst of the most beautiful scenery that I ever saw, more beautiful than I ever conceived. To-day it is slightly raining, and the high Alps are wrapt in clouds. But yesterday morning was bright and clear, and the chain of the Bernese Alps stood sharp against the sky—the Jungfrau, Wetterhorn, and all the rest dazzling one with their everlasting snow. We went up the lake in a steamer to Interlaken and got up to a height which commands the lake of Brienz, where we were some twelve English miles nearer to the high mountains. But it is not near so beautiful a scene as from my bedroom window at this place: and verily I bless God for having made so fair a scene.... I long to see an Alpine pass and glacier. But the days are gone when I should have eagerly climbed every height, and thought each day wasted in which I had not walked twenty or thirty miles. I feel that one ought to come to Switzerland at a much earlier time of life than I have done, at a time when one is more alive to the wondrous scenes of Nature, the rock, the mountain, and the flood, when one's health and body are more fresh and vigorous, and one is less alive to petty annoyances. However, I will not complain, and I am glad to find that, though my hair is falling off and going grey, I yet feel much of youthful ardour and freshness return when I breathe this fresh and sparkling air, and look on these scenes which are all Nature's own, and bid defiance to man's art to alter them.'

To Scott he wrote later:

'Tell Mrs. Scott that I cannot less well appreciate the scenery of Cumberland and Westmoreland from having been in Switzerland. Indeed I am pleased to find that *really* beautiful scenery interests one the more, the more one sees. It is not the actual scale, but the relative proportions and colour, and a thousand nameless things, that make beautiful scenery. If she challenges me to say that Cumberland is as *sublime* as Switzerland—there I must demur. To be in the heart of the Bernese Alps (much finer they, *me judice*, than Mont Blanc), to see and hear avalanches "momently falling," to look on *real* peaks, thousands of feet above you, when you are yourself at twice the elevation of any Cumberland hill, shining in the smoothest, brightest, purest covering of eternal snow—in relief against a dark-blue sky, or at sunset passing through a hundred hues, from pure white through the gradations of yellow, orange, roseate red (a quite indescribable colour—so delicate, so rich), and then again fading into silver white, heightened by the moonbeams: this, with all their beauties of form which the pencil cannot give, far less words, renders the Bernese Alps from the Faulhorn the sublimest scene I ever hope to see.'

It is strange that, possessing so keen a sense for the beauties of Nature, and so deep a love for History and Art, Liddell very rarely travelled abroad. After his marriage, he seldom left England, except under Doctor's orders. He visited Athens only once, when he was cruising in the Mediterranean for his health; and, more strange still, he never visited Rome, though his Roman History seems to show close familiarity with its topography.

# CHAPTER IV

HEADMASTERSHIP OF WESTMINSTER, 1846-55

IN entering upon his work at Westminster in September 1846, Liddell began a very important period of his life, comprising many successes indeed, but many grave cares and anxieties.

He brought his bride to their new home in the ancient low-roomed house on the east side of Dean's Yard, adjoining the archway which leads into Little Dean's Yard. This house had originally formed part of the Prior's lodgings, but had for long been assigned to the Headmaster, and its walls were hung with the portraits of former occupants, including the famous antiquary Camden, who had been Headmaster in Elizabeth's reign, 1593-99. Since that distant time, no one had been chosen for the Headmastership who had not been educated at the school; and the selection of a non-Westminster was an innovation which, though admitted to be necessary, was a severe shock to the venerable traditions of the place. All the chief school buildings, as well as the Headmaster's house, were part of the ancient Abbey, lying close against it on its southern side. The schoolroom was formed out of a portion of the Monks' dormitory; the Abbot's refectory was the dining-hall of the forty Queen's Scholars. They had in olden times been lodged in the Abbey granary, but had been transferred in 1732 to a new dormitory, begun while Atterbury was Dean, from a design furnished by the Earl of Burlington based upon an earlier design of Wren's, which stretched along the western side of the Infirmary garden. The cloister garth was the boys' fighting green; the Abbey was their chapel. The school was without property of its own, and was entirely dependent on the Dean and Chapter, who were not accustomed to be over-generous, or to spend much anxious thought upon the special requirements of the boys. The neighbourhood was bad; and, to reach the chief playground in Vincent Square—an open space of about ten acres—many low streets had to be traversed. The river indeed provided a place for recreation not yet rendered perilous by crowded steamboat traffic; but the Thames then received the whole drainage of London, and its tidal waters were by no means without their drawbacks.

Liddell was encouraged by a cordial welcome from all persons connected with the school, and his own reputation augured well for the success of his rule. Buckland, but lately made Dean, was, as we have seen, most ready to back him to the utmost in all that he attempted, and was himself profoundly dissatisfied with the existing state of the school. Arthur Stanley describes a conversation with Buckland in the previous January, as they were travelling down to Oxford together:

'He talked a great deal and very sensibly about the reform of Westminster School, the abuses of which he described at great length, particularly in the physical department—counterpanes in the dormitory not washed for eleven years, school not cleaned since Queen Elizabeth died, tyranny and cruelty among the boys, three of whom he had been instrumental in expelling. All this he meant thoroughly to look into, and thought of writing a pamphlet on the subject, and made me give him a detailed account of great parts of the system at Rugby.'

In Mrs. Gordon's *Life of Buckland*, the College is thus described:

'Buckland found that Dean Atterbury's dormitory, after over a hundred years' use as bedroom, sitting-room, and playroom, was in a most dismal condition, with the walls blackened by smoke, and here and there hung with moth-eaten green baize curtains; the tables and lockers seamed and scarred in all directions; and the floor —. Taking his children to see the place, their father asked, "Well, children, what's this floor like?" The answer was prompt, "The fossil ripple-marks in our hall at home." [A fossil slab of ripple-marks now in the Oxford Museum.] The floor was only cleaned once a year, so that its rough surface was not to be wondered at, as the boys did a great deal of cooking there amongst their other diversions.'

Many of the Chapter too, if not all, shared the Dean's sympathy with reforms, and Liddell speaks particularly of the sub-Dean, Lord John Thynne:

'Who is a *real* gentleman (as they say in Ireland), a most agreeable, kind, good man, who will do all that lies in his power to promote the good of the school and my wishes.'

The great body of Old Westminsters also desired to encourage the new Headmaster; and the entries of new boys were eminently satisfactory. But the task before him was not an easy one.

'I shall have to begin,' he writes, 'with some very unpleasant business. I shall have to turn off people who consider themselves excellent servants of the College. I shall have to make myself many enemies. But nothing can be done without this. I shall have the concurrence and support of all Westminsters whose opinions are worth having. I shall be warmly seconded by Buckland and Weare, and by all the electors, so I shall, in reliance on all this favour, boldly throw down the gauntlet, and make a clean sweep.'

The existing ushers gave place to new men of Liddell's own choice, all of whom were admirably fitted for their posts; the Rev. Stephen J. Rigaud, a double First Class man and Fellow of Exeter College, the Rev. James Marshall, of Christ Church, and the Rev. B. F. James, of Exeter College. Rigaud five years later became Headmaster of Ipswich School, and afterwards Bishop of Antigua. Mr. James spent the whole of his working life at the school, and died soon after his retirement. Mr. Marshall remained at his post for nearly thirty years, and still possesses, in the dutiful affection of many generations of Westminster men, their grateful appreciation of a very noble ideal of faithful service and pure and lofty aims. With such assistants many changes, which would otherwise have been difficult, were made comparatively easy. Stricter discipline and more industry were enforced; the work of the Forms was re-cast; proper provision was made for the teaching of French and Mathematics, and Wordsworth's Greek Grammar and Edward VI's Latin Grammar took the place of the antiquated Westminster manuals.

The Under-master, the Rev. Thomas W. Weare, cordially welcomed all improvements. He had been, as has been said, a fellow-student of Liddell's at Christ Church, and his lengthened experience of Westminster, as boy and master, gave a special value to his advice and assistance. To him belonged by custom the entire management of the College; and it was his wish to co-operate with his new chief in introducing such changes as would adapt the College life to modern requirements without impairing its ancient autonomy. Two great blows had recently been aimed at its traditions by Samuel Wilberforce, during his short reign as Dean, and both had been parried. He had proposed that a master should reside actually in the College building, so as to live among the Queen's Scholars, and to exercise a constant check upon their independence. Such an intruder would have found himself stirring a hornets' nest. Wilberforce had also made a determined effort to abolish the Latin Play; but this had been met by a unanimous protest from the whole body of Old Westminsters, addressed to Dean Buckland soon after his appointment. Reforms such as these, dictated by a spirit unfamiliar with the ἦθος of a Public School, would have no place in the plans of the new Headmaster and his colleague the Undermaster. But they heartily supported the Dean and Chapter in their proposal, already made in June 1846, to carry out certain structural alterations in the College building. Below the great Dormitory, the only home of the Queen's Scholars by day and night, there was a spacious cloister, inaccessible to the boys, but open to the College garden, and used by members of the Chapter and their families as a sheltered walk, or a serviceable tea-room at garden parties. This area it was now proposed to enclose, and to form within it large rooms which would afford proper accommodation as day quarters for the Queen's Scholars. The Dean and Chapter were not willing to advance the necessary funds for this improvement, but they issued an appeal to Old Westminsters and others; and within a short time the new rooms were constructed, and a Sanatorium was also built at the south end of the College, containing adequate provision for sickness, and a home for a resident Matron, who was to look after the boys' linen, and tend them when on the sick list. This was a vast improvement. Hideous indeed was the Sanatorium, and hideous and gloomy beyond words were the new apartments of the College. Buckland had no aesthetic sensibilities, and was fond of corrugated iron; and it was thought fair that if the boys inhabited the cloister, they should at least be deprived of the privilege of a sight of the green grass and stately plane-trees of the garden. The windows of the new rooms were accordingly placed high up, and were glazed with an opaque substance which excluded even the sky. They were prison chambers; but the boys became accustomed to them, and they led at once to the disuse of the Dormitory as a day room. Liddell's own sense of what was beautiful or decorous must have caused him many a sigh over such ugly and mean quarters. In the College Hall, too, the ancient open fire in the centre of the floor, its smoke escaping through the louvre in the roof, gave place to a square iron erection of a singularly inartistic character, which however had one decided merit, in that it provided two clear and bright fires admirably adapted for the making of toast. Many were the laments of the boys over the abolition of the old fire-place: but when about forty years later this iron structure was in its turn replaced by a more worthy successor, it had so far established itself in the affections of the boys that its loss was the theme of plaintive epigrams at the Election dinner. 'Ah,' said Liddell to his neighbour as he sat there as Elector, 'they lament its loss now: but you should have heard how they abused me when it was first put up!'

The great schoolroom, also, many years after worthily restored, was now stripped of its ancient benches, picturesque in their decay, and hewn and hacked by the knives of many generations, and in their place was fitted spick and span modern oak furniture with iron supports, supplied at small cost from the neighbouring depôt of the National Society. It was very ugly, but much more convenient for Form-work.

The life of the boys within the walls of College had been from time immemorial very independent. Authority was in the hands of the ten 'Seniors,' the Captain and three monitors at their head. There were curious customs of all sorts, many of them unsatisfactory survivals, and the life was rough; and for the ten junior boys, who were Fags, not only rough but hard. Most of the menial offices of the College were performed by them, and little time was left for their school work. The allowance for the food of the Queen's Scholars was so inadequate that they paid a considerable sum each Term for breakfasting at the boarding-houses, and a great deal of evening cooking went on at the three fires in the long Dormitory. These evil economies were now to a great extent abolished; proper meals were provided in the Hall, and additional service, the latter indeed at the expense of the boys, or rather of their parents. An annual charge was also made in the bills for the improvements to the College buildings, till the whole expense was paid off. This tax outlasted Liddell's time.

It will be well to insert here an account of the new Headmaster's work at Westminster, from the pen of the Rev. James Marshall, who writes with an authority and knowledge possessed by him alone. It gives a very interesting picture of Liddell's position, and an appreciative estimate of his character:

'When Mr. Liddell came to Westminster, the school, as is well known, was at a very low ebb. There were even vacancies in College for want of a sufficient number of boys qualified by continuance in the school to make up the statutable complement of forty. Mr. Liddell had from the first caused it to be fully understood that he would only accept the Headmastership on the express condition that he should bring his own assistant-masters. Irritation was naturally to be expected on the part of the gentlemen who retired, and of their many and warm friends. Some disquiet from this cause was also more widely spread. The Old Westminsters were a manly, warm-hearted, outspoken body of gentlemen and scholars, devoted to their school, and jealous of its traditions; a little exclusive, perhaps, from a genuine doubt whether anything outside Westminster could equal what was within it.

'I am glad of the opportunity of acknowledging one very kindly and characteristic tradition. At the annual dinner of the Old Westminsters it was the custom to invite the Masters as guests. It was also the custom, on that occasion, for those Masters who were clergymen, to wear cassock and bands, and the pudding-sleeved gown. We edified the passers-by in St. James' Street by stepping across the pavement in this guise, and passing into the Thatched House, where we dined in the room of the Kitcat Club.

'This important constituency welcomed a Headmaster of such high academical distinction, of such weight of personal character, and, I think I must add, of such a presence; but were at the same time somewhat dismayed at seeing that four out of the five Masters were non-Westminster men. The Old Westminsters were not free from the inconsistencies that are usually found in large and irresponsible bodies. They were anxious for improvement, and at the same time nervously alarmed lest any actual step taken in that direction should impair the characteristic spirit of the school. Their attitude therefore, or at least the attitude of many of their number, was one of watchfulness rather than of unreserved confidence.

'Meantime, the criticisms on the Dean and Chapter were free and frequent, and sometimes bitter. This criticism the Abbey authorities naturally resented. They were willing to do all that they thought could fairly be required of them. Dean Buckland in particular entered *con amore* into the plan of structural alterations designed for the better accommodation of the Queen's Scholars. But they were plainly determined to resist indefinite encroachments on the part of the school:—and with some reason, for a school, be it where it may, has a capacious maw which is not easily satisfied.

'The new Headmaster felt his position very keenly; the more so, perhaps, because his personal influence at Oxford had been unquestioned and extraordinarily great. He was fully alive to his responsibilities, and grieved that, in discharge of them, he was sometimes forced to run counter to the feelings and opinions of men whose regard he valued and whose position he respected. He was by no means one who wore his heart upon his sleeve; but once, in course of conversation, with a very resolute, but at the same time a sadly pained expression, he took upon his lips the words "I have set my face like a flint."

'This prejudice was gradually but not slowly dissipated. The restoration of the Play had a very reassuring effect. It had been intermitted in 1846, and a question had been raised about its continuance in future. This was set at rest by Dean Buckland's answer to a memorial presented by the Marquis of Lansdowne, and signed by nearly all the Old Westminsters then living. Accordingly in December 1847, Hervey Vaughan Williams, the Captain, in his dress as Queen's Scholar, with the usual courtly addition of knee-breeches and silk stockings, stepped forward on the Dormitory stage to tender the new Headmaster a greeting in the old well-recognized form. And when, in the Prologue, he thus struck the dominant note—

> Gaudere multos, qui nunc audiunt, puto,
> Quod prodit in scenam iterum nostra fabula ;
> Gaudemus et nos ; anno namque proximo
> Omissa multos terruit, haud iniuria :

the burst of applause which followed ; the pleasurable excitement or rather enthusiasm shown by so many refined and intelligent faces ; and, in the older men, the look of kindly encouragement for boyhood, made up a scene not soon to be forgotten by those who witnessed it.

'Prince Albert, to whom Mr. Liddell was domestic Chaplain, was present at a fourth special representation of this Play, and afterwards at that of 1851.

'The school increased in numbers and was in a fair way of recovering its old connexion. Many, some of high rank, several of great distinction, again sent sons to their old school. It was seen that Mr. Liddell, though not an Old Westminster, was in the best sense of the term a Public School man; and that, while he would prune unsparingly erratic and mischievous growths, he would leave untouched the free, manly, and honourable stock of the Public School spirit. He was too wise a man to sacrifice a use because of an abuse.

'The tide continued for some time steadily to rise; but counteracting forces came gradually into play. It is worthy of the great position formerly occupied by the school that the checks to its prosperity should be closely connected with the great movements of national thought.

'One of these, which is still in full force, had already made itself felt in Reform, Catholic Emancipation, and Free Trade. 'The "Spirit of the Age," which with the "March of Intellect" was a phrase much in vogue at that time, was emphatically one of inquiry. That a thing had been was no presumption that it should be. In that respect the age might be represented by Dr. Arnold, of whom it was said that he always awoke in the morning with the idea that everything was an open question. This was actually the case at Westminster School from the time of Mr. Liddell's appointment. Everything connected with it was a subject of discussion with a view to possible alteration or abolition. The subjects and mode of instruction, the discipline, the constitution of the College, the relation of the school to the Chapter, to the Universities, and to the Public, were all in their turn brought under the microscope, and had to await the result of the scrutiny; and, to crown all, it was extremely doubtful whether Westminster School was to remain at Westminster, or to migrate to another site. All these uncertainties were perfectly well known in London, and consequently among the boys. This knowledge made discipline none the more easy, and would have had a very prejudicial effect, but for the cordial union among the Masters, a union which was naturally based on the warm regard and high admiration which was felt by all for their chief. All wise policy for a School, as for a State, must be far-sighted. It was impossible to plan for the future, when all the elements which entered into the combination might be swept away at six months' notice.

'There is no doubt that Mr. Liddell chafed against these limitations, which in every direction hampered his designs. He was a strong man with his hands tied. But no sign of impatience appeared. There was no cooling of his interest in the boys, no diminution of the care with which he superintended the work of the school or discharged his own special office of the teaching of the Sixth Form. Of the manner of that teaching I naturally had no experience; I can only speak of results. Boys used to pass from my Form into the Sixth. Occasionally their answers to examination questions would pass through my hands; and I have noticed how boys' minds have been enriched by even a short period of intercourse with the Headmaster.

'For the school in general a system of periodical examinations was devised and gradually developed under Mr. Liddell and his successor, till it became theoretically almost perfect. Practically fewer papers and questions, and greater strictness in exacting answers, would perhaps have been better for the lower Forms. The arrangement was such that favouritism was impossible; and, after the minute and unsparing criticism of the Public School Commission of 1864, there was no question of the justice with which the boys had been classified or elected into College or to the Universities; nor, it may be added, a hint that a single shilling of the funds administered by the school authorities had been misapplied. Meantime every idea of material improvement was met by a *non possumus*. The restoration of the ample and nobly proportioned schoolroom, the provision of class-rooms, and an almost unique school Library and adjuncts, works which have since been so successfully carried out, could not even be attempted while the tenure of the school was uncertain, and while there was no arbitrament possible between the claims of the school and Chapter on one another. It was sometimes forgotten that the Dean and Chapter were Trustees for their own body as well as for the school. Unfair judgments were passed upon them. When the school was empowered to manage its own affairs, it was found that the service of the Queen's Scholars in Hall could not be conducted on the same lavish scale as before.

'The second great movement which impeded the prosperity of the school was the attention which began to be paid to matters affecting the health of individuals and the public. The Duke of Buccleuch's Sanitary Commission, which was favoured by Prince Albert and Sir Robert Peel, reported in 1844, two years before Mr. Liddell came to Westminster. There was a growing feeling in favour of the country in preference to town for the residence of boys. The feeling was increased by an unhappy event which soon followed.

'Dean Buckland had lost no time in devising a scheme for pipe-draining the precincts, which was to be carried out by the sanitary authorities. In the preliminary soundings, notwithstanding all precautions, a source of malaria was tapped, with its most disastrous consequences. Typhoid fever attacked the Dean and two of his family, and was fatal to two young and promising boys who had lately been elected into College. Two Canons' daughters also died. The terrible disease entered the Headmaster's house, and Mrs. Liddell was for ten days in imminent danger. Her alarming illness naturally excited general interest and sympathy. Consequently the accidental and temporary unhealthiness of Westminster became known far and wide; and the impression made was so deep that it did not disappear when the cause of the disease had been removed. It was useless to point out that the school had been before, and afterwards continued to be, remarkably free from serious illness.

'Still the belt of building towards the South and West kept spreading, and the river, before the main drainage of London was taken in hand, became year by year less attractive. Mr. Liddell, who had been profoundly moved by the visitation of fever, seems gradually to have become convinced of the impossibility of maintaining a great residential school at Westminster. I have heard him express that opinion in very strong terms; and I think that he welcomed preferment to the Deanery of Christ Church not only for its own sake, but also because it relieved him from a position of great perplexity.

'The strain upon his powers must have been very great, and was not sufficiently estimated at the time. Besides the administration of a Public School under special embarrassments, and the teaching of the Sixth Form, he before long imposed upon himself the difficult and responsible task of preaching at intervals to the boys. This was full work for one man. But he was also on the Oxford University Commission, which was very industrious in its sittings. The revision of his Lexicon was a constant drain upon his time, and with it he was engaged in the severe labour of combining in an orderly narrative his researches into Roman History. And London society would not forgo its claim on one so fitted to adorn it, who was living in its very midst. Yet with all this variety of care and exertion, there was rarely any appearance of hurry, still less of irritation; but uniformly the same dignified composure of demeanour. It is no wonder that, after nine such years, his health should have broken down, and that he should have had medical orders to recruit himself during two winters in Madeira, soon after entering upon the duties of the Deanery.'

After mentioning the Lexicon and the Roman History, Mr. Marshall refers to Liddell's literary style:

'It has this quality of excellence, that it never draws attention to itself. This purity of diction is characteristic. He would have boys and men say what they mean, and mean what they say, and was ruthless in stripping off the *purpurei panni*. An undergraduate in his paper work at an Oxford examination had introduced, *à propos* of nothing, a fine expression derived from Hooker, and ultimately, I imagine, from the Schoolmen, "The angels fell by reflex thought." Mr. Liddell used to describe, with some gusto, the state of imbecility to which the unfortunate man was reduced, when he was asked in *viva voce* to explain the meaning of his words.

'The same nervous simplicity extended to his Latin style. The prologues which he wrote to be spoken before the Westminster Play exemplify his power of compelling a somewhat intractable language to express exactly what he felt. One specimen is appended; a description of the famous Exhibition of 1851:

> Ergo anno iam peracto bis millesimo
> Mire aedificatum vidimus Palatium,
> Cui non rigebat mole saxea latus
> Firmique solido roboris fulcimine,
> Sed vitrea sic micabat pulchritudine,
> Et paene incredibili artificis sollertia,
> Tanquam si nebula mane consurgens novo
> Gelata medio constitisset aethere.
> Sed inerat aedi si quid usquam splendidi
> Si quid magnifici, si quid ignoti prius
> Ars hominum efficere posset atque industria;
> Denique natura si quid olim cautius
> Terrae in latebris condidisset abditis,
> Si quid sub alto condidisset aequore,
> Sive in inaccessis montibus, id inerat quoque[1].

---

[1] Another instance may be quoted in the elegiac lines which told of the 'Adelphi,' a play originally acted at the funeral games of Aemilius

'Mr. Liddell's speech had, of course, all the refinement of breeding and culture, but it breathed of the North in the greater richness of the vowel sounds, and the more distinct articulation of consonants. The aspirate made itself felt in such words as "who," "when," and "where." I have often thought that the greater play thus habitually given to the lips made them more expressive than their owner quite realized. He certainly had the power of saying much without words. For instance, one of his pupils at Christ Church, a man of mark, was observed to be preparing his work for lecture with a care that was by no means usual in his case. Being rallied by his friends, he said, "Well, you know, I can't stand Liddell's look when I am breaking down." This silent punishment, be it observed, was for those who did not use their gifts, not for those who had no gifts to use.

'His sermons to the boys were strong, clear, and sometimes severely simple. One in particular deeply affected them, when he spoke of their schoolfellows, some lying beneath the "bleak Crimean shore," others upon it with their brave comrades in arms enduring privation and toil, and living in hourly familiarity with death. In the year 1851 he preached before the Queen a sermon on faith, hope, and charity,

---

Paullus, and at Westminster in the December following the death of General Wolfe (1759) and the death of the Duke of Wellington (1852). The 'swing' of the verses still lingers in the memory after an interval of forty-six years.

>     Fabula quae prodit nata est dum maxima Roma
>         Prosequitur Paulli funera moesta sui;
>     Dein nostram redit in scenam, volventibus annis,
>         Ut Wolfi exsequias Anglia tristis obit;
>     Tertia sors restat—vocat illam tertius Heros—
>         Te, Wolfi, maior, maior et Aemilio.

which was afterwards published by command. That perhaps gives the best idea of his spiritual insight and reach of intellect, and suggests the thoughts on which he most loved to dwell.

'In his preaching there was the same withdrawal of self as in his writing. This was not mere literary method, or good taste; it was the result of genuine Christian humility, which shrunk from display, but was deeply rooted, and was part of the staple of his inner life. I venture to assert, against all possible contradiction, that no estimate of the late Dean's character can be just and full, which does not take this gracious quality into account.

'It is unnecessary for me to speak of Dean Liddell's reputation for learning. But, great scholar as he was, his noblest lessons were taught less by what he knew than by what he was. Those who were brought into close relations with him, especially minds that had the plasticity of youth, learned by the mere association to loathe what was mean and cowardly, to covet earnestly the best gifts, and to be true in thought and word by the strength of Him who is the Truth.'

This admirable testimony to the Headmaster's work and character may be briefly supplemented by some reminiscences of those who were boys under him.

1. One vivid impression, which length of time has not wholly effaced, was that of awe. The new comer, called up to stand before him and the Under-master, both dressed in full canonicals, with bands, cassock, and Geneva gown, and to answer questions with the object of having his place in the school

determined, experienced the unpleasant sensation of sinking into his shoes, before a presence so majestic, a voice so deep, a manner so reserved. And this first impression was not transitory. It was renewed every Saturday morning, when the Headmaster went round the school, visiting Form after Form, and reading out the week's order of merit, the 'principes' as the list was called from the winners of the top places. This review of the week's work was a severe and alarming scrutiny, and idlers met with stern rebuke. Yet even while they dreaded his advent, the boys learnt to attach immense importance to his brief words of comment, and to be greatly encouraged by his praise. There was indeed much gentleness underlying his austere demeanour. On one occasion when he had to rebuke a boy of good ability who, week after week, had fallen below his proper place in Form, his voice faltered, and his eyes moistened, as he spoke in fatherly condemnation of the folly and wrong of this continued idleness. He never spoke in anger: he never lost perfect self-control. He had learnt the value of self-command. In a letter from Westminster to an intimate friend who had been appointed to the Headship of a College at Oxford, he wrote with the frankness of old acquaintance on the importance of calmness in dealing with young people:

'Perhaps you will not take it ill if I take the liberty of an old friend to add a piece of advice. Several persons who formerly knew you at ——, in talking over with me the chances of the election, doubted the propriety of electing you, because (they said) you did not exercise sufficient control over your temper in dealing with undergraduates. I am afraid I cannot boast of a very good temper myself. But I am fully aware—and try to exercise what I feel—of the great and primary importance of perfect coolness and deliberation in speaking to and dealing with young persons. I know not whether, and how far, what I have heard is true. If it is not true, then what I say is naught. If it is, you are (I am sure) candid enough to set what I say down to the right and only motive.'

But gradually, to the feeling of awe was added that of affection, as the boys rose in the school and came under his personal instruction in the Sixth Form. For he was an admirable teacher: thorough, clear, suggestive, stimulating; exacting in the care which he demanded in the preparation of book-work, but singularly interesting in the instructiveness of his comments and the wide range of his illustrations. He was not a mere textual scholar, but an historian and statesman. His Juvenal lesson still lingers in the memory, as a model of what a lesson should be; the boys were not only well drilled in the text and allusions, but were referred to the best modern satires, and indirectly led to an appreciation of much of the noblest English literature. He was fond of poetry, and taught the elder boys to recite it well. During a portion of the year, there were 'speeches' in the great schoolroom on Friday mornings, at the end of the lesson, in the presence of all the boys, when the members of the Sixth Form stood up by the Headmaster's table, and repeated passages of English poetry which had been previously selected. On one occasion, when the present Vicar of St. Peter's, Bournemouth, had recited the whole of Gray's 'Elegy' with faultless taste and without a single mistake, an emphatic 'Thank you, Fisher' gave an apt expression to the feeling of all the listeners, and a more than ample reward to the reciter.

In those ancient days, a rudimentary knowledge of Hebrew was most wisely required of the elder boys who were candidates for the Universities. Liddell taught this subject in a very interesting manner, although it was generally believed that he had acquired all his knowledge in the short interval between his appointment as Headmaster and his entering on his office.

2. The challenges, or examination for admission into the College, were a severe tax upon the Headmaster's powers of endurance. According to modern custom, the candidates would be tested by an examination lasting a few days or a few hours: but in those more leisurely times the competition extended over two months, occupying almost daily the interval between morning school and dinner; the minor candidates, as they were called, were pitted one against another in pairs, engaging in a curious conflict partaking somewhat of the nature of the old academical disputations. Short passages of Greek or Latin, previously selected by the Headmaster from the Greek Epigrams or Ovid's Metamorphoses, were construed, and then the lower boy,

called the challenger, asked his opponent certain questions founded upon the words or sentences in the passages. If the upper boy, the challengee, could not answer them, and the challenger himself answered them correctly, the former lost his place, and became in turn the challenger. So the contest went on, till the stock of questions was exhausted. In some challenges, the number of questions was limited, in others it was not; and two boys who had been carefully drilled in the Greek and Latin grammars would keep up the contest throughout a whole day, from early morning till nine at night. It was a mode of examination which demanded rigid grammatical accuracy, and the Headmaster, who presided, had to be continually on the alert to note every question and answer, and to give a prompt decision on all doubtful points. Around him stood the 'Helps,' elder boys who had prepared the combatants for the fray, and acted as advocates for their several clients. When a question arose as to the exact meaning or derivation of a word, the large dictionaries were referred to; and Liddell and Scott was of course the authority for Greek. Sometimes discussions would arise even as to the correctness of this august volume, and 'Helps' would boldly venture to quote Scapula or Schrevelius against the new Lexicon. But Liddell was always good-tempered and always reasonable, and enjoyed the keen advocacy of the boys. It used indeed to be told—but this was an amusing libel which no one really believed—that when an admitted error was pointed out, Liddell would say, 'Ah, yes, Mr. Scott wrote that paragraph.' This tradition, however, gives a point to the following anecdote, which is narrated on the authority of the actual writer of the bold effusion. Once a year, on the Friday before the election to the Universities, it was customary for the Headmaster to come into school, carrying a bowl containing Maundy money, the little silver coins which were supplied from the Royal Mint. He would then call upon the boys to gather round him, and to read epigrams upon Theses announced a few hours before. These epigrams—supposed to be the boys' own composition—were rewarded by gifts of the silver pence; the very best gained four coins: a four-penny, three-penny, two-penny, and penny piece; the others were rewarded by a less complete set. Upon one occasion, when the challenges had revealed some mistake in the Lexicon, the thesis for school epigrams happened to be '*Scribimus indocti doctique.*' A boy delivered the following epigram:

> Two men wrote a Lexicon, Liddell and Scott;
> Some parts were clever, but some parts were not.
> Hear, all ye learned, and read me this riddle,
> How the wrong part wrote Scott, and the right part wrote Liddell.

The audacious poet survived the venture, and gained not only a hearty laugh, but a full complement of pence, from the Headmaster.

On another occasion, soon after the schoolroom had received its new and mean furniture, the thesis *mutandus locus est* was given out, and produced the following epigram from the pen of one of the senior boys, now a dignified Registrar in Chancery:

> 'Mutandus locus est,' and those who rule
> Act up to this; improvements come in swarms.
> They change the ancient customs of the school,
> And will not even leave to us our forms.
> Instead of those old desks with many a name
> Carved over, they would bring us to propriety
> By filling school—unutterable shame—
> With benches from the National Society!

Another delightful epigram—on the same thesis—was read by a very small boy:

> I was placed in the 'fourth' when I came here,
> By Mr. Liddell and Mr. Weare;
> But I've done pretty well, so I think I've some claims
> To be placed in the 'fifth' under Mr. James.

It is evident that liberty of speech was not then curtailed at Westminster.

3. The moral tone of the school was undoubtedly raised under Liddell's rule, and the manners grew less rough, as the conditions of life were made more comfortable. It was of great benefit to the boys to be guided by masters who were thorough gentlemen, and entirely imbued with the Public School spirit. They all trusted the boys, were ready to accept their word, and would take no unfair advantage of them. There are no memories of Liddell which are not associated with a chivalrous sense of honour; and boys instinctively grew to be honourable and truthful themselves.

One who can speak from the most intimate knowledge of him writes:

'What I should like brought out is his great aversion to *exaggerations* about anything, and his love of *exact* truth. I think of late years at Westminster he scarcely ever punished except for a lie, and then he had no mercy. There was nothing that disturbed him so much as to feel that any one was not speaking the exact truth to him; he never trusted them again. I have heard that boys used to say they could not tell Liddell a lie and look him in the face; and I have heard him say, "I can call no man a gentleman who can act a lie, even if he does not tell it." He was truth itself, and even what is called "humbug" he could not endure.'

The Under-master taught the Queen's Scholars the same lesson. The latter was indeed, perhaps, over-sensitive on one point. Upon entering College from his house, he would always give a prolonged warning by putting the key noisily into the lock, and turning it in a very leisurely fashion; or if he passed through College in the day-time, he would cough, or rattle his bunch of keys, to enable the boys to know that he was near. Perhaps they sometimes took advantage of this courtesy; but on the whole, it was respectfully appreciated.

The institution of special school services in the Abbey had much influence on the religious life of the boys, and brought the Headmaster into a new relation to them. Before Liddell's time, they had attended the Abbey simply at the usual morning and evening services on Sunday, and never in full numbers. Leave out was always granted to boys who had friends in London, from noon on Saturday till Sunday evening. Many, therefore, were always away from the Abbey services, and the remnant sat in their accustomed places in the choir. The sermons were preached by the Canon in residence, and had no special reference to the needs and difficulties of boys. Liddell resolved to have an occasional service for the school alone, at which he might himself preach. He accordingly got leave from the Dean and Chapter to use the Abbey on the first Sunday of each month, at eight o'clock in the morning. The whole school then attended, and no leave of absence was granted. There was no music, but the prayers were read by the Under-master, and Liddell preached from his stall. They were, as Mr. Marshall has already stated, very remarkable sermons: simple, direct, stately, dealing with the incidents of school life, and the current events of the history of the day. They made a deep impression on the boys. One— on the death of the Duke of Wellington, and of Liddell's favourite pupil, Hervey Vaughan Williams— he printed for private circulation, with the line from Tennyson as its motto, 'The path of duty is the way to glory.' At other times, though he would not print his sermon, he would, at their earnest request, put it into the hands of the elder boys, and they would copy it for themselves: a good test of the value they attached to it. The services were greatly liked, and did much good; but the hour was uncomfortably early, and the stopping of 'leave out' was a tiresome incident of them. In the winter, moreover, the Abbey, then untouched by any system of heating, was piercingly cold, even dangerous to delicate boys without great coats and before the breakfast hour: and it was but dimly lighted with a few wax candles. One can still recall the chill and the darkness, and the prayers unrelieved by music or singing, and then the magnificent English and sonorous tones of the preacher. Perhaps the sermons gained in impressiveness from the fact that 'Early Abbey,' as it was called, came only once a month.

4. The Latin Play, performed before the Christmas holidays, was, from the point of view of the Queen's Scholars, the greatest event of the year. The erection indeed of the theatre in the actual Dormitory threw all domestic arrangements into confusion for some weeks beforehand, and the constant rehearsals were perhaps to some extent a hindrance to school work. But larger considerations happily prevented any change in the time-honoured custom dating from Queen Elizabeth's reign; and the crowded and enthusiastic audience assembled in the narrow and uncomfortable theatre showed the very wide interest taken in the performance by the *élite* of London society. The Prologues were, as a rule, written by the Headmaster, and specimens of Liddell's felicitous Latinity have been already given. The Epilogues were humorous satires on the foibles of the day, and were usually the work of some Old Westminster of scholarly tastes. Many possess sterling merit as specimens of Latin adapted as a vehicle for the expression of modern ideas, and for

their refined and delightful humour. The Chartists, the Peace Congress, and the 'Bloomer' dress furnished the themes of three of the best Epilogues during Liddell's time. In the last of these, Thais, Pythias, and Dorias come upon the stage dressed in half-masculine costume, to the horror of their former lovers. Thais invites Thraso to cross the Atlantic with her to America, and is met with the reply:

>Ah! me mare terret;
>Ipsaque tu terres, horrida imago *maris*!

Mrs. Dexter, Mrs. Bloomer's representative in England, threatened an action at law for the ridicule thrown upon the cause she advocated; being especially annoyed at the lines (probably the only ones at all intelligible to her):

>Bloomer tu, Dexter an audis,
>Nil opus hic inquam est dexteritate tua.

By a strict etiquette, the Play was always omitted on the death of a Royal personage. The Queen Dowager died on December 2, 1849, when all the preparations for the year were well advanced, the theatre erected, and the tickets issued. What was to be done? The Queen's Scholars audaciously took the matter into their own hands, and wrote a letter to the Prime Minister, Lord John Russell, who was an Old Westminster, entreating him to represent to Her Majesty the disappointment and inconvenience which would result if the Play were abandoned. They also wrote to Colonel Phipps, the Queen's private secretary. Through these two persons, both of whom took it for granted that the application was made with the full sanction of the school authorities, Her Majesty was approached, and most graciously and considerately allowed the performance of the Play, provided it did not take place on the day of the funeral. The matter then came, for the first time, to the Headmaster's ears, and the triumph of the boys was short-lived. He interposed without a moment's delay, and wrote as follows to Colonel Phipps:

'I regret extremely to find that the Queen's Scholars of St. Peter's, Westminster have thought fit to apply to Her Majesty to sanction the performance of the usual Latin Play, while the remains of Her late Gracious Majesty the Queen Dowager are still uninterred.

'It is probable that the application was understood to be sanctioned by the Dean of Westminster or myself. It was however made without our knowledge; and if we had been consulted we should certainly not have allowed it to be made.

'It is the feeling of all the authorities of the school, as well as of many old Westminster men, that this would not be a proper occasion on which to break through an old custom of respect paid by the Royal foundation to the Family of the Sovereign. The personal excellence, as well as the exalted station of Her late Majesty, demand this tribute. We therefore, with all gratitude for the consideration shown by Her Majesty, and especially for the extremely kind and gracious way in which Her pleasure was conveyed, beg leave to decline the permission which She has accorded.'

The Play was accordingly most properly omitted; and in the Prologue of the following year a fitting reference was made to the death of the Queen Dowager.

5. The Headmaster had already, in the previous year, run counter to the wishes of the boys in another matter of great importance in their estimation—the Eton and Westminster boat-race. This contest had begun in 1829; and, in spite of the disparity in the numbers of the two schools, Westminster had been victorious in four out of the eight races which had already taken place; and in 1846, on the course from Putney to Mortlake, had gained so decisive a victory that it was arrogantly asserted by the boys that if Eton were beaten again she would probably refrain from challenging her adversary in future years. So in 1847 there was a general enthusiasm in favour of the race; a new boat was built by Noulton and Wyld; it was named after Mrs. Liddell, and launched by her; and on July 29 the race was rowed on the ebb tide from Barker's rails to Putney. But the fates were adverse, and Eton gained an easy victory.

Liddell, however, felt grave misgivings as to the expediency of such a contest. To row so long a course was a severe tax upon the physical power of the boys; too much time was spent in preparation, and too much interest was devoted to the event: and the necessary publicity of a contest on London waters was in itself an evil. Dr. Williamson had felt similar scruples, and had prevented the race from taking place in 1838, though he had allowed it in subsequent years. And now it was definitely abandoned; not without many regrets on the part of the boys and the old members of the school, but with the full concurrence of the authorities. In 1860, under Dr. Scott, an Etonian Headmaster, an attempt was made to revive the contest on a shorter course; but after four years' experience it was finally given up. The London river had by this time become too crowded and dangerous for practice; and Eton was overwhelmingly superior in numbers.

So the work went on, busily and hopefully. The school grew in numbers and in reputation; there seemed every prospect of its steady advance. Then came the first great blow and crushing anxiety. The fever which desolated the precincts did not spare the school; two of the Queen's Scholars died, as has been already mentioned, and Mrs. Liddell lay for ten days unconscious, at the point, as it seemed, of death. Through the skill of Dr. Watson, and the assiduous care of Dr. Acland, who was hastily summoned from Oxford to watch by her bedside, her life was happily saved.

But the effect of this outbreak upon the fortunes of the school was immediate. The entries in 1846–7 had been 47. Three years afterwards they were 37, and in the succeeding years, 30, 32, 34, 37, and 23 respectively. The rumour of unhealthiness, founded upon this one outbreak which could be traced to a definite source of infection, spread abroad among the public: boys were withdrawn and the numbers would not rise. Cholera, too, came to London in the summer of 1849, and the Headmaster was obliged hastily, and on his own responsibility, to postpone the meeting of the school in September. This act brought him into collision with the Dean of Westminster, who thought he had exceeded his powers, and usurped the Decanal authority; and a correspondence ensued, containing among others this severe letter from Buckland:

'The tone of your last letter, which I received at Woburn Abbey, where I had not access to our statutes, and in which you "express what you think should be the proper rule for your conduct in such matters," makes it imperative that we should come to a distinct understanding as to the duties of our respective offices in this College. . . . You say "you believe the Headmaster always has regulated the length of the holidays without reference to the Dean." I have inquired of the Chapter Clerk, whose recollections are most exact, whether in his father's time any extension of the customary weeks of vacation was *ever* made by the Headmaster without permission first obtained of the Dean. His reply was, *Never*, except when the Sovereign commanded it. I therefore think that your recent extension of the holidays, on account of the cholera, without consulting the Dean (whom a letter might have reached in twenty-four hours in any part of the kingdom if sent to the Deanery) was a virtual, if not a direct violation of our statute, Cap. 14, *de vitanda aëris contagione*. . . . As you refer to the practice of other collegiate schools, I must inform you that in my own case, as a scholar of Winton

College, Dr. Huntingford, of his sole authority as Warden, gave me leave of absence for six weeks of ordinary school time; and that on my waiting on the Headmaster, Dr. Goddard, of whom I had asked no permission, on the eve of my departure for these six weeks, he said to me that had he been Warden, or possessed power to prevent it, I should not have had this indulgence. In the case of Rugby, which you refer to, and where you say Dr. Arnold stipulated for *absolute power* as the condition of his accepting office, I consider such a foundation by a private individual (and governed by lay Trustees, not one of whom is necessarily resident, nor accustomed to collegiate or academic habits) to form no parallel to the collegiate establishments of Winchester, Eton, and Westminster; and if Dr. Arnold (my friend and relative), whose transcendental love of liberty induced him to admit of no law within that school but his own will, and tolerate no superior to himself, and to stipulate, as a condition of his accepting office, that there should be in Rugby School no control superior to his own:—if he had been nominated under similar conditions by the Dean of Christ Church or Master of Trinity, and proposed to the Dean of Westminster as the successor of Dr. Williamson, I must have exercised my veto, and would not and could not have assented to such a stipulation without violating my oath to keep the Statutes of our College. The effect of your proposal "that the boys ought to look to the Headmaster as supreme" would amount to a reversal of the past and present order of authorities recognized by the tradition of all Old Westminsters, viz. that within this College we know but three authorities, the Sovereign, the

Dean, and the Headmaster; and to substitute a new order of precedence, consisting of the Sovereign, the Headmaster, and the Dean. I should consider my assent to such an abdication of my proper place to be a betrayal of that office which has been entrusted to me by the Sovereign, and nothing but the mandate of our Royal Visitor, reversing our statutes, will induce me to abandon a tittle of my rights, in a manner that would degrade myself and all my successors.'

To this stormy epistle the Headmaster returned a gentle answer, pointing out that he had regarded the question as one of *expediency* and not of *right*, and that it had been practically impossible to consult the Dean before deciding on the matter, which it was imperatively necessary to settle without any delay.

Gradually the conviction grew that the only real remedy for the school, if it was to retain its ancient character of a Boarding school, was to be found in its removal to the country. Schemes were then discussed by which such a fundamental change might be carried out. Prince Albert gave the assistance of his warm sympathy and co-operation, and various sites, including Cooper's Hill and Caversham, were visited. At one time it was contemplated that the school should be removed at the public expense, so as to make room for a magnificent avenue which, beginning at Buckingham Palace, should end at the Victoria Tower, the Abbey standing out on its north side. But there were insuperable difficulties in the way of every scheme; and the Public Schools Act has finally settled the question of the retention of Westminster, on its existing site, as a great London school.

The Headmaster's hands were always full of work. In addition to the ordinary burdens and anxieties of his post, he had the unending task of correcting and enlarging the Lexicon. Moreover he undertook to write, for Mr. Murray, a *History of Ancient Rome*. This work was first published in 1855, in two volumes. It was soon afterwards abridged into a School History, and in this form has ever since retained its place on Mr. Murray's list as 'The Student's History of Rome, to the Establishment of the Empire.' That it so maintains its position, though it has never been revised or brought up to date by the introduction of the results of modern research and discoveries, is a strong testimony to its sterling merits. It is a thoroughly useful book[1], well illustrated, well arranged, and admirably written. Mr. Marshall thus speaks of its opportune publication:

'The History of Rome had its own seasonableness. Niebuhr had revolutionized the scheme of Roman History. But his influence had nearly spent itself. Scholars began to weary of disquisitions which, however learned, acute, and brilliant, resulted after all for the most part in conjecture. They craved to realize the full-blooded life of the

[1] An Italian translation of the larger History reached its sixth edition as long ago as 1886.

Roman State without being worried by perpetual suggestions of doubt and discussions of hypotheses. Mr. Liddell's history came opportunely to satisfy this want. He did what could only be done by a writer of historical instinct and sound judgment, who was saturated with knowledge of his subject. He gave a masterly summary of what was ascertained respecting the original races which coalesced in the Roman people, and the evolution of their not less complicated political system. I recollect the pride and interest which I felt when I was allowed to read the MS. of the chapter which describes the Senate, and there for the first time found a clear, concise, yet adequate account of the constitution and functions of that memorable assembly.'

This book was the only historical work that came from Liddell's pen. But he was always deeply interested in the study of history; and his friends at Oxford had been anxious, several years before, to encourage him to devote himself seriously to the subject. In 1849 he was strongly urged to apply for the Regius Professorship of Modern History, vacant by the death of Dr. Cramer. From his intimate friend J. M. Wilson, who had succeeded him as Professor of Moral Philosophy, he received the following letter:

'MY DEAR LIDDELL,

'I passed through London a week ago, and was sorry to hear that you were absent. I wished to see you, having a strong desire that you should come to Oxford as Professor of Modern History. Is there any probability of this? I cannot tell you how much we want you here. I am certain your being here (or coming among us as Arnold did) would be of the greatest service to us. I should take twice the interest in my own lectures if I had any one to speak to respecting them, but I have no one. Depend upon it you can have no better sphere of work than Oxford is at present, and your coming would be life to not a few. I wish I could induce you to make application for the Professorship. I cannot help thinking that you might easily procure it; and the railroad would make coming and going easy.

'Very truly yours,
'J. M. WILSON.'

He felt himself, however, quite unable to act on the suggestion, and the Professorship was accepted by his friend H. Halford Vaughan, whose brilliant lectures deservedly attracted very large audiences. They are now so completely forgotten that it may be interesting to read what Liddell wrote about them to Vaughan himself:

'I hear on all hands the highest encomiums on your lectures. Conybeare of Christ Church, for instance, writes me word that, though he was himself prevented from hearing them, "he has talked of them with many clever men of various political views and has only heard one opinion of them." "All," he adds, "seem struck with the great beauty of the language, with the imagination and wide illustration, as well as the philosophical power of mind shown in them." "Suggestive" is a term popularly applied to them. There is also a general wish as well as (I may as well tell you) a general expectation to see at least your first two lectures in print. People say they want to have an opportunity of reading what gave them so much pleasure in the hearing; and some did not go to *hear*, in the hope that they should be able to *read*. Unless you have some reason against printing, I think you would gratify many persons by so doing. I hear also from Conybeare the following, which agrees with what you wrote me word of, viz. "the large attendance perhaps frightened some of the Hebdomadal Board. From whatever cause, there is an agitation carrying on by Greswell and others against the Modern History School: they argue that it will beat Natural Science out of the field. Daubeny and Acland refuse to join this illiberal crusade".'

In a short sketch of Vaughan's life written many years later Liddell describes the lectures as well deserving the success which they at first attained:

'He read me portions of them at Hampstead, and I well remember a most graphic picture of the household of William the Conqueror and his rollicking sons. But before long he got tired of the work, showed great caprice and irritability in his intercourse with his friends at Oxford, and finally resigned the Professorship into the hands of Goldwin Smith in 1858.

'Vaughan's personal appearance was striking. His features were large, well-defined, and mobile, especially his eyes. They revealed at one time bright enjoyment of some humorous thought or word, or admiration of some strong and vigorous sentiment; at another time they were fixed on you with an intensity of expression that seemed to pierce to your very soul. He had an immense "fell" of rough hair, of which his father the judge once said, "To my certain knowledge the masons refused to buy Halford's hair to mix with their mortar; it was, they said, too coarse." This gave a sort of wild Olympian character to his head.'

It will not be necessary to say much about Liddell's labours on the first Oxford University Commission. The Commission was issued under the great seal in August 1850, and held its first meeting on October 19 in that year. The Commissioners were—S. Hinds (Bishop of Norwich), A. C. Tait (Dean of Carlisle), F. Jeune (Master of Pembroke), H. G. Liddell, J. L. Dampier (Vice-Warden of the Stannaries), Baden Powell (Savilian Professor of Geometry), and G. H. S. Johnson (Fellow of Queen's). The Secretary was Arthur Stanley, and the Assistant Secretary Goldwin Smith. No fewer than eighty-seven meetings were held, and from only one of these was Liddell absent. It was through their work together on this Commission that Liddell's friendship with Stanley ripened into that close and affectionate intimacy which only closed with Stanley's death.

The strain of this work, coming as an addition to his duties as Headmaster, was lightened by the great interest which he took in the question of University Reform. He had for many years been convinced of the necessity of remodelling the constitution of the University by getting rid of the supremacy of the Heads of Houses, and giving real power to the great body of residents engaged in education. Early in life he had written a pamphlet on the subject; and his long collegiate and academical experience had convinced him that the unenlightened and even reactionary rule of the Hebdomadal Board made all improvement at their hands impossible. He had observed the action of the Heads of Houses in the various theological controversies of his time, and had had ample evidence of its unwisdom. The chief reforms recommended by the Commission were—the revival of the Ancient House of Congregation, upon a reformed basis, as an effective Legislative body; a reconstruction of the Professorial system, so as to give it a leading place in the educational machinery of the University; the relaxation of the obligation to take Holy Orders as a condition of the tenure of Fellowships; the removal of local and other restrictions on the tenure of scholarships and Fellowships; the abolition of the distinction between Nobleman, Gentleman Commoner, and Commoner; and the introduction of a new class of students not belonging to any College or Hall.

These recommendations were the result of prolonged deliberations; and they expressed a unanimity only arrived at after much discussion. In a letter to Vaughan, Liddell writes:

'You know very well that all the more important of these recommendations were compromises, and that perhaps not one—certainly not myself—of the Commissioners would wish to see them adopted exactly as they stand. But the spirit and tendency of them was (I think) approved by all.'

Mr. Vaughan, owing to his position as Professor, and his long intimacy with Liddell, carried great weight with the Commissioners.

'Your answers formed the text of our debates, and I carried propositions *in general terms* founded on your proposal for remodelling Congregation and the Hebdomadal Board. Your arguments in favour of Lodging Houses told.'

The subsequent changes in the constitution of the University as embodied in the Act of 1854, and the Ordinances of the several Colleges, were based upon, but were by no means identical with, the recommendations of the Commissioners.

It was obvious that the contemplated alterations in the tenure of Fellowships and scholarships would affect materially the relations existing between Westminster School and Christ Church. Ever since Queen Elizabeth's time, boys had been elected annually from the College at Westminster to studentships at Christ Church; and these studentships stood on the footing of Fellowships, in being tenable for life subject to certain conditions. The Commissioners recommended that the studentships should for the future be divided into two classes, corresponding to Fellowships and scholarships at other

Colleges; and that a certain number of the junior studentships (or scholarships) should be set apart for Westminster candidates, and should be tenable no longer for life, but for a period of seven years. This change would alter the whole status of the Westminster students. It was not likely that so radical a proposal would be welcomed at the school or at Christ Church. Indeed, among all the Oxford potentates, Dean Gaisford had stood alone, if not in irreconcilable hostility to the Commissioners, certainly in contemptuous disregard of them. 'From the Dean of Christ Church,' says the report, 'alone of all the Heads of Colleges, no answer was received to any of the communications of the Commission.'

When Liddell was appointed Commissioner he deemed it an act of courtesy to write to Gaisford and acquaint him of the fact. The reply was somewhat chilling:

'MY DEAR SIR,

'Though you desire me to refrain from acknowledging your letter, I must write shortly to say that I can express no opinion as to the propriety of your accepting the office of Commissioner in the projected visitation of the University; but as to the Commission itself I feel, in common with almost every one both at Oxford and Cambridge, that it is a measure which can be productive of no good, and may eventually breed discord and disunion, and destroy the independence of those bodies.

'I am, yours faithfully,

'T. GAISFORD.'

The changes in the constitution of Christ Church, including the alteration in the tenure of the Westminster studentships, did not take effect till 1858. Indeed, owing to unexpected delay in the sealing of the Ordinance, the boys chosen from Westminster in that year were, to their surprise and delight, elected on the ancient footing, and were the very last to be inscribed on the venerable roll of 'Students of Christ Church,' as it had existed from the time of King Henry VIII.

The domestic life of the Headmaster, which had begun so brightly, was not without its sorrows and anxieties. The terrible fever of 1848 has been already mentioned. In 1853 came scarlet fever: two of his children suffered from it, and with his second son, a child nearly three years old, it proved fatal. He died on November 27. The trouble was the greater, because Mrs. Liddell was not allowed to share in the nursing of her child, or indeed to be near him. The doctors had insisted on her absence. So the burden of the trial fell on Liddell himself, and he shared by day and night the labours of the nurse.

'Nothing can be done,' he writes to his mother, 'but to support nature and trust in God. He has so far taken his food very well, and if he continues to do so we may continue to hope.'

Of his wife he says:

'She must not come near our dear angelic little child. I can call him by no other name—so good and patient and gentle he is. I am sitting by him now, while the nurse goes out to get a little air, and every quick-drawn breath goes to my heart. One does not know how one loves them, till a time like this comes.'

To H. H. Vaughan, he wrote later:

'My presentiments were too just. On Sunday the 27th, just a week after you saw me, my dear, dear little boy died. It was a miserable week, each day bringing many alternations of hope and fear. I buried him on Wednesday, and resumed my labours. But I was so worn out by watching and anxiety, added to my usual work, that I fell ill on Saturday; and, though I am much better to-day, they have said that I *must* leave town, and remain quiet for a few days at least. My wife is not allowed to return home. One of the other children has had the same direful disease, but (thank God) favourably. The other two are well.'

To Acland he wrote just afterwards from Tanhurst, a house on Leith Hill kindly lent by Mr. Justice Vaughan Williams, father of the present Lord Justice:—

'I cannot even yet believe that we shall never see again on earth his fair face with those gentle bright blue eyes and silken hair. A more healthy strong child never was. A more docile obedient child never was. I hardly can remember when it was necessary to speak a second time. His winning pretty ways are stamped in our memories, I believe, for ever. His thoughtful happy disposition made him the favourite wherever we went; and I verily believe the grief of my father and mother is hardly inferior to our own. You will pardon these babblings of fondness. But I watched him alone through that dreadful illness, and it relieves me to write so to those who can and will, I know, feel with me.'

Those who were then at the school will remember how the boys shared in their Headmaster's sorrow, and how touchingly he thanked them, when they spontaneously requested that the annual Play, for which all preparations had been made, should not take place.

The burden of responsibility, and the conviction of the impossibility of raising the school to a high level in numbers and prestige, so long as it remained in London, disposed him, in 1854, to seek some other sphere of work; and he was near to accepting the Mastership of Sherburn Hospital in the county of Durham. But happily no such retirement was necessary. On June 2, 1855, Dean Gaisford died, and there was scarcely a doubt that Liddell would be his successor. He first received definite news of the appointment in the following letter from his old pupil the present Earl of Wemyss, then Lord Elcho.

*June* 6, 1855.

'MY DEAR DEAN,

'I went to Lord Palmerston this morning, to urge your appointment. He told me that he had heard so much in your favour, that he had taken the Queen's pleasure about it the day before yesterday, but that his time had been so fully occupied yesterday, that he had not had time to write to you. Upon my asking him if *I* might announce this to you, he begged of me to do so, as it would save his writing to ask you to call upon him to-morrow morning at 11.30, at which hour he wishes to see you. He added, in his jocose manner, "you may tell him likewise, that I hope he will excuse my having named him to the Queen, without having previously obtained his consent." I can assure you that nothing could have given me greater pleasure than to be thus the means of communicating intelligence so pleasing to my old tutor and friend. I rejoice most sincerely at your appointment, as I feel confident that in your hands Christ Church will hold out every possible inducement to us to send our sons there, in the full confidence that you will turn them out *gentlemen* and useful members of society.

'Yours ever,

'ELCHO.'

Then came the hurry of the remaining weeks of the Summer Term, and at last the leave-taking. Those who were then boys at the school will recall the presentation in the big schoolroom of the silver vase which was their parting gift, and the addresses read by the captain of the Queen's Scholars and the head Town Boy—addresses which Liddell afterwards carefully docketed, and preserved to the end of his life among his most treasured papers— and then the supper at the Headmaster's house. There was genuine sorrow in saying Farewell: for the boys were very proud of their splendid Headmaster; and Mrs. Liddell had endeared herself in a thousand ways to the whole school, having taken a kindly interest in all their doings. The actors in the annual Play owed her a special debt of gratitude for the pains and taste which under the guidance of Sir Charles Newton she had expended upon the due arrangement of their classical dresses; and those of them who had acted female parts, for the lessons she had taught them as to their gait, restraining their stride within feminine limits, and teaching them the management of their arms. To many of those then present it was a parting for life, but some looked forward, in just confidence and with delightful anticipations, to a renewal of the friendship before long within the walls of Christ Church.

# CHAPTER V

### DEANERY OF CHRIST CHURCH, 1855-91

'I WISH I could convey to you the *cheer* which followed the announcement by Lord Palmerston of your appointment in the House. It said more than I can say, and would have gratified you, I am sure.' These words of a member of the House of Commons expressed a feeling very generally shared by all who were interested in the welfare of Oxford, and especially in the welfare of Christ Church. The distinguished career and European reputation of the new Dean, and the important services which he had lately rendered to the cause of University Reform, made his appointment not only obvious and proper, but also very widely acceptable. At Christ Church itself, however, there prevailed an old-fashioned conservatism, which had regarded with dislike and apprehension the changes recommended by the Commission, and which dreaded the experience of the rule of one who had been a prominent member of that body.

'The expectation of us all,' writes the Bishop of Gibraltar, 'but I cannot say the hopes, were fixed upon the able and distinguished Headmaster of

Westminster. Many of us at that time were strong conservatives as regards the affairs of Christ Church, and little wished to have one who was a liberal, and had been an influential member of the University Commission, to be our ruler. Moreover, he was personally unknown to all but the seniors.'

It speaks well for them and for him that he received a generous and courteous welcome from all the residents, and entered upon his new office amid every expression of cordial goodwill. The Sub-Dean, Archdeacon Clerke, kindly offered the use of his house while the Deanery was being prepared for its new occupants. The Chapter of that time comprised many distinguished men, but representing very different opinions, and various types of Churchmanship. The Sub-Dean had been chaplain to Bishop Bagot, and was a delightful example of the courteous, old-fashioned, tolerant Churchman, just touched by the Oxford Movement, but cautious in accepting its lead. He was now serving Bishop Wilberforce as faithfully as he had served his predecessor, but probably with some bewilderment of mind. Next to the Sub-Dean, though much his senior in years, came Dr. Barnes, then in venerable old age. He had been appointed to a studentship sixty-five years before, had filled the various college offices, had been a Canon since 1810, and during the great war had served, from 1796 to 1802, as Major of the University Volunteers. Dr. Pusey, the Regius Professor of Hebrew, had been Canon since 1828. He was at the height of his influence, and brought the weight of long experience and high academical position, in addition to his unique ecclesiastical authority, as a force to be reckoned with in all matters relating to reform at Christ Church. Dr. Bull, the Treasurer, enjoyed, in addition to his Christ Church preferment, another Canonry at Exeter, a Prebendal Stall at York, and the delightful Vicarage of Staverton, Northants, his usual summer residence [1]. He had been Tutor and Censor in bygone days, was a courtly gentleman, a refined scholar, and a shrewd man of business. Dr. Jelf, who had been Tutor to the King of Hanover, was Principal of King's College, and much occupied in his London duties. He was a kindly, reasonable, and friendly man. Dr. Jacobson was the Regius Professor of Divinity. His opinions were definitely

---

[1] Dr. Bull's preferments are summed up in a once well-known epigram:—

> 'In a coach with Will Whip, ere the use of the Rail,
> To Town I once travelled; and inside the Mail
> Sat a Canon of Exeter; on the same perch
> Sat a Canon of Oxford's Episcopal Church.
> Next came one who held (I own the thing's small)
> In the Minster of York a Prebendal Stall;
> And last came a Vicar all comely and fair,
> With a Vicarage snug and some hundreds a year.
> Now good reader you'll think that the coach was quite full—
> No, there was but one traveller, *Dr. John Bull*!'

An old Christ Church student may perhaps venture to express his dislike of the modern fashion of addressing members of our Chapter as 'Canon' so and so. A title of very indefinite and often of infinitesimal value thus takes the place of a specially honourable designation; for it has been customary for the University to confer the degree of D.D. upon Canons of Christ Church by Decree of Convocation. Dr. Pusey was *never* called 'Canon' Pusey.

liberal, and in favour of University Reform. Dr. Ogilvie, the Regius Professor of Pastoral Theology, had been chaplain to Archbishop Howley, and associated, in far distant times, as Tutor of Balliol, with the radical changes which created the greatness of that college. He was now quite without enthusiasm for reform, and inclined to resent all novelties. Dr. Heurtley, the junior member of the Chapter, was the Margaret Professor of Divinity, a gentle, holy man, of the old evangelical school, not without strong conservative convictions, but never unmindful of Christian charity.

It was a heterogeneous body: with none of its members, except Dr. Jacobson, was the new Dean likely to be in warm sympathy. Yet to the Dean and Chapter then belonged the whole government of Christ Church; the students had absolutely no power or authority. Though the Censors and Tutors were responsible for the discipline and the tuition of the undergraduates, they were without a voice in all questions relating to the property or the general administration of the House. The Dean and Chapter were the sole governors. As an illustration of the subordinate position then occupied by the students, it may be mentioned that the High Table on the dais in the Dining Hall, at which the Dean and Canons sat twice a year upon the annual 'Gaudy' days, was habitually occupied not by the Tutors, but by the undergraduate noblemen, or 'Tufts,' who ranked as Doctors, and thus sat daily above their preceptors at their common meal.

It was a strange survival from the sixteenth century, and was not likely to endure much longer. In relating the story of Dean Liddell's rule, it will be necessary to note briefly the inevitable changes by which the educational staff obtained their proper position in the government of their College.

The old pre-eminence of Christ Church in the Honours Schools had not been maintained in recent years, and the new Dean was likely to have an uphill task in once more establishing it. Dean Gaisford had not given much encouragement to competition by members of the House for academical distinctions, though he was a steady and strenuous supporter of all good work done by them within its walls; and his profound scholarship and untiring industry could not but make a deep impression on all the abler men who came under his influence. He had been in many respects a great ruler, strong in sturdy independence and simple straightforwardness; his authority was undisputed, and on the whole he had guided the fortunes of Christ Church with dignity and success. But kind as he was at heart, he was not distinguished for urbanity of demeanour:—an epigram used to contrast him with his contemporary, the courtly Warden of All Souls:

> Gaisford and Sneyd each other's lectures seek,
> The one learns manners, and the other Greek.

The story of his appointment to the Greek Chair illustrates this characteristic, and may be given in Liddell's words:

'In 1810, Gaisford had published an edition of

the Grammarian *Hephaestion*, which established his reputation as one of the chief Greek scholars of the day. In the next year, the Professorship of Greek became vacant by the promotion of William Jackson to the Bishopric of Oxford. The choice of his successor lay between Elmsley and Gaisford. Dean Jackson had retired from his high office to seclusion in the village of Felpham, near Chichester. But he was still consulted by Lord Grenville (the Chancellor) and other great men in London on all Oxford appointments. There could be no doubt as to which of the two distinguished scholars would have his recommendation. The old Dean did not hesitate to put Gaisford forward. He sent for his former pupil to Felpham, told him to get a copy of his *Hephaestion* bound in the best style, and to send it with a letter, which he dictated himself, to Lord Grenville. He obeyed, and in due course received from his Lordship the gratifying information that the Prince Regent had been pleased to place the Regius Professorship at his disposal. The story went that he replied—not this time from the dictation of Cyril Jackson :

"My Lord,—I have received yours, and accede to the proposal.      Yours,
                              " T. Gaisford."

'He held the office till his death in 1855, and justified his appointment by the various excellent editions of Greek authorities which he published. He never gave lectures.'

Dean Liddell adds :

'I had been recommended by Lord Palmerston to succeed Gaisford in the Deanery of Christ Church.

Who was to succeed to the Professorship? I remember that Charles Clifford of All Souls was deputed by the Prime Minister to consult me about it. "Won't you take it yourself," he asked, "and relieve us of all further trouble?" I declined the offer, partly because I knew there were better Greek scholars than myself in the University, partly because I thought it inexpedient that the Professorship should be attached to the Headship of a College. "Well then," Clifford said, "you must see Lord Palmerston, and tell him who you think ought to be appointed." Consequently I was summoned to an interview with Lord Palmerston, and mentioned several names— Scott, Newton, and Jowett. As to Scott, I said there was (in part) the same objection that I felt in my own case; he was Head of a College. Newton and Jowett were, I thought, both of them inferior to him in Greek Scholarship. But Newton had earned a high reputation in one department of Greek literature—in inscriptions—a department which had hitherto received scanty encouragement in Oxford, and I thought this gave him a strong claim. "Oh yes," said Lord Palmerston, "I know that man; ask him whether he will accept." I did so; but Newton was unable to relinquish his post at the British Museum for a Professorship which was at that time worth only £40 a year paid by Christ Church. In the end Jowett was appointed. As Professor, he devoted himself chiefly to the task of familiarizing English readers with the master works of Greek philosophy, or providing what Mark Pattison irreverently and wrongly called "cribs." His translations of Plato and Thucydides are masterly transfusions of Greek thought and language into

English. They may be read as if they had been originally written in the vernacular tongue.'

It is interesting to add that, in 1893, when the Greek Chair was again vacant, some correspondence with reference to Jowett's successor passed between Mr. Gladstone and Dr. Liddell, who was then, like Cyril Jackson in 1811, living in dignified retirement, in a quiet country home.

The first important question which the new Dean had to face was the reform of the constitution of Christ Church in accordance with the recommendations of the Royal Commission. The Commission had clearly pointed out the evil arising from the close system of nomination to studentships by the Dean and Canons, from the inadequate emoluments of the students, and from the absence of all participation by them in the government of the House and the management of its property.

'At Christ Church,' says the report, 'the students, those from Westminster excepted, are nominated by the Dean and Canons in turn, the Dean having two turns. It is true indeed that many of these dignitaries, especially the Dean, have taken pains to make creditable appointments; but it is notorious that studentships are often given as a matter of favour, and that the relations or friends of Canons are likely to be preferred.

'The Dean and Canons have only to surrender their patronage, and to invite the best scholars in England to compete for their studentships. . . . The studentships should be divided into two classes, corresponding to the fellowships and scholarships of Colleges. Means should be found to increase the value of the studentships, especially the senior studentships, in order to enable Christ Church to compete fairly with other Colleges. It is not unreasonable to expect that something should be done by the Chapter, whose own income is very large, if not while the present vested rights subsist, yet on the occurrence of vacancies.'

The Commissioners proceed to suggest the suppression, for this purpose, of the two canonries unconnected with professorships; the suspension of election to twenty studentships pending the settlement of the new Ordinance; and the reservation of a definite proportion of junior studentships for Westminster School.

The Ordinance of 1858, which effected the first change in the ancient foundation of King Henry VIII, was framed on these lines. The Dean and Canons were still to be the sole governing body, the sole administrators of the property; but in place of the large body of students appointed—except the Westminster men—by a system of private nomination, there were now created twenty-eight senior studentships and fifty-two junior studentships, twenty-one of the latter to be connected with Westminster School. All the rest, both senior and junior, were thrown open to public competition. The senior students would rank as fellows of Colleges—but without the real position and authority of fellows—the junior students, as scholars. The Canonries were reduced from eight to six. In order to ensure an effective and impartial electoral Board, the election of students, whether senior or junior, was placed in the hands of the Dean, six Canons, and the six senior members of the Educational Staff. Thus, for the first time, the students had equal powers with the Canons in this important matter; and the system of private nomination was abolished for ever. But the appointment of the College Officers (Censors and Readers) still rested with the Dean and Canons; and their authority, in all matters connected with the property of the College, was in no respect curtailed.

This change effected an important and most salutary reform. But it was naturally unpalatable, for various reasons, to many of the Canons. The proposals of the Commissioners were often and fully considered at Chapter meetings, but unanimity did not prevail. Towards the close of their discussions, Dr. Pusey saw the uselessness of offering further resistance.

'I shall not write to the Commissioners,' he told the Dean, 'a single voice will not be heard by unwilling ears. I have done what I could towards retaining the old Christ Church. *Fuit Ilium.* The Commissioners, with yourself and Dr. Jacobson, will be responsible for the new. I shall be very glad if the Commissioners' plan should work better than I hope of it. . . . The Act has deluded us with a show of power of negativing propositions which we think disadvantageous to the College. I shall not keep up an ineffectual struggle, though I must think that we have been treated ill.'

The Dean replied:

'With regard to the Ordinance, it is matter for difference of opinion. *Old* Christ Church is, so far as I can see, in a state of decay, and must (if not restored) fall into decrepitude. The measure proposed for restoring it may be good or bad. It can hardly reduce it lower than it is. Neither you nor I may see the success which I hope for. But I cheerfully accept the responsibility.'

That success, however, was only partial. The changes then effected were not destined to be final. It was not likely that this newly-created body of senior students, comprising the whole educational staff of the College, and recruited yearly by the election of able young men from other Colleges who had no traditional reverence for old Christ Church, would acquiesce in holding an anomalous position, immeasurably inferior to that of fellows elsewhere. It was inevitable that a movement should soon begin to alter the status of the students, and give them a recognized place in the administration of the corporate property. After much controversy, and many negotiations between the Chapter and the students, a body of Referees was appointed in February 1866, who were to decide all matters at issue. Archbishop Longley and Sir John T. Coleridge were named for this purpose by the Canons; Sir Roundell Palmer by the Dean; Sir William Page Wood and the Hon. Edward Twisleton by the students. Their recommendations were embodied in an Act of Parliament, 'The Christ Church

Oxford Act,' which was passed in 1867. By this Act the government of the Foundation, and the disposal and management of its possessions and revenues, were vested in the Dean, Canons, and Senior Students. Certain powers with respect to the Cathedral Church, its services and ministers, were reserved to the Dean and Chapter, and ample revenues were set apart for a Chapter Fund. The Act made careful provisions for the various complications resulting from the composite nature and divergent interests of the new Governing Body.

'The Dean,' writes the Bishop of Gibraltar, 'had a difficult part to play, as he was head of both the contending parties. That the revolution, for it was no less, created no discord or ill-feeling was due in a large measure to the impartial and conciliatory attitude which he took throughout.'

It was also due—it should be added—to the generous acceptance by the Chapter of their altered position.

So matters remained till 1877, when Oxford was again thrown into the crucible, and the Parliamentary Commission, of which Lord Selborne was chairman, made drastic changes in the character and tenure of College emoluments. Under statutes which became law in 1882, the names of 'senior' and 'junior' student were abolished; the latter became scholars; the former, under the ancient title of students, were divided into two classes, official and non-official, with different conditions of election and tenure.

U

Such, in brief outline, were the successive changes in the constitution of Christ Church which Dean Liddell witnessed, and for which he was largely responsible. He was not indeed on more than one Commission. He refused—though pressed—to serve on the executive Commission which followed upon the first, for the purpose of framing or approving the new Ordinances. This refusal was chiefly based on the ground that it would be undesirable for the new Dean, just entering on his office, to be hampered by duties which would have a distinctly party character, and would necessarily involve much unpleasant controversy.

'The more I think of it' (he writes to Vaughan) 'the more unwilling I am to begin my reign at Oxford conjointly with an office of Commissioner. Is no one else to be found?'

In 1876 he was again invited to serve on the Commission which Mr. Disraeli's Government proposed to issue, and to allow his name to appear in the Bill which was to be introduced at the beginning of the session of 1877. He was then in quite an altered position in the University. He had but lately served for four years as Vice-Chancellor, and had won the respect and confidence of all parties, and his acceptance of office would, as he was assured by Lord Salisbury, 'singularly add to the strength of the Commission and the value of its work.' Lord Salisbury's invitation was privately backed by influential members of his party.

'I am sure,' wrote Sir John Mowbray, 'your acceptance of the post will inspire confidence in every quarter, Conservative and Liberal.' But after much consideration the Dean declined the offer; mainly, it is believed, on the ground that his acceptance would deprive the Commission of the services of a distinguished Oxford man who had more leisure than himself for the task, and who would, in the Dean's judgment, be of more use as a Commissioner. No doubt he was also influenced by his unwillingness to embark once more, at the age of 66, on the strife and vexation connected with University reforms, of which he had already had his full share.

Dean Liddell's name will be for long associated with the buildings of Christ Church. On becoming Dean he was for the first time in his life able to indulge his artistic tastes on an adequate scale, and without the restrictions which had hampered him at Westminster. First, of necessity, came his new home, the Deanery. It needed many alterations. To his refined taste are due the panelling and decorations of drawing-room and hall, the opening out of the long gallery on the first floor as an additional reception-room, and the construction of the stately staircase, called the 'Lexicon' staircase, because its cost was defrayed from the profits on that book. Much delay took place before the Deanery was fit for occupation; a fire at Baker's factory in Lambeth destroyed all the new woodwork just as it was on the point of completion. However, early in 1856 the work was almost finished. On February 12, he wrote to his mother:

'As I sit in this now very beautiful house, and admire all that has been done, I feel sensible how worthless it all would be, if we had not kind parents and kinsfolk and friends to join us in admiration; and so it is with birthdays and all that brings joy in this life. . . . Painters and paperers still linger, but we are now very nearly done, and hope to throw open our doors for an evening musical party next week. They are intending to get up the 'Macbeth' music, with choruses, some glees, and other music, by the help of some of the young men and some ladies, if they are not too prudish to join. The gallery will be a good place for sound, forty-four feet long, opening by a wide archway upon the stairs, so that a great number may be present—not to mention the drawing-room. I wish you, like my father, had seen the house before it was done, in order that you might appreciate what has been done. We have spent all my father's magnificent present upon the sideboard, which I hope he will soon come to admire. It is really, I think, or rather will be (for it is not finished), *most* beautiful. I have not yet got anything with your present for my library, for that room at present remains untouched.'

About a fortnight later he adds:

'The house is all but finished, and now nothing remains but the pleasant task of showing it to our friends and—paying the bills. We begin with two musical evenings on Thursday and Saturday next, without any dinner parties. All the College will be asked on the two nights, and all whom we know among Heads of Houses, &c., are asked. We very much wish you could all be here. *You* could sit and hear it all quietly in your own bed-room, if you

CHRIST CHURCH CATHEDRAL IN 1813.

*To face page* 148.

did not feel equal to venturing into such a crowd; for what will, I hope, be your bed-room opens into the gallery where the music will be performed. So, about 8 o'clock on Thursday evening, think of Madam making her first curtsey at the head of her own stairs in Oxford. This is a strange place for rumours. It has been reported that Mrs. Liddell is getting up private theatricals, and that Dr. C—— permits his daughter to personate one of the witches, while the Dean is expected to represent Macbeth!'

Next came the work on the Cathedral; a re-arrangement of the interior urgently needed, but not intended to be final. Not till seventeen years later was an adequate restoration of the building attempted. But the over-crowding of the congregation, who were confined within the restricted space of the choir itself, led to much irreverence; and some alterations were imperatively necessary. Old Christ Church men will remember the daily scene in Chapel in those ancient days; the choir cut off from the body of the Church by the heavy organ-screen; and within its narrow limits the mob of undergraduates seated on rows of benches which faced westward, and crowded up against the altar rails; the high barrier of stalls concealing the view of the choir aisles[1]; the 'Prick bills' walking up

[1] Keys, the Dean's Verger, was stationed at the entrance to the choir, and kept a stout dog-whip with which to belabour any dogs which—as not unfrequently happened— followed their masters into Chapel. Keys lived in the south transept, and his beer store was in a cupboard just below the pew, on the north side of the choir, in which the Deanery ladies sat. Dog-whip and beer were both summarily ejected by Dean Liddell, to the old verger's great annoyance.

and down, pricking in the men on to their lists as
they managed to identify them; the singing men and
boys, on 'Surplice' prayer-days, bracketed out aloft
under the shadow of the Norman arches, the men
on one side, the boys on the other; the slovenly
undevotional service, whether English Prayers on
Sundays and Holy Days, or Latin Prayers on other
occasions, when the sonorous tones of Dean Gaisford
overpowered the responses of all other worshippers.
Mr. Ruskin indeed has idealized the scene in his
'Praeterita,' and his description does justice to his
fine imagination, and deserves to be quoted:

'In this choir, written so closely and consecutively
with indisputable British History, met every morning
a congregation representing the best of what Britain
had become, orderly, as the crew of a man-of-war,
in the goodly ship of their temple. Every man in
his place, according to his rank, age, and learning;
every man of sense or heart there recognizing that
he was either fulfilling, or being prepared to fulfil,
the gravest duties required of Englishmen. A well-
educated foreigner, admitted to that morning service,
might have learnt and judged more quickly and
justly what the country had been, and still had
power to be, than by months of stay in court or
city. There, in his stall, sat the greatest divine of
England—under his commandant niche, her greatest
scholar—amongst the tutors the present Dean Liddell, and a man of curious intellectual power and
simple virtue, Osborne Gordon. The group of
noblemen gave, in the Marquis of Kildare, Earl
of Desart, Lord Emlyn, and Francis Charteris, now

Lord Wemyss, the brightest types of high race and active power; Henry Acland and Charles Newton among the senior undergraduates, and I among the freshmen, showed, if one had known it, elements of curious possibilities in coming days. None of us then conscious of any need or chance of change, least of all the stern Captain, who, with rounded brow and glittering dark eye, led, in his old thunderous Latin, the responses of the morning prayer.'

Nevertheless, it was high time that a change should be made. The arrangement of the interior, as it then was, dated from the reign of Charles I, when Brian Duppa was Dean, and the seventeenth-century woodwork was of interesting design and worthy of preservation. It was as far as possible kept. But the organ-screen was removed, and the organ placed on the floor of the south transept. The stalls of the Dean and Canons were shifted to a position westward of the third bay of the nave, so that almost the whole length of the church, as it then existed, was made use of for service. The seats were all re-arranged, and the lofty barriers at the sides of the choir removed; the choir itself was assigned to the bulk of the undergraduates, the Censors sitting among them; the Tutors and other graduates, as well as the noblemen and gentlemen commoners, sat westward of the transepts; and under the central tower were placed the choristers. The pulpit occupied almost its present position, and the Vice-Chancellor's throne (now relegated to the Latin Chapel) was placed opposite to it. The sounding-board of the pulpit added dignity to the episcopal throne, placed below the altar-steps on the south side. It is stated that the whole of this reconstruction was contrived out of the old woodwork, none of it being removed from the church, and no new materials introduced. The effect as a whole was good, and the services were vastly improved. More care was taken in selecting chaplains capable of intoning their part, and the choristers were diligently trained by Dr. Corfe, the organist. The church was no longer a by-word.

Dr. Corfe was at this time sorely plagued by one of the choirmen, whose 'alto' singing was miserably bad. He came to the Dean. 'Mr. Dean, I really cannot have that man singing any longer: he spoils the whole choir. If only he sang "bass," it would not so much matter; but such an "alto" is intolerable.' 'Very well, Dr. Corfe,' said the Dean, 'I will deal with the matter.' So the choirman was sent for. 'Dr. Corfe complains of your singing, and says he cannot have you sing "alto" any longer; but that it would not be so bad if you sang "bass." For the future, therefore, be good enough to sing "bass".' 'But, Mr. Dean,' rejoined the man, 'I cannot sing "bass".' 'Well,' answered Liddell, 'I am no musician; but sing "bass" you must. Good morning.' And for many a year afterwards, as can be but too well remembered, the man sang 'bass,' till he was finally shelved.

On ordinary week-days, Latin Prayers were always said at the College services. They were not abolished till the end of 1861, when the present Bishop of Gibraltar and Dean of Durham were Censors. It was supposed that the substitution of English for Latin would encourage devotion, but it is doubtful how far this has been the case; and certainly there was a loss in the abandonment of the time-honoured book in its dingy brown binding, with its long S's that led the unwary astray (one Chaplain always read 'sumas' as 'fumas' in the Litany), and its quaint rendering of the Psalms, some verses of which must always linger in the memory. Who, that ever heard them, does not remember the Dean and Censors repeating with stentorian voice that mysterious verse:

'Similisque factus sum onocrotalo gaudenti solitudine, ac buboni agenti in locis desertis;'

or the *in saecula saeculorum, Amen*, rolled out in tones which made them sink into Lord Dufferin's memory, to be used, some years afterwards, as the most fitting ending for his famous Latin speech in Iceland [1]?

On Sundays and Holy Days there were Surplice Prayers; the Holy Communion was celebrated once a month after the Choral Matins: its proper place, no doubt, but involving a service of nearly two hours' length before breakfast. College sermons were not known; but when the Dean or a Canon preached in his turn before the University, the sermon always took place at Christ Church and not at St. Mary's. This ancient privilege has been surrendered since

[1] See *Letters from High Latitudes*, ch. vi. p. 68.

1869, as a necessary result of the introduction of ten o'clock service with sermon, for the members of the House and for the general public. It was a privilege for which Dean John Fell contended fiercely in 1673, and it was then ordered, after reference to the King and Council, 'that from henceforth every Canon of Christ Church should (*quatenus* a member of the University) preach at St. Mary's, and (*quatenus* Canon) at Christ Church.'

This rearrangement of the church was carried out under the Dean's close supervision, with the assistance of an architect, Mr. Billing. It was a thoroughly congenial task, and he was constantly engaged in it, superintending every detail. Even in the middle of August he was found in Oxford, having travelled up specially from Bamborough Castle to see that all was going right.

'I spent the greater part of yesterday morning' (he writes on August 17, 1856), 'in the church, going through all small details, so as to prevent, if possible, the necessity of my return. But it is very fortunate that I came. There would have been several enormous blunders. When work is going on, one ought always to be on the spot. The whole really will look very well. But I wish you could have seen it when it was quite clear and open. They have begun fixing the seats now.'

The work was pressed on, so as to be finished before the re-assembling of the College in October; but the Dean was not allowed to witness its completion. On September 30 came the beginning of

CHRIST CHURCH CATHEDRAL, 1856-1870.

*To face page* 154.

the serious illness which kept him away from Oxford for many months. He had been visiting an estate in Leicestershire, and on that day writes to his wife:

'I renewed my cold by my Market Harborough trip, and Acland says I had better stay in bed. It is very tiresome, as I had fully calculated upon being up to welcome you. Nor have I been able to superintend the finishing of the church, as I desired.'

These improvements in the interior of the Cathedral were intended to be of quite a temporary character. They had not been costly, had been hastily completed, and left very much to be done when a favourable opportunity should arise. That opportunity was not found until the new Governing Body had been created under the Ordinance of 1867. It was of happy omen for the future relations between the Chapter and the students, that a cordial acceptance was given to a proposal made by the senior resident student, the Rev. T. Chamberlain, for the appointment of a Committee to confer with the Chapter on the question of the restoration of the Cathedral. This resolution was passed in March 1868. There were difficulties to be faced at first; but a year afterwards matters had so far advanced that Mr. G. Gilbert Scott was asked to prepare plans and estimates. An appeal for funds was next made to the general body of Christ Church men. The Governing Body subscribed £1,000 from their corporate funds; the Chapter, a like sum from the Chapter Fund; the Dean promised a private subscription of £500; and the other residents gave according to their means or inclinations. In the summer of 1870 the first contract with the builders was signed, and two years later the work was practically completed, at a cost of more than £17,000.

Those who were privileged to serve on the 'Restoration' Committee under the presidency of the Dean will gratefully acknowledge the debt due to his untiring attention to every detail of the work, and to his exquisite artistic taste and well-balanced judgment.

It was not indeed so much a 'Restoration' as an 'adaptation' of the church to its twofold purposes, to serve as the Cathedral Church of the Diocese, and the College Chapel. Before Dean Liddell's time, the first of these two objects had been for long almost unrecognized. There was an episcopal throne indeed, which was occasionally occupied, and there were Canons' Prayers on week-days, scantily attended. But the requirements of the College had always been first considered. The Cathedral Church was within the College gates, and was therefore only accessible at the pleasure of its Head. The Dean, moreover, claimed to be his own Ordinary, and the Bishops had met with scant courtesy from former Deans. Even in Dean Liddell's earlier years, the Bishop, on his rare visits, would slink into his seat from the side aisle as though he were almost an interloper. But after some years of diligent care in the improvement of the services, the Cathedral, made more convenient for a mixed congregation by the reconstruction of the interior in 1856, had become well attended by the general public, and there were larger demands upon its space at the Sunday services. The work undertaken in 1870 brought the church, in all essential points, into its present condition. The interior of the fabric was thoroughly cleaned, the whitewash brushed off, and the original surface exposed. The quaint seventeenth-century screens, which shut off the chapels north of the choir from the north transept, were removed. They were of unusual design, shaped as inverted arches, so as to form, with the Norman arches above them, complete circles with solid masonry, only partly pierced, below. The plain two-light windows which Brian Duppa had inserted throughout the church, and had filled with Van Ling's glass, were removed, and somewhat commonplace Perpendicular windows took their place. One only of these curious windows remains. It was spared in compliance with a general request of members of the House, and may be seen at the west end of the north aisle of the nave. It represents Jonah under the gourd, and the city of Nineveh in the distance. The east window, then of Decorated tracery, and filled with gaudy French glass recently given in commemoration of the tercentenary of the foundation of the College, made way for a charming reconstruction of the eastern end in accordance with indications of earlier work discovered by the architect. Portions of the French glass may still be seen distributed among the clerestory lights of the south transept. This transept, one bay of which had long been desecrated by its use as a Verger's house, was now brought wholly into the church; and a curious chamber, which extended over the slype, was carefully rebuilt in accordance with traces found *in situ*. A light screen of open iron-work, wrought by Skidmore of Coventry, was carried round the nave and choir, so as to mark off the central portion of the church for Collegiate use without excluding the general congregation from full enjoyment of the service. At the west end of the nave an additional bay was built, replacing one of the three destroyed by Wolsey; it was intended that it should be called Dr. Dowdeswell's bay, the cost being defrayed by a sum of money bequeathed some years before by that member of the Chapter. And when, before the restoration was completed, the Canon's house which separated the Cathedral from the Great Quadrangle became vacant, an approach to the church was made from the terrace through a double archway. This was completed in 1872, and now forms the chief entrance. The central tower arcade was also opened to view; its Norman arches had been long hidden by the floor of the ringing chamber. But the bells were now removed altogether from the church, and a new belfry was constructed for them above the Hall staircase. There they were placed in a plain wooden case, irreverently called the

CHRIST CHURCH CATHEDRAL AFTER RESTORATION.

'Tea-chest,' which was some years afterwards hidden from view by the construction, from the designs of Mr. Bodley, of the stunted tower with four corner turrets, which rises at the south-east corner of the Great Quadrangle. It was Mr. Bodley's wish to surmount this lower tower by a lofty campanile of wood and copper; it is hoped that this design may yet be carried out.

It remained to furnish the interior in a manner worthy of the building. The stalls and seats in the central portion were made of dark Italian walnut from Mr. Scott's designs. The floor of the choir was laid with rich marbles, surrounding designs in Maltese inlaid work. The Bishop's throne, a Diocesan memorial of Bishop Wilberforce, was also designed by Scott. Gradually other enrichments were added by various donors; the place grew in beauty year by year. The altar frontal, and the richly-bound Bible of 1674, were the gifts of Dean Liddell's three eldest daughters.

The Cathedral was indeed an object of his unceasing care, and is a worthy monument of his taste. And he desired to throw the building open as widely as possible to the public, and to have the services conducted with care and reverence. Although with no liking for any of the extreme developments in doctrine or ritual which were becoming so common, Dean Liddell was in hearty sympathy with every attempt made to meet the demand for more frequent and more reverent services. A weekly celebration of Holy Communion was introduced in 1865; to this was subsequently added a celebration on Thursday mornings. Diocesan gatherings of various kinds were encouraged during the vacations, when the church was not needed for College purposes. Bach's Passion music was rendered for the first time on March 20, 1873, by the three choirs of Christ Church, Magdalen College, and the Chapel Royal, Windsor. Later in the same year Bach's Christmas music was rendered there, and the Church has again and again been used for such special services. If, a few years before Dean Liddell's time, a writer in the *Ecclesiologist* could describe the service at Christ Church as 'the most slovenly and irreverent that we have ever witnessed in any English Cathedral,' it may now claim to rank among the most beautiful, even in a University which boasts of New College and Magdalen Chapels.

Another important architectural work is associated with the earlier years of Dean Liddell's rule. For some time past the Chapter had been accumulating funds for rebuilding an ancient part of the College, and, in a communication to Lord Palmerston in 1854, they expressed a hope that the undertaking would soon be begun. Many Christ Church men will remember the Chaplains' Quadrangle, the scene of innumerable bonfires, formed by the Old Library (the monastic refectory) on the north, Wolsey's kitchen on the west, the cloister and passage to the meadow on the east, and on the south a low range of venerable buildings where the Chaplains and Auditor had rooms. A narrow archway led

THE GREAT QUADRANGLE, CHRIST CHURCH.
*From a Drawing made in 1850.*

eastward from the cloister to a somewhat mean block of buildings erected after the fire of 1669 by Dean John Fell, which fronted the Broad Walk. It was now resolved to pull down Fell's Buildings and the south side of the Chaplains' Quadrangle; and in their stead was erected the long range of Meadow Buildings, from the designs of Mr. Deane of Dublin, whose firm, then Deane and Woodward, had been the architects of the University Museum. The style is Rhenish Gothic, and the exterior elevation still perhaps invites criticism; but the interior arrangements are excellent, and rooms have been provided for a large addition to the numbers of the College. The work was completed in 1865, some of the rooms having been occupied in the previous year.

The Great Quadrangle in its turn required to be dealt with. No material alteration in its architecture had been made since the time of its completion under Dean John Fell, when the whole of the north side was built. At the same time Wolsey's work had been curiously transformed by the addition of an Italian balustrade running round the whole range of buildings, including even the Hall; and the earth excavated from the centre of the Quadrangle had been piled up to raise the broad terrace, so that the bases of the shafts which were to support the vaulting of Wolsey's projected cloister were hidden below the level of the terrace walk. There had apparently been no uniformity of surface in the area of the Quadrangle before Fell's time; the whole place was till then unfinished; and a staple with ring for fastening horses was to be seen near the Deanery door as late as 1870, thus indicating that it could be reached on horseback in olden days. In 1842 the terrace had been very handsomely faced with grey Cornish granite. Now—under Dean Liddell—the crumbling surface of the soft Oolite stone of which the Quadrangle was built, long disintegrated by rain and frost, was renewed with a harder stone from the Taynton quarries wherever necessary. The shafts designed to carry the vaulting of the cloister received—with perhaps an almost over-conscientious reproduction of Wolsey's unfinished project—the slightly curved stones to show the intended springing of the vaulting; the arches, which had been smoothed to the wall face, were renewed round the Quadrangle, and even introduced on the north side, where they had never existed before, and the terrace was lowered about fifteen inches to disclose the bases of the shafts. This change in the level of the terrace revealed the foundation of the external buttresses of the cloister. It was decided, but not without much hesitation, to leave them exposed. The balustrade, some parts of which had lately fallen in a storm, was removed, and battlements took its place. Beneath them was carved a line of shields, illustrative of the long history of the House. The Hall received its pinnacles, and its splendid proportions were disclosed by the removal of the masking wall which connected it at its eastern end with the corner tower. Over

Kill-Canon a small tower, originally intended by Fell for astronomical purposes, but never carried up beyond the line of the balustrade, was now completed.

There remained the Chapter House, and the mutilated cloister, of which Wolsey had ruthlessly destroyed the western side, to be restored as far as possible to their original beauty. The cloister garth was cleared of a mass of earth which had accumulated there during three hundred years. The removal of the soil not only enabled the proportions of the cloister itself to be appreciated, but also exposed to view some puzzling foundations of conventual buildings, possibly of the lavatory. The northern side of the cloister had long been used as a muniment room, for which purpose it was quite unfit, as Anthony à Wood complained two centuries before. All documents were now removed; the tracery of the windows was renewed throughout the cloisters to its original Perpendicular character; the *lierne* vaulting of the roofs was restored; and over the doorway of the Chapter House—a most interesting remnant of an earlier building—the bold experiment of a loftier vaulting in oak was successfully accomplished. The Chapter House—an exquisite specimen of early English architecture—had been strangely disfigured in the seventeenth century. A party wall had been built across it, dividing it into two nearly equal portions, and the flooring of the inner part, which was used for Chapter business and hospitable dinners, had been raised within a few feet of the bases of the shafts of the tracery which clothed the walls and the graceful eastern window with its five pointed lights. Beneath this floor a cellar had been formed, where the Chapter wine was stored. All these monstrous obstructions were now swept away, and the noble proportions of the room were once more shown.

Such were the principal architectural works associated with Dean Liddell's epoch. It is a matter of regret that the Meadow Buildings were not called by his name: but his statue—the gift of Sir John Mowbray and Mr. Vere Bayne—stands above the Kill-Canon archway, on its northern side. On the south side of the same archway is a modern statue of his great predecessor, John Fell. It was the gift of Liddell, as his initials indicate [1]; and it takes the place of the earlier statue of the same famous Dean, familiar to many generations of Christ Church men, and often subject to indignities at their hands, which now rests in quiet seclusion in the garden of Nuneham Park, bearing the following inscription from Liddell's pen, recounting its chequered history:

'Effigies quam aspicis viri optimi qui cur homuncionibus quibusdam displiceret ipsi nesciebant in Aede Christi minio semel atque iterum illita hoc in recessu requiem obtinuit A. D. 1887.'

Certainly to no other Dean than Fell did Christ Church owe so large a debt, in the reconstruction

---

[1] The inscription is:
JOHANNI FELL
H. G. L.
DECANO DECANUS
MDCCCLXXVII.

THE GREAT QUADRANGLE AFTER RESTORATION.

*To face page 164.*

and dutiful preservation of its buildings, as it has owed to Liddell. And as Fell planted the Broad Walk with its double line of seventy-two elm trees, so to Liddell is due the new avenue which leads from the gate of the Meadow Buildings to the river, superseding the narrow, damp, and unsavoury path which skirted the west side of the meadow by the Trill Mill stream [1].

[1] This walk was formally opened in 1872 by Princess Louise. The crews of the Eights assembled in the Deanery Garden, and walked in procession from the Meadow gate to the Barges, carrying the flags of their respective colleges.

# CHAPTER VI

DEANERY OF CHRIST CHURCH (*continued*)

MUCH more is needed for a successful ruler of an ancient, learned, and numerous society than artistic taste and high intellectual gifts. The Dean of Christ Church has to maintain the efficiency of a Cathedral establishment and of a great collegiate foundation. He has to gather round him, and guide with constitutional, but not arbitrary authority, a body of students comprising brilliant representatives of every department of academical study; and over a very large number of undergraduates he has to preside as the upholder of discipline, the encourager of industry, and the rewarder of merit. Firmness, tact, discernment, consideration, courtesy, are all necessary elements of success in so prominent a position; they largely create that authority without which chaos is likely to prevail, and that confidence which alone makes authority welcome. But confidence is proverbially a plant of slow growth; and a Headmastership has rarely, in Oxford experience, been found a good training for the Headship of a College. It was only by degrees that Dean Liddell, who never lacked authority, gained the full confidence of every member of his House; it was only by degrees that respect changed into regard, and regard ripened into affection.

There were difficulties at first. The unfortunate selection by the new Dean of a Tutor who did not understand how to deal with undergraduates made discipline for a time an arduous task. His own enforced absence for two consecutive winters in the island of Madeira was a serious interruption to his work, and kept him almost a stranger to many whom he desired to know. Fortunately his place, during the winters of 1856–7 and 1857–8, was well filled by the Sub-Dean, Archdeacon Clerke, who was deservedly popular, and held the reins of government with steady hands, ably supported by the Censors. A letter written by him to the Dean in February 1858 will remind old Christ Church men of an incident of not unfrequent occurrence in former days, and will bring to their memory one whose name has been happily associated with the fortunes of the House since 1842, and who still, as senior Student of the Foundation, occupies a warm place in the affections of present and former members of Christ Church.

'Our winter is now passing away. We are having a most mild one altogether; but have had enough snow to set the *boys* here at work one night at the old amusement of blocking up Kill-Canon. They are inclined to be more noisy than they were last Term, but I have not much to complain of. Our new noblemen seem to be a well-conducted set, and I hope we may improve, not spoil them. I am bound to speak well of Prout as Censor[1]. He shows firmness, and knows how to manage men, and they seem to respect him.'

From time to time—as happens in every College —troubles and anxieties with regard to discipline would arise; the most serious in Liddell's time was as far back as 1870; but the absolute calmness and impartiality of the Dean made such disorder comparatively easy to deal with. The Bishop of Gibraltar, who was Censor from 1861 to the end of 1869, describes his experience of such incidents:

'After I had become Censor, and for the eight following years, I was brought into constant and intimate relations with the Dean. The discipline of the House rests with him and the Censors. The two Censors divided the Term between them, the Senior Censor being responsible for the first, the Junior for the second half. It was the custom for

---

[1] Mr. Prout was Junior Censor, having been unexpectedly called upon to take the office on Mr. Lloyd's retirement. The Senior Censor at this time was the brilliant scholar and quaint humorist Osborne Gordon, a man of singular power and wide popularity. He had been in office for several years under Gaisford, and was not perhaps quite in sympathy with Liddell's views, though he always loyally supported his chief. He left Christ Church in 1861, having accepted the College living of Easthampstead.

It may be interesting to add a complete list of the Censors during Liddell's time as Dean. O. Gordon, till 1861; G. Marshall, till 1858; C. Lloyd, 1858; T. J. Prout, 1858-61; C. W. Sandford, 1861-9; G. W. Kitchin, 1861-3; T. V. Bayne, 1863-77; H. L. Thompson, 1870-77; H. Salwey, 1877-82; E. F. Sampson, 1877-94; H. S. Holland, 1882-4; R. E. Baynes, 1884-7; W. Warner, 1887-92.

the Censor in office to call upon the Dean every morning before ten o'clock, when lectures began, and to confer with him on any matter affecting the discipline, studies, or other interests of the undergraduates. On looking back on those interviews, I see the Dean standing at his desk, busily engaged with his great Lexicon. What struck me most in him on these occasions was his perfect self-control, and his inflexible justice. Once or twice I had to report serious breaches of discipline. Trying, disappointing, and disheartening as those outbreaks of lawlessness were, the Dean was always calm, never made an error of judgment, was never provoked into a harsh act, or even into a harsh word.'

*Harsh*, perhaps, never; but *stern* words often, at least in his earlier days. Many men who were undergraduates during his long reign would, if asked their impression, recall this special characteristic, that he was stern. It was not that he was naturally severe; we know that he was gentle and tender-hearted; but he was shy and reserved; there were traditions of the Decanal office not associated with suavity of demeanour; he was the official mouthpiece when fault had to be found; and he was always sparing of praise. The result was that the more industrious members of the College sometimes felt that they scarcely received their due meed of commendation and encouragement, while the less deserving experienced justice at his hands, untempered by leniency. 'Collections' at the end of Term brought an ordeal not pleasant to be faced by the indolent or the unruly. The green baize covered table; the row of Tutors who knew each victim's failings, and had often told him of them; the Dean seated at the north end of the table, with the terminal report before him;—and then the examination badly done; the fatal record of lectures unattended, or other and graver misdeeds; at last the plain unvarnished words of rebuke which fell from the Dean's lips: this was no agreeable experience, and left no happy memory behind. And with many an undergraduate, this was almost all he knew of the Dean, this terrible review in Collections three times a year. Men did not understand that beneath that cold and imperturbable presence there lay hid sympathy and tenderness which would have gladly found expression under different circumstances. Sometimes the Censors had the painful duty of bringing young men before the Dean at his own house for severe punishment or serious warning. The same impression was left on the culprits after their alarming interview. On one occasion an awkward mistake occurred. There were two brothers of the name of L——, one of whom was a model of propriety, the other somewhat of a scapegrace. The latter was one morning to be brought before the Dean by the Censors. They had instructed the Dean as to the nature of the offence, and the character of the rebuke to be administered. The door opened, and an undergraduate appeared, to whom the Dean spoke at once, not mincing his words. But, on looking round, the Censor to his dismay perceived that the wrong Mr. L—— had by some mischance answered the summons to attend: the good and not the bad brother was in the room. As soon as possible he intervened: 'I think, Mr. Dean, a mistake has been made; this is not the gentleman we wished to bring before you, but his brother.' 'Oh,' said the Dean, as he put up his eyeglass, and spoke in his coldest tones, 'the Censors have always spoken well of *you*. Be good enough to pass on to your brother what I have said to you. You may go.' And out the man went, but not in an amiable mood. On another occasion a junior student who had gained high University distinctions, and was of absolutely blameless character, called upon the Dean to enter his name as a candidate for the crowning reward of a successful career—a senior studentship. As he entered the study the Dean, without at first completely turning from his desk, addressed the astonished undergraduate with marked severity: 'We're not going to have this sort of thing . . . and a student too; it makes it worse!' Then he looked round, and seeing who his visitor was, he bluntly added, 'Oh! they've sent the wrong man. Pray be seated, Mr. Paget.' For the person so assailed was no other than the future Dean, who thus learnt a lesson which has perhaps been of use to him in later years.

A less strong, less dignified, less majestic figure would have suffered from this sternness of demeanour; but Liddell's straightforward simplicity and aristocratic bearing atoned for much, and, especially in his later years, he was universally venerated, while his manner became gentler, and his whole attitude towards undergraduates grew to be more fatherly, sympathetic, and genial. And when some young man who had gone through the experience of undergraduate days at Christ Church was exalted to the position of Tutor, he came to appreciate much that he had not known before, and to regard the Dean with profound and affectionate respect. He discovered that his chief always made the most generous allowance for errors of judgment and immaturity of knowledge in the young Tutor; that he gave to him the utmost encouragement and the wisest guidance; and that he always supported the authority, even if privately he could not always commend the discretion, of every member of the educational staff. And so as the years passed, and Censors and Tutors came and went, there was one judgment which never faltered, one experience which extended over many generations; a pillar of strength on which all came to rely with implicit confidence and grateful unanimity.

In 1868 an occurrence of an unusual kind led to some perplexity. A Roman ecclesiastic, who afterwards obtained an undesirable notoriety, spent some time in Oxford, and was in the habit of frequenting undergraduates' rooms at Christ Church, and trying to unsettle their minds. Dr. Pusey was much concerned at this, and wrote more than once to the Dean on the subject. His letters, even at this distance of time, have an interest of their own. In June 1868 he wrote:

'I understand that a very clever Roman controversialist, Father —— of Pau, who has taken Mr. Comberbatch's duty at the Roman Catholic church for a time, is visiting a good deal with our undergraduates and talking controversy with them; not particularly with such as think and believe as I do, for we might counteract his influence, but with others who understand less the ground upon which they stand. I fear that the effect of these visits will (as I have said with regard to Dr. Newman) be to produce unsettlement among our undergraduates, who are no match for a clever controversialist. Possibly you have heard this before. But if any persons leave the Church of England for Rome, my friends and I are the persons blamed; whereas I suppose the intercourse with a controversialist who unsettles minds which have probably thought very little seriously on any subject, is probably the result of his friendship with the Roman Catholic undergraduates.

'Of course, I do not look for any answer. I hope that, the Long Vacation being so near, what I fear may not be. But Father —— has been very successful among the English residents at Pau, and has, I understand, drawn away a good many. I understand that he has all the tact of a man of the world, and can adapt himself admirably to different minds. He seems to be especially addressing himself to this House, where the young men invite him to their rooms. You alone know whether anything can be done, except in the way of helping any who get perplexed and come to one.'

The Dean answered this letter, and heard again from Dr. Pusey:

'I had heard that Father —— was introduced not by the Roman Catholics but by an undergraduate who as yet calls himself a Presbyterian, and is, I suppose, a Roman Catholic in all but the declaration, which he promised not to make till of age. I did not mean to throw any blame; only, if you did not happen to have heard it, to mention it, because I knew that the blame would come on me and my friends, and, if possible, that it might be prevented. I have had too sad experience in those cases for twenty-three years not to know what occasions them. I do not think that I have ever taught anything about the necessity of belonging to the Church, having been always happy about good Dissenters, who were acting according to their consciences, as belonging to the soul, though not to the body, of the Church.'

In a later letter he adds, more generally:

'I trust that it is not so grave a matter as was stated at first, but something passing.

'Evil, in this imperfect world, lies close to all good. I do not decry genuine free inquiry, because some abuse it to scepticism; or progress, because some understand by it casting aside truth; so neither is reverence for authority an evil, because some follow authority which God never gave them. Nor can I be responsible for those whom people please to call by my name, whereas they themselves say, that we, the old Tractarians, were well enough for our day, but they have got beyond us. I learned what I learned from my mother; the Catechism, the Holy

Scriptures, our Divines, the Fathers, to whom we were directed. If people, like *some* of the young clergy, take Rome for their model, I am not surprised when they go there.'

The Dean adopted the simple expedient of instructing the porters not to allow Father —— to enter Christ Church; and his stay in Oxford soon afterwards came to an end.

Throughout the Dean's long reign, the number of undergraduates was well kept up. In 1855 there were about 200 of them on the books; in 1891, about 280. The rooms were almost always full; and though some old Christ Church families transferred their allegiance to other Colleges, the bulk of them remained faithful. One great change, which the first University Commission had strongly recommended, the Dean witnessed and approved: the abolition of the distinction between Noblemen, Gentlemen Commoners, and Commoners. Whatever might have been the justification, in older days, for the formal recognition of differences of rank among undergraduates, it was by now an anachronism, and did harm; especially when young men were admitted to the enjoyment of peculiar privileges, whose intellectual equipment was below the ordinary level, and who were not even nominally employed in reading for a degree. When Gentlemen Commoners appeared at Collections, and were examined in Creasy's *Fifteen Decisive Battles of the World* as the staple of their Term's work, it was time that their order should cease to exist within the walls of Christ Church. They had degenerated into an idle clique of wealthy men, enjoying certain immunities, but bringing no corresponding advantage to the College[1]. It was far best that all such distinctions should vanish. This reform was effected under the Ordinance of 1867, in which it was enacted that:

'There shall be no distinctions in respect to academical dress, designation, College charges, or College payments, among Undergraduate members of the House, not being Junior Students nor Exhibitioners within the House.'

The regard graciously shown to Mr. Liddell by Her Majesty and Prince Albert during the whole of his life at Westminster was continued after his preferment to the Deanery, and in Michaelmas Term 1859 H.R.H. the Prince of Wales became a member of Christ Church. He resided at Oxford for two years, living at Frewin Hall, but regularly attending Chapel and lectures, and occasionally dining in hall. In 1863 the Crown Prince of Denmark came into residence, the present Dean of Durham acting as his Preceptor; but his career at Oxford was interrupted by the breaking out of the war between Denmark and Prussia on the

[1] Some years before, Osborne Gordon had sent a Gentleman Commoner, who was devoid of classical tastes, to a course of lectures on 'The Atmosphere,' with a promise to examine him in Collections, and find out what he had learnt. 'Well, Mr. ——,' said Gordon, 'what is the atmosphere composed of?' After much hesitation the man replied, 'Zinc.' 'Thank you,' said Gordon, 'that will do. Good morning.'

Schleswig-Holstein question. In 1872 H.R.H. Prince Leopold was entered on the books. He lived for three years at Wykeham House, and afterwards had rooms assigned to him in Canterbury Quadrangle, which he occupied during occasional visits to Oxford.

The matriculation of the Heir Apparent was naturally attended by exceptional ceremonial. The Dean has described it in a letter to his father, dated October 18, 1859:

'I had not time to write last night, after our grand doings with the Prince of Wales. He came down in a royal carriage (not by special train) at about four o'clock. I received him on the platform, and followed him to his house. The Vice-Chancellor and Proctors then called to pay their respects; then the Mayor and two Aldermen with an address; I standing by and introducing them. Then I went down to Christ Church, where we had the gates shut, and all the men drawn up in the Quadrangle. At five he came, and the bells struck up as he entered. He walked to my house between two lines of men, who capped him. I went out to meet him, and as we entered the house there was a spontaneous cheer. All through the streets, which were very full, the people cheered him well. Then I took him up to the drawing-room, and entered his name on the buttery book. He then retired with his Tutor, Mr. Fisher, and put on a nobleman's cap and gown in the gallery, and returned to receive greetings as the first Prince of Wales who had matriculated since Henry V. He was also introduced to the Sub-Dean and Censors. I then *walked* him across the

Quadrangle, and across the streets to Pembroke College, where we found the Vice-Chancellor waiting at the door. He took him upstairs, and there matriculated him in due form. This morning at eight he came down on foot from his house to chapel. His Governor is Colonel Bruce, brother of Lord Elgin, a very nice person indeed; and his Equerry Major Teesdale, one of the heroes of Kars, a very pleasing young man. Now you will ask, how it all went off. Very well, *very* well. Colonel Bruce came down to see me this morning, and said everything was done *à merveille*, and that the whole ceremony was a kind of model of how to do this sort of thing, and that the Queen and Prince Consort would be highly gratified by the account which he should send. The Prince himself is the nicest little fellow possible, so simple, naif, ingenuous and modest, and moreover with extremely good wits; possessing also the royal faculty of never forgetting a face.'

One may venture to assert that those two years passed at Oxford by the Prince were very happy years. He did not read for a Degree, but he attended courses of lectures in history and kindred subjects. It may be permitted to describe one of these; a scene still imprinted on the memory. It was a private course given to the Prince by the Regius Professor of Modern History, Mr. Goldwin Smith, who was then residing at New Inn Hall; and the lectures took place in the dining-room there. Nearly opposite to the Hall was an ancient gateway, belonging originally to St. Mary's College, and at this time forming the carriage entrance to the Prince's residence. Through this gateway he would pass at the hour of lecture, and quickly cross over the street. He always wore a nobleman's cap and gown, and was attended by his Tutor, Mr. Herbert Fisher, and by an Equerry or, sometimes, his Governor, Colonel Bruce. He took a seat at one end of the room, with his Tutor and Equerry on either hand; and at the other end, nearest the fire, sat the Professor. On the side by the windows was gathered a small and specially selected group of four or five Christ Church undergraduates, who had been invited to make an audience, and afford the Prince a sense of companionship. All took notes, as the lectures went on; and they were well deserving of the compliment. The text-book was the *Annals of England*, and the Professor began with the earliest sections; and he would sit with one leg folded over the other, and talk delightfully, in his brilliant epigrammatic style, about the various subjects which were suggested as page after page was turned.

The record of the distinctions gained by members of Christ Church in the Honours Schools was no doubt—for many years—far from being a brilliant one. This was a great disappointment to the Dean. He had entertained sanguine hopes that the opening of the studentships to public competition would ensure not only a constant supply of able Tutors, but also a body of junior students who would benefit largely by their instruction and take high degrees; and that thus the intellectual tone of the whole College would be sensibly raised. To a certain extent this was effected, but only to a certain extent. The junior students were not sufficiently numerous to make any deep impression upon the whole society; nor was it likely that in the undignified scramble for clever lads in which all Colleges were then—as now—engaged the chief prizes would fall to Christ Church, which had not the reputation of being a reading College. Westminster indeed always sent up its best men; but its numbers were small, and these were often but of moderate ability. Many exceedingly good men were elected as senior students and became Tutors, though the unduly large proportion of clerical studentships considerably narrowed the field of choice. It was a grave disaster that one of the first two elected for this purpose, Mr. G. R. Luke of Balliol College, whose rare intellectual gifts and chivalrous devotion to his work made from the outset of his career at Christ Church a profound impression upon colleagues and pupils alike, perished by drowning in March 1862, in the third year after his election. The loss was irreparable, and was keenly felt by the Dean.

'He was far more hurt and pained'—writes Dean Kitchin—'than I ever saw him touched by anything, when the news reached him of the sad accident which deprived Christ Church of the splendid scholarship and enthusiasm of Mr. Luke. "How full of misfortunes Christ Church has been," he cried, "οἱ δὲ χείρονες μένουσι, the best are taken from us." He was quite overcome with grief; for he not only had a high regard for Mr. Luke, but had hoped that through this infusion of new blood the old heart of Christ Church was waking up into fresh action, and that the former classical distinction of the House was coming back under Mr. Luke's enthusiastic teaching and influence.'

It should also be borne in mind that Christ Church has always been frequented by undergraduates who belong to the richer landed gentry of England. Such men have their future secured; for many there are large estates to which they will in due course succeed; they have not the same motive for exertion which rouses poorer men. Many are always content with a Pass degree; to others, the various avenues to the Honours degree through the non-classical schools offer an attractive course; and a large number of industrious students may make good use of their time, and yet not be found in the highest classes. There was plenty of thorough, sound, and conscientious work done within the walls of Christ Church, which produced no high distinctions; and a harsh verdict was sometimes quite unjustly passed upon the College, and upon its stately chief. One such attack was made in the newspapers as early as December 1859, when the Dean had but recently recovered from the serious illness which kept him away from Oxford for two consecutive winters, and before the new Ordinance, from which so much was hoped, had had time to bear any fruit. Not only were strictures uttered against the College, but personal reflections were cast upon the Dean himself, who was accused of following 'the trail of preferment,' a ludicrously inappropriate charge. Liddell was naturally pained, as his private letters show; but he declined to make any reply to the anonymous foe. Two generous answers were, however, written: the one by the Master of Pembroke, his late colleague on the Commission, and the other by his close personal friend, Arthur Stanley.

It had been a great joy to Liddell, that on the death of Robert Hussey, the first occupant of the Chair of the lately founded Regius Professorship of Ecclesiastical History, Stanley had been appointed as his successor. Though the appointment was made in December 1856, it did not involve the immediate residence in Oxford of the new Professor, who was then Canon of Canterbury, for the Canonry of Christ Church which had been annexed by Act of Parliament to the Professorship had not yet fallen vacant. But on Dr. Bull's death in February 1858, the vacancy occurred, and Stanley came into residence at Christ Church in the Summer Term of that year. From that time till his appointment to the Deanery of Westminster in the autumn of 1863 he was Liddell's close neighbour, his loyal colleague in the Chapter, and his chivalrous ally in academical disputes. His house was that which had been built by Dean Fell for the Canon of the third stall. It stands between Kill-Canon and

Peckwater, and now forms part of the lodgings of the present holder of the Chair (Dr. Bright); having been enlarged by the annexation of portions of the residence of Dr. Barnes, upon his death in 1859.

No other friend exercised so much influence as did Stanley over Liddell's opinions, or had so great a share of his confidence and affection, except perhaps the shrewd and caustic Scotchman who succeeded Liddell as Professor of Moral Philosophy, and afterwards became President of Corpus, the Rev. J. M. Wilson.

It was a happy chance that Stanley came back to Oxford just at the time when Liddell was beginning to feel keenly his isolation, and to long for the support and sympathy of a friend. We have seen that to his colleagues in the Chapter his attitude as to reforms at Christ Church was by no means acceptable. Dr. Jacobson alone could be counted as his supporter on that body. And in the University the leaders of opinion were still of a strongly conservative type; liberalism in academical politics, and liberalism in theology, were alike distasteful. The earlier elections to the new Hebdomadal Council had not been of good augury for the cause of progress. The co-operation of an old friend, and particularly of a friend who had shared all the labours of the University Commission, was a source of great delight and encouragement to the Dean. He had warmly advocated the appointment. 'Of all offices,' he wrote, 'this is the office for him; and of all men he is the man for the office.' But people at Oxford did not think so. At the outset of his new career Stanley was destined to find himself on the unpopular side. Those who had the good fortune to be at Oxford then, and to share his friendship, will remember how triumphantly he overcame the initial difficulties of his position; how singular a power he exercised in the University pulpit and in his Professorial chair; how rich a centre of universal hospitality his house was made. They will recall the fascinating talk, the playful wit, the radiant sympathy and charity, which brought together in delightful intercourse the cultivated London guest, the formal Oxford Don, and the shy undergraduate, in the pretty seventeenth century drawing-room, with the large water-colour drawing of Mount Sinai over the fireplace, and just above the mantelpiece the line of figures representing the opening procession of the States-General, with Mirabeau (as the host delighted to point out) walking at the head of the 'tiers état.'

Stanley stood manfully by the side of the Dean in the Chapter, which body, as he told his mother, contained 'very explosive elements.' The mutterings of the storm over the Jowett stipend were beginning to be heard, and in the selection of senior students by the new body of electors, already mentioned, serious differences of opinion prevailed. And in academical matters the same comradeship was found. There were many battles on behalf of liberty to be fought in the Hebdomadal Council; and important elections, such as that for the Boden Professorship of Sanskrit, where great principles were involved, brought the need of skilful handling of forces. The Jowett question came before the University in its various phases. Among these was the proposal to endow the Chair from University funds; this was thrown out. Then came the futile prosecution of the Greek Professor for heresy, in the Vice-Chancellor's Court, by Dr. Pusey, Dr. Ogilvie, and Dr. Heurtley. This was doomed to failure from the outset. Stanley preached a famous sermon before the University just at this time, on Sexagesima Sunday, 1863, in which, without directly referring to the event which was present to the minds of all his audience, he spoke of the evils of theological controversy, and laid down certain rules for abating it. The first rule was the obvious but most necessary maxim, 'Never condemn a book unless you have read it.' He announced and enforced this with marked emphasis. On that same evening the present writer was in Stanley's drawing-room, and happened to take up a volume on Church history which had just been published. He ventured to ask his host what sort of a book it was. 'Oh, it is not worth much, it is not worth much.' And then, with a smile of inimitable archness, he added, 'but indeed I haven't read it[1]!'

[1] The details of the long controversy relating to the endowment of the Regius Professorship of Greek have been intentionally omitted. They may be read in the memoirs of Dr. Pusey and of Mr. Jowett. For the final offer of Christ Church to raise the payment to the Chair from £40 to £500 a year the Dean was largely responsible.

With the support of the Dean, in the Summer Term of the same year, Stanley had proposed Charles Kingsley for the honorary degree of D.C.L. This proposal was resisted by Dr. Pusey, who charged Mr. Kingsley with the heresy of universalism, and also with having written *Hypatia*, a book not fit 'for our wives and sisters to read.' In the midst of the distressing controversy which this strange accusation involved, came the sad death of the Dean's infant son, Stanley's godson, only eight weeks old.

Stanley wrote at once:

'Most truly and deeply do I feel for you—for you both. The recollection of that former loss was what made us all so fervently rejoice in this new gift— so graciously sent, as it seemed; so graciously, let us hope, taken away. What can I do for you— I or my sister? Anything that you wish, to ease you or Mrs. Liddell of any part of the coming burden, as it now will seem, of what before seemed such a bright prospect. I sent you a note this morning about the wretched affair of Monday. How different, oh, how different is the vexation, grief, and anxiety of things in which one's own failings and the failings of others are involved, and the pure peaceful sorrow, however keen, that hangs round the death-bed of a little child! May God be with you! May you long be spared to us! You must have seen how much more closely the events and trials of the last year have drawn us together; how great and constant a support you have been to me.'

From Dr. Pusey, the other party to the Kingsley

controversy, there came at the same time a letter to Mrs. Liddell:

'MY DEAR MRS. LIDDELL,

'Human sympathy avails but little. Yet you will let me express mine at your quick bereavement of the little one whom God lent you for so short a time. It is a sore trial; only our good Father knows how to make all work together for good. I can to this day see the little one whom I lost above thirty years ago, just as she sat smiling then. I know then your sorrow. One comfort alone there is, that God, in His eternal love, created them just to appear in this redeemed world, and made them members of Christ and His own children, and then removed them spotless for that mansion which He ever in His love intended for them, where they behold Him and are blessed in sight of Him. It must be a beautiful band of souls which, born into this world of sin, were so taken away before they could know sin. He loved your child, whom He created out of love, better than you could love him; and has provided for him, as He knew to be best. God comfort you!

'Yours very faithfully,
'E. B. PUSEY.'

The Oxford atmosphere was indeed charged at this time with controversy, and Stanley's chivalrous temper would not allow him to keep silence when the reputation of a friend or the credit of an unpopular cause was at stake. The Dean always shrank from such conflicts. Liddell had preached the sermon at Stanley's ordination many years before: and often in conversation with friends would Stanley quote the words which in 1870 he printed in the preface to his *Collected Essays*. He there wrote:

'Nor can I forbear to call to mind a solemn warning which, at one of those moments in life when even slight things are remembered, fell from a distinguished preacher, afterwards a dear and honoured friend, who, addressing a band of youthful candidates for ordination in the Cathedral at Oxford, after enumerating the great realities of theological study and of practical life which ought to occupy the thoughts of an English clergyman, added impressive words to this effect: "Avoid controversy, if possible. Few have ever entered into controversy without repenting of it. I might enforce this by many arguments. But I will content myself with repeating what I have already said: few have entered into controversy without repenting of it".'

Liddell, on reading these words, wrote as follows:

'Let me thank you for your *Collected Essays*, which I shall read again with instruction and delight. Especially let me thank you for the kind and generous notice which you have taken of words uttered by me—ah! how many years ago—words which I little expected to see revivified at the end of so long a period. When I wrote and spoke them, I had not in my mind such controversies as you have been engaged in. I was thinking of the ordinary run of young clerics in country parishes, where solid work and study of a positive and healthy kind are more likely to produce charity and largeness of mind than devotion to controversy with nonconformists more narrow-minded perhaps than the young clerics themselves. Of course, controversial writing is necessary, and (properly conducted) most beneficial.'

Stanley's friendship was very precious to the Dean; and when the time came, in 1863, for the inevitable change to Westminster, he wrote an urgent letter of entreaty that he would even then consider the possibility of remaining at Oxford. Unfortunately, through Stanley's absence from England, the letter did not reach him before his final choice was irrevocably made.

'I apprehend from your language that if the Deanery of Westminster falls vacant, you *know* it will be offered you. Well, I heartily regret it, partly for selfish reasons, no doubt: but partly because I really think you would be both more useful and happier in your Chair at Oxford. Life in London, no doubt, has its bright side; but *to live perforce for eight months in* WESTMINSTER *is* (*experto crede*) not an enviable lot. Preaching in the Abbey will give you a wide scope of influence; but I know not how far your physical powers will be adequate to fill that vast space; and I much question whether any influence you may there exert will, in reality, be nearly so great as that which you have at Oxford. There, at best, you will infuse a flavour or a fermenting action into the mass; at Oxford you create the flavour and the fermenting leaven itself. You will have a seat in Convocation. But that is a barren honour; and I think you will soon come to the conclusion that the time spent in that body of debate, not action, is wasted time. Nor will you be more at Her Majesty's service at Westminster than at Oxford; nay, not so much. For being bound to eight months' residence, and desiring (as you will desire) some time for travel, the time at your command will become more limited than at present it is[1].'

When the matter was publicly announced, together with Stanley's approaching marriage with Lady Augusta Bruce, another letter from Liddell expressed exactly his feelings:

'On your intended marriage I do most heartily and exultingly congratulate you. Since you lost her whose complete union with you was to me one of the most touching and lovely traits I have met with—even in you—I felt there was something wanted "to free the hollow heart from paining"; and I felt that, under the circumstances, even in your case that something must be a wife. May Lady Augusta be all that you wish, and you all that she hopes!

'But here, alas! my congratulations end. Neither for you, nor for us, nor for any one, can I look with pleasure on your leaving your living work here for the dead mass that will meet you at Westminster. —— thinks it an excellent appointment, because it will remove you from Oxford. So, no doubt, think the ——s and ——s, and "hoc genus omne."

Hoc Ithacus velit et magno mercentur Atridae.

Pardon my unavailing regrets. You receive no more honourable testimony than the universal sorrow

---

[1] This and the two following letters have been already published in Mr. Prothero's memoir of Dean Stanley.

of your friends and the joy of your non-friends at your promotion—though "promotion" I cannot call it.'

One more letter must be quoted; a letter written immediately after Stanley's farewell sermon at Christ Church on November 29, 1863:

'My best and dearest friend,—How have you torn open afresh all the wounds which the news of your departure caused! I can scarcely see to write—for tears.
  'And how nobly have you avenged the friends who would fain have continued you in the office of teaching good and giving true glory to God in this place. I wish for no other punishment upon those who have closed our pulpits against you (for the present—not for long, I am confident), than that they should have heard you to-day.'

Never again, however, till the first Sunday in Lent 1871 did Stanley preach before the University. Dean Liddell entered on his office as Vice-Chancellor in October 1870, and resolved to redress this injustice without delay. He nominated Stanley to preach the annual sermon on the Jewish Interpretation of Prophecy in the ensuing Lent Term, having appointed Dr. Liddon to preach on the previous Sunday morning. He writes to his father:

'Both sermons have been a great success. Liddon's was what is called the "Humility" sermon, always preached on the Sunday morning before Ash Wednesday. He delivered a very fine discourse to a very crowded church, though the Dean of St. Paul's, who was present, pronounced it *not* one of his best. Stanley's sermon yesterday afternoon was a noble sermon. The church was again crowded. He began by saying that he should not enlarge on the *Principles* of such interpretation, because he had spoken on that subject the last time that he had addressed a University audience, *nine years ago!* These last were not his own words. Since that time, except two sermons in Christ Church Cathedral, he has been silenced, so far as the University is concerned. The Archbishop of York, who was present, said it was a perfect scandal to the University that it should be so.'

In Michaelmas Term 1872 Stanley was nominated by the Board appointed for the purpose as one of the Select Preachers for the ensuing year. Dean Liddell was still Vice-Chancellor, and in virtue of his office was chairman of this Board; and each name, after receiving his approval, had to obtain the sanction of Convocation. It must be acknowledged that at this time Stanley had deliberately brought himself into even more than usual antagonism with Churchmen, by his proceedings in connexion with what was called the 'Westminster Communion,' and by his fierce denunciations in the Lower House of the 'damnatory clauses' of the Athanasian Creed, and his contemptuous criticism of those who by explanatory notes would attempt 'to draw out the teeth of this old lion, who sits there in his majesty, and defies any explanation to take out his fierce and savage fangs.' But the more sagacious leaders of the Church party, though offended and distressed, saw the unwisdom of contesting his appointment. It was left to Mr. Burgon, and four other members of Convocation, to lead the opposition and summon the non-residents to vote. Some characteristic letters—afterwards published—were written by Burgon to Liddell as Vice-Chancellor, and received from him short but courteous replies, simply pointing out that the opposition to Stanley was in effect a vote of censure on the Board of nomination, and on himself in particular. The effort to prevent the appointment ended in failure; it was carried by 349 to 287 votes. As a final protest against 'the unfaithfulness to the truth of God which the University manifested by its vote,' the Dean of Norwich (Dr. Goulburn) resigned his post as Select Preacher.

On receiving the news of the result Stanley wrote to Liddell:

'You will have known, without my saying it, that I was more anxious for you than for myself, and more anxious for the University and the Church than for either of us. And now it seems like a sudden return into an unlooked-for haven of peace.

'For me, I can truly say that even if there had been any personal annoyance—which there was not—it would have been a hundred-fold repaid by the kindness of my friends. Even the single vote of Dr. Lushington will be to me "a joy for ever[1]." I wish that I could find some means of expressing my gratitude. I fear there is none, except to do the

[1] Dr. Lushington, at the age of ninety-one, travelled from London to record his vote for Stanley.

best I can to justify the appointment. This, as well as so much else, I owe to you. May God bless you for it, and preserve you long among us. By accident, according to a long engagement, I had to give a lecture last night to a very homely audience in Southwark, and took the Bishop of Manchester with me. After the lecture, as you will see briefly reported in the *Times*, in a capital speech he took up the event of the day. It was the first allusion to it, but the audience quite understood, and the cheers were a good echo of those in the Oxford Theatre.'

It has been shown that in the Chapter at Christ Church there were men of very various types of character, among whom there were likely to be many serious differences of opinion. And so it was with the new Governing Body established in 1867. A skilful guidance was needed if collisions were to be averted and business profitably transacted. Dean Liddell was pre-eminently good as a chairman. His personal dignity was itself a sufficient assertion of authority. He was fair to every one. He never spoke much, but never allowed debate to wander. He focussed opinion, and at the right moment elicited a decision, often drafting a resolution which happily embodied the gist of the conclusion at which the discussion pointed. He was very patient of tedious speakers, and would solace himself by taking out his gold pen, and after wiping it carefully on the sleeve of his gown (his invariable practice) would draw wondrous landscapes on the pink blotting paper which lay before him, while the stream of talk

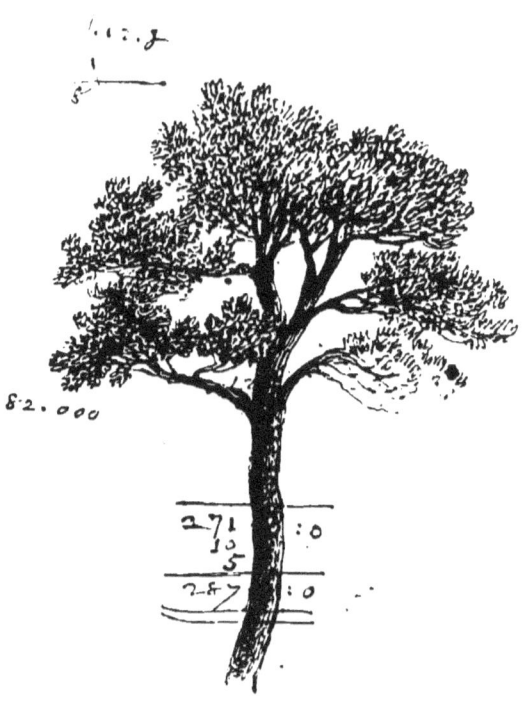

flowed on. Churches, castles, bridges, ruined keeps and ivy-clad walls, woodland and river scenes, in endless variety, were the outcome of dreary sessions of the innumerable committees which Oxford crowds into the afternoons of its all too brief Terms. Many hundred sketches from his pen are still treasured up by his friends; he would leave them on the table at the end of a meeting, and some admirer would carry them off, and well worth preservation they were.

The services of so excellent a chairman and so practical a man of business were constantly in demand for University and civic matters, and involved many engagements in addition to the duties within the walls of Christ Church. The citizens claimed his assistance to guide them in the difficult work of the drainage of Oxford; and he took a very deep interest in the questions which arose from time to time in relation to the prevention of floods in the Thames valley. His counsel was always sought for: so great and universal was the respect paid to his methodical and business-like habits, and to his sound and unbiassed judgment.

Work such as this was entirely congenial to the Dean. He liked to have to deal with practical matters; they were a recreation, by their very contrast to his other duties. In the midst of his letters to Scott about minute corrections in the Lexicon, one comes upon questions, equally minute, concerning the drainage of a town near which his correspondent happened to be spending his vacation.

He requires to be informed as to whether the town has been lately drained, and by whom; what is the population of the area dealt with; what is the length and size (sectional) of the main outfall sewer, and what the size of the secondary sewers; what has been the expense per head of the works; and whether the engineer employed has given satisfaction in point of attention and economy. And when the unhappy lexicographer had replied as well as he could to such unexpected and bewildering inquiries, he received another long letter, containing an elaborate contrast between two classes of engineers —those who deal with water-works, and those conversant with drainage schemes. On one occasion Sir Henry Acland brought to Christ Church a learned German professor who was very anxious to have a sight of the famous writer of the Lexicon. On inquiring for him at the Deanery, they were told that he was in Christ Church Meadow. They went thither, but he was nowhere to be found. On asking a workman whether he had been seen there, 'Oh, yes,' said the man, 'he has just gone down the drain.' An adjacent man-hole was then approached, and in answer to a call, a loud voice was heard from below, and soon the majestic head emerged from the lower depths. The German professed himself more than satisfied, and declared that he had never before seen a famous scholar amid such peculiar surroundings.

In the drainage of the Thames valley Liddell had taken a deep interest from the time of his return to Oxford in 1855. Many evils attended the frequent recurrence of winter floods, but it was difficult to find a remedy. At last, after committees had spent many years in discussing various schemes, Sir John Hawkshaw was instructed to prepare a report; and the plan which he recommended in 1882 involved very considerable undertakings. A new and more direct channel was to be cut for the Cherwell at its junction with the Thames; and Iffley Lock was to be removed. This last proposal would render necessary the dredging of the river above Iffley, and many subsidiary works.

It was natural that the proposed abolition of Iffley Lock should provoke fierce opposition, not only from all lovers of the river, but also from the City authorities, who owned the water-works and dreaded the consequences of the lowering of the water-level. But the favourable reception which the scheme as a whole met with at first, and the generous promise of subscriptions from residents in Oxford and riparian owners, emboldened the Dean, in company with the Master of Balliol, Mr. Jowett, then Vice-Chancellor, to enter into a formal agreement with the Thames Valley Drainage Commissioners, by which this body undertook to carry out Sir John Hawkshaw's scheme in its entirety for a sum of £14,000, payable by instalments spread over three years. For this sum the Vice-Chancellor and the Dean made themselves personally responsible. The scheme, however, was only partially executed. The new mouth to the Cherwell, now called the Vice-

Chancellor's Cut, was opened; but in the face of the strong opposition aroused, it was found impossible to complete the work of the removal of Iffley Lock. The Dean and Mr. Jowett had paid £3,600 to the Commissioners, and had no legal claim to be re-imbursed; but the subscribers consented to the repayment to them of this sum, and the balance of the money subscribed was returned. The result of the work has been to carry off the flood-water from the Cherwell valley with greater rapidity than before; and although Iffley Lock still remains, the Thames valley has experienced considerable benefit from the widening of the weirs, which enables the flood-water to pass away more quickly.

Among the recommendations of the first Oxford University Commission had been the establishment of a class of students unattached to any college or hall, but in all other respects members of the University, and subject to proper supervision in regard to studies and discipline. Of this scheme Liddell had always been an advocate, and it was largely due to his personal efforts that it was carried into effect in 1868 and successfully developed. The Dean of Durham, who was the first Censor of the *Scholares non ascripti*, writes gratefully of the help which he gave:

'Liddell was the true founder and friend of that body. All the success of the movement, first recommended by him, was due to his clear-headed advice and guidance. For he always stood by these poor lads, and did much to create a friendly feeling for them in the Hebdomadal Council and among the leading members of the University. This it was that carried the feeble society through the difficult years of its childhood, and indeed assured to it its present permanent state.'

With his warm approval the ancient Congregation House adjoining St. Mary's Church was fitted up as a place for the common worship of the non-collegiate students; and when in later years it was found practicable to build proper accommodation for them, he cordially supported the Master of Balliol in promoting the erection of the present convenient block of buildings, adjoining the Examination Schools, where a handsome library and lecture-rooms, as well as offices for the Censor and his staff, have been provided at considerable cost.

To describe with any completeness the public services of Dean Liddell in matters affecting the interests of the University would almost entail the writing of a history of Oxford for a period of more than thirty-five years. During the whole of his tenure of the Deanery, with one short interval, he was a member of the Hebdomadal Council, for he was first elected in 1855 to fill a chance vacancy, and from 1858 to 1891 he served upon it without interruption. With that Council rests the initiative of all academical legislation. For all the changes—many of them of a very important and even fundamental kind—which were effected during that long period he was largely responsible, for he exercised a remarkable influence over the deliberations of the Council, and gradually emerged from the position of a party representative and came to be regarded by the whole University with a singular respect. He combined the knowledge, experience, good sense, courtesy, and impartiality which are invaluable on all important deliberative and executive bodies. He became a Curator of the Bodleian Library in 1860, just at the time when his close personal friend H. O. Coxe was appointed Bodley's Librarian. To both Coxe and his successor, the present Librarian, he gave loyal and constant support. In the records of the Library indeed no great reforms are associated with his name; but he seems to have been always on the side of progress, and to have supported the late Master of Balliol in developing the resources of the Library and rendering its vast stores more accessible to scholars. He was also instrumental in transferring some of its artistic treasures to the University Galleries.

It should be added that from 1857 onwards he was a Delegate of the University Museum; a Curator of the University Galleries from 1858; a Delegate of the Press from 1861. For many years he was a Commissioner under the Local Government Board Act, and a Curator of the University Chest. In all these offices his services were of the utmost value; but it would be wearisome to describe his work in detail. It will suffice, as an illustration of its character and importance, to quote two letters written by men who are well qualified to estimate his merits, shown in two very different spheres of labour, both congenial to him. Mr. Lyttelton Gell, for many years Secretary to the Delegates of the Press, thus describes his services on that body:

'The Dean first attended the Board on June 14, 1861, and the last meeting at which he was present was on December 18, 1891. It was only during the last quarter of this period—from the autumn of 1884—that I had personal experience of his invaluable influence upon the Board; before that time my impressions are gathered from frequent reference to the Press records.

'To the undergraduates of my own generation the Dean had been *the* Vice-Chancellor—an Olympian figure, far removed; and it was not until after some experience of Boards and business in London that I had the opportunity of realizing week by week across a narrow table his remarkable sagacity both in literary and in business problems.

'In his earlier years the Press had owed much to his initiative; but to me, meeting him first in Press business when he was already past seventy, the Dean appeared not so much then as an initiator, but rather as the pivot about which affairs revolved, as the Nestor who was steeped in accumulated experience, and whose judgment as to the wisest way of handling the staff, of transacting business, and of dealing with administrative questions, was invariably accepted. He understood the value of method, and of reference to fixed and pre-determined principles in the conduct of large affairs. Consequently one learnt to lean upon him as a rock of consistency, as the man who would stem the hasty stampede from a settled policy, and arrest the snap-decisions which are the weakness of a Board so constituted. He represented a certain tradition which embodied the experience of a remarkable knot of Delegates by whom the Press, as we know it, had been built up and prepared for its immense and profitable expansion dating from Jowett's Vice-Chancellorship. Henry Smith, Mark Pattison, and the present Dean of Westminster had not long disappeared from the Board when my experience began; and (omitting all reference to existing Delegates) the Bishops of Salisbury and Hereford, Archdeacon Palmer and Alfred Robinson, were then still amongst their number. The Dean was very tenacious of certain forms and methods which then governed the conduct of the Delegacy; and though to one fresh from business in London they seemed at first rather restrictive, yet I soon valued his wise insistence upon "the customs of the Board." The periodic arrivals of a new Chairman or new Delegates, necessarily inexperienced in the business referred to them, and sometimes inspired with all the self-confidence and precipitation which ignorance of wider considerations begets, fully justified the Dean's attitude; and fortunately his authority was such, and his impartiality so absolute, that he had but to state that such a course or such a precedent should be followed, for every one to acquiesce.

'His judgment was as sound in the literary as in the administrative sphere. He not only discerned what was good from what was bad, but also he had consistent views as to what (apart from the question of intrinsic merit) it was wise for the Delegates to publish, and what not. Further, he knew the book which was worth improving, and many a proof-sheet profited by his taste and accuracy. To him, as Chairman of the School-books Committee, assisted by its Secretary, the present Dean Kitchin, the excellent little "Clarendon Press Series" owed much of its value. Himself a consummate critic, he helped to plan the volumes and to annotate them, and often revised the proof-sheets with his own hand. He was especially interested in the school editions of the great English writers which marked an epoch in educational views. English Literature indeed, like English Philology, always evoked his keen sympathy. He was assiduous in his care for the progress of the *New English Dictionary*, though perhaps his practical views made him uneasy at the expansion of its scale; and he always regretted that the University had become pledged to so huge an expenditure without more precise information as to the state of the materials at the outset of the negotiations with the Philological Society in 1877. Looking back upon my recollections of his attitude towards the various projects which came before the Board, it seems to me that he attached a greater value to work in Teutonic Philology than to Latin and Greek scholarship. The labours of Skeat, Earle, Sweet, Brachet, and Vigfússon were certain of his special sympathy, and to Vigfússon in particular he was a never-failing friend.

'Towards one of the greatest of the Board's undertakings, the Revised Version, he always seemed to maintain a considerable reserve. The financial arrangements with the Revisers were made while he presided as Vice-Chancellor, so that there is every reason to assume that he concurred in the enterprise, though I entertain the impression that he was dissatisfied with the result, at any rate as regards the New Testament.

'I had heard from the Dean, when he began to consider his retirement, that the Press would be the last of his University responsibilities which he would lay down; and in fact the last University Board which he attended was that of the Press Delegacy, upon which he had through more than thirty years rendered such invaluable service. I met him in the Bodleian Quadrangle as he arrived, and he told me that when the meeting rose his final labour for the University would have been accomplished.

'Oxford memories are so short, that most people nowadays take the Press for granted, and imagine that its reputation has always stood where it does, that it has always turned out plenty of important and well-printed books, and always contributed from £5000 to £10,000 a year to the University Chest. As a matter of fact, these thirty years represented a revolution. At the outset of the Dean's experience the Press was comparatively a small concern. Its publications were few and far between, and the possibility of deriving a regular annual income from the Press for University purposes was not established until Jowett's Vice-Chancellorship, 1882-6. Similarly there was a certain disposition to take the Dean for granted, and to assume his qualities and his influence as part of the order of things. Doubtless his own modesty and his reluctance to assert the authority which he possessed tended to this result. His influence was often almost intangible, the mere outcome of his presence.

For he was one of those men who affected everything for the better, morally and practically, out of sheer high principle, without any vanity, antagonism, or self-seeking. Other people might claim the actual credit for what the Dean had in reality rendered possible. It is absolutely not conceivable to imagine him claiming for himself the credit of anything, a characteristic which makes it all the greater pleasure to indicate the remarkable value of his services. He remained Olympian—too high-minded to be touched with combativeness, or jealousy, or self-assertion, too shy and reserved to be eager to urge his own opinion, or even to express it unless it was essential, yet too wise and public-spirited to stand aloof, if his judgment, saturated with long experience, told him that the right decision was trembling in the balance.'

The name of Vigfússon recalls a pathetic history, which is best told in the Dean's own language.

'About the year 1864 I received a letter from Mr. (now Sir George) Dasent, desiring to interest me in the publication by the Clarendon Press of an Icelandic Dictionary. Mr. Cleasby, brother of Mr. Justice Cleasby, had lived many years in Scandinavian lands, and had made large collections for the purpose of a Dictionary of the most ancient and most classical tongue of the Norse nations. Mr. Dasent was well known as a Norse scholar; and he proposed to himself to arrange Mr. Cleasby's materials and see the book through the press. To do the rough work and assist in the arrangement he had engaged a young Icelandic scholar, who had studied philology at Copenhagen and taken his Doctor's degree at that University, by name Gudbrand Vigfússon. The work was proposed by me to the Delegates of the Press, and accepted by them. It entailed much vexation and no little labour on us, which fell chiefly on *me*. Vigfússon came to Oxford, and was practically left to deal with Cleasby's work single-handed. He found it in great part a chaos, and he often told me that he could have done his task better and with less labour had he started *de novo*. He was a thorough scholar, worked like a horse, and was altogether a capital fellow. But his English was very defective, though he did not like to acknowledge this, and was apt to be more diffuse than necessary. For many weeks he used to come to me every morning at ten, with some pages which he had prepared, and I worked at them with him for an hour. This regularity of work was interrupted sometimes by official duties, and vacations came when it was necessary to revise his work by post. But I continued to toil through every page, often twice; and after much trouble the book was eventually published in 1874. The short preface which I wrote is dated 1869.

'After the completion of the Dictionary I saw little of Vigfússon. He became acquainted with York Powell, the present Professor of Modern History at Oxford, and assisted by him published the "Sturlunga Saga" at the Clarendon Press.

'Poor fellow! he died of a liver complaint in 1889. I visited him while he was being nursed at the Sarah Acland Home in Wellington Square. He fully appreciated the attention and comfort of the Home. He left me by his will the gold ring which was the symbol of his Doctor's degree at Upsala. I wore it constantly, and intended that on my death it should be given to York Powell. But I have unfortunately lost it. It flew from my finger when I was stripping rhododendron bushes of their seed-vessels in the garden at Ascot, and I failed to find it.'

It should be added that shortly before his death, Vigfússon presented, with other books, an Icelandic Bible (Bishop Gudbrand's, 1584) to the Library of Christ Church, accompanied by a memorandum written by Mr. York Powell, but signed by himself. He says:

'These books I wish in my lifetime to give to the Library of Christ Church, there to be preserved and remain as a remembrance of my grateful feeling towards Christ Church and those of her members herein named in especial. First to the Dean, for his well-timed protection in 1867, without which the Icelandic Dictionary would undoubtedly have broken down, and also for the constant, untiring, and experienced supervision which he gave to the Dictionary from first to last; which I wish to record, though he himself would be unwilling to have it known; for no one knows, and no one can ever know, how much the Dictionary, as it stands, owes to the Dean of Christ Church.'

Then, after mention of the kindness and assistance given him by Dr. Kitchin and Mr. York Powell, he says:

'By a strange coincidence, all three are Christ Church men.' And he concludes, 'I wish this memorandum to be affixed to Bishop Gudbrand's Bible, and therein to remain, as a record of my deep-felt gratitude. G. V.'

To the value of the Dean's services at the University Galleries, no one is better qualified to bear testimony than one of his younger colleagues on that Board, the Rev. Dr. Woods, late President of Trinity College, who writes as follows:

'Among the many services for which the University has reason to be grateful to Dean Liddell, not the least important is the work which he did as Curator of the University Galleries—work which I have heard him say was one of the pleasures of his life. For more than thirty years he was an active member of the Board, and to his initiative and administration were largely due the improvements effected during that period. He was appointed Curator shortly after his return to Oxford, on the death in 1858 of Mr. Sneyd, Warden of All Souls College. The University Galleries were at that time a recent institution. The building, one of Cockerell's finest and most original works, had been opened in 1845, and its interior must have presented at first a somewhat bare appearance, though the original models for the principal works of Sir F. Chantrey, presented by his widow in 1842, served to furnish part of the lower floor, and portraits from the Bodleian Library, many of which have since been returned, were hung in the Picture Gallery above. The deficiencies of the new institution were, however, soon supplemented. During the ten years which immediately succeeded its opening, more than eighty oil-paintings (including good examples of Sir Joshua Reynolds and of the Dutch and early Italian Schools) were acquired by donation or bequest. The growth of the collection of prints and drawings was even more rapid. In 1845 the priceless series of drawings by Michael Angelo and Raffaello was purchased by a public subscription (towards which the second Earl of Eldon contributed £4000), and placed in the Galleries. This gift was supplemented by a loan from the Bodleian Library of the fine collection of German and other prints and drawings which had been bequeathed to it in 1834 by Mr. F. Douce; while in 1855 Mr. Chambers Hall, in addition to a previous gift of pictures, presented a large number of prints and drawings, including a valuable series of Rembrandt etchings.

'On his appointment then as Curator in 1858 Dean Liddell found the University Galleries in possession of a fair collection of pictures, and of a large mass of prints and drawings, many of them very recently acquired, and merely put away in cupboards to await arrangement. It is obvious that the rapid growth of the collections must have far outstripped the possibility of properly dealing with them at the time. The first duty of a Curator under these circumstances is to make himself acquainted with the contents of his collections, and there can be no doubt that the Dean spent much time over his work. Notes in his handwriting on the wrappers of the Douce prints and Rembrandt etchings show that he worked through them more than once, and quite towards the end of his time at Oxford I remember how clear and accurate was his knowledge of many of the prints and drawings. Without his knowledge and taste and trained eye it would have been doubly difficult to make any progress with the arranging, cataloguing, and mounting which were so urgently needed. At that time there were only three Curators besides Bodley's Librarian, who was constituted an official Curator so long as the Galleries contained any work of art belonging to the Library, and who naturally concerned himself mainly with the safe custody of these objects. Dean Liddell's colleagues in 1858 were Dr. Cardwell, Principal of St. Alban Hall, and Dr. Wellesley, Principal of New Inn Hall. Dr. Cardwell was then old, and Dr. Wellesley, though a man of fine taste, as is evident from the important collection of prints and drawings which he made, does not seem to have spent much time or trouble on the Galleries, so that the chief burden of the work must have fallen on the Dean. Considerable progress, however, was made in the direction of sorting, cataloguing, and mounting many of the prints, though the Curators were hampered by the small means at their disposal. A short catalogue of the pictures was also prepared by Mr. Joseph Fisher, the first keeper of the Galleries, who held his office for forty-five years. On the death of Dr. Wellesley in 1866 (Dr. Cardwell had died in 1861) the Dean became the senior Curator, and the Board was strengthened by the appointment of Dr. (now Sir Henry) Acland, and Professor Rawlinson. For the next eighteen years the Board continued unchanged. Sir H. Acland's life-long friendship with the Dean, and their common interests and tastes, enabled them to work together with exceptional cordiality; while Professor Rawlinson undertook the responsible office of Treasurer. The effect of the new *régime* soon became apparent.

One matter which Dean Liddell, himself an amateur of considerable force, had much at heart was the dissemination of a knowledge of drawing. In the autumn of 1866 a temporary home was provided at the Galleries for the recently established School of Art. Classes were held by Mr. Macdonald, and were largely attended. On the establishment of the Ruskin School of Drawing in 1871, a portion of the basement of the Galleries was fitted up for the use of the evening classes of the School of Art; and much encouragement was thus given to the study of drawing by boys and girls of the artisan class. A still more important service to the study of art at Oxford was the appointment of Mr. Ruskin as the first Slade Professor of Fine Art in 1869. By the regulations made under the Declaration of Trust, the lectures of the Professor are to be given at the University Galleries, and the Curators are represented on the Board of Electors to the Chair. Mr. Ruskin's acceptance of the Professorship was due principally, if not entirely, to the influence of his friends Dean Liddell (who was chairman of the Board of Electors) and Sir Henry Acland. It will be remembered how great was the enthusiasm with which Mr. Ruskin's lectures were welcomed. Many members of the University date from that period their first awakening to a sense of the beauty of Italian Art, and it may be doubted whether the interest of the University in painting and sculpture has ever again been so keen or so widely spread as it was then. No one felt more strongly than did the Dean how great was the advantage to Oxford of having Mr. Ruskin among its teachers; and later on, when his connexion with the University was severed, to no one did his loss mean more than to the Dean. I have heard him more than once refer with deep feeling to his sense of the personal loss to himself. Another matter with which the Dean and Sir Henry Acland were closely connected was the gift, in 1868, of £1200 by the present Earl of Eldon to supplement his father's benefaction. This sum was to be applied in the first place to the maintenance and illustration of the series of Michael Angelo and Raffaello drawings, and secondly to the purchase of books, prints, and photographs illustrating Italian Art. One result of this benefaction was the preparation and issue in 1870 of Sir J. C. Robinson's catalogue of the drawings. Other additions made to the collections, and improvements effected at the Galleries, during the years 1866-84 might be mentioned. The two surviving Curators certainly look back with satisfaction to the work done by them during that period under the chairmanship of Dean Liddell.

'In 1884 a great change took place in the constitution of the Galleries Board, by the appointment of six additional Curators. The reason for this change was the increasing importance of the study of Classical Archaeology, and the need felt of having this subject adequately represented on the Board. The Dean continued as chairman of the enlarged body; and was chairman also of a committee appointed in 1885 to consider (1) what works of art in other University buildings would find a more fitting place in the Galleries; and (2) whether the present space was sufficient for the full and proper exhibition of the works of art at present in them. The recommendations of this important committee virtually laid down the lines along which subsequent changes have moved. The appointment of Mr. Percy Gardner to the Chair of Archaeology in 1887 was followed by the transfer to the Galleries of the Arundel Marbles and the establishment of an Archaeological Library. The difficulties caused by the conflicting claims of the Chantrey Collection and the continually increasing number of casts were partially met by a small extension of the Galleries, two new rooms on the ground floor and one on the basement being added in 1890. With all these changes Dean Liddell had much to do, and appeal was made to his judgment at every turn. Meanwhile the other and older work at the Galleries, in which the Dean felt perhaps a more direct interest, was not neglected. The Michael Angelo and Raffaello drawings were admirably repaired and remounted, and have gained a new lease of life. Many pictures which required careful reparation were successfully dealt with, and on the redecoration of the picture-gallery in 1891 the pictures were rearranged, and a provisional catalogue of them was prepared by two of the Curators. In 1886, on the appointment of Mr. Herkomer to the Slade Professorship, a new studio, built after the Professor's own design, was added to the Galleries. To Professor Herkomer's munificence is due the fine portrait of Dean Liddell which now hangs in the Galleries. It was painted by him shortly before the Dean's departure from Oxford.

'The time was now at hand when Dean Liddell was to give up the work which he had so long and so successfully carried on at the Galleries. The last meeting of the Curators which he attended was held on November 25, 1891. Reference was made to the fact that he would still continue to be a Curator, and it was ordered that the thanks of the Curators for his services in the chair be entered on the minutes.

'It will have become evident that any account of the Dean's work at the Galleries virtually means a history of the Galleries during the twenty-five years of his chairmanship. But the personal aspect of his work must not be altogether passed over. His younger colleagues could not but be conscious that they were associated with a remarkable man. He had a commanding personality, clear convictions, and a sound judgment. His wide experience and knowledge of men and affairs always made themselves felt in a discussion, though he often delayed giving his opinion until he was asked for it. I had frequently occasion to consult him during the last few years of his time at Oxford, and I shall always gratefully remember his help and kindness. Beneath a certain brusqueness of manner there was great considerateness for other people. I remember, when it became necessary to appoint a deputy-keeper owing to Mr. Fisher's age and infirmities, with what great delicacy the Dean made the communication to him. The Dean was capable of strong attachment to those with whom he habitually worked, and I know that he loved the Galleries and everything connected with them. It will probably be long before any one man again does as much for them as was done by Dean Liddell between 1858 and 1891.'

In this interesting account Dr. Woods describes the appointment of Mr. Ruskin to the Slade

Professorship of Fine Art as having been brought to pass chiefly through the influence of Dean Liddell and Sir H. Acland, and he mentions the Dean's pleasure in welcoming Mr. Ruskin as a teacher of Art at Oxford. Mr. Ruskin's admiration for Liddell in earlier days has already been referred to. Their friendship had begun while Ruskin was an undergraduate[1], but had been interrupted by his absence from Oxford and visits to the Continent. With the publication of *Modern Painters* Liddell had not been concerned; he had not even heard of it as likely to appear. Many years afterwards (in 1879) he told Mr. Ruskin of his first sight of the volume:

'Thirty-six years ago I was at Birmingham, examining the boys in the great school there. In a bookseller's shop window I saw *Modern Painters, by a Graduate of Oxford*. I knew nothing of the book, or by whom it was written. But I bought it, and read it eagerly. It was like a revelation to me, as it has been to many since. I have it by me, my children have read it; and I think with

---

[1] In a letter written in 1837, Liddell thus describes Ruskin: 'I am going to drink tea with Adolphus Liddell to-night, and see the drawings of a very wonderful gentleman commoner here who draws wonderfully. He is a very strange fellow, always dressing in a greatcoat with a brown velvet collar, and a large neck-cloth tied over his mouth, and living quite in his own way among the odd set of hunting and sporting men that gentlemen commoners usually are. One of them, for instance, rode to London and back the other day in five and a half hours, a hundred and eight miles. However, he got rusticated for his pains, so he had better have stayed at home. But Ruskin does not give in to such fancies as these, and tells them that they like their own way of living and he likes his; and so they go on, and I am glad to say they do not bully him, as I should have been afraid they would.'

a pleasure, a somewhat melancholy pleasure, on those long past days.'

The first volume was published in April 1843; and Liddell, when he penned the words just quoted, must have quite forgotten that after buying the book and studying it carefully, he ventured, after the appearance of the second edition in 1844, to note down and forward to the author some criticisms and corrections. He seems to have commented unfavourably on the style in which the volume was got up, and to have made various suggestions as to phrases and modes of expression, and some criticisms on the main thesis of the work. His letter is, unfortunately, not to be found; but the nature of his comments may be gathered from Mr. Ruskin's reply:

*October* 12, 1844.

'MY DEAR SIR,

'I was on the very point of writing to beg for your opinion and assistance on some matters of art, when your invaluable letter arrived. I cannot tell you how glad and grateful it makes me; glad for its encouragement, and grateful for its advice. For indeed it is not self-confidence, but only eagerness and strong feeling which have given so overbearing a tone to much of what I have written. I *need* some support, considering the weight and numbers of those against me; and you will, I am sure, believe me when I say that I looked to none in the whole circle of the friends whom I most respect, with so much anxiety as to you: though I never ventured to hope for more than *pardon* from you for one half of the book, even if (which I little anticipated) you should take the trouble of looking over it at all. You may judge, therefore, of the infinite pleasure which your kind letter gave me; and, from the respect which you know I felt for all your opinions (even when I, in my ignorance, was little capable of understanding them, and felt most inclined to dispute them), you may judge of the deference I would yield to them now, when a little more acquaintance with high art has brought me into nearer sympathy with you. I wish there were something in your letter which I could obey without assenting to, that I might prove to you my governability. But alas! there is nothing of all the little that you say in stricture which I do not feel and which I have not felt for some time back. In fact, on looking over the book the other day, after keeping my mind off the subject entirely for two or three months, I think I could almost have anticipated your every feeling; and I determined on the instant to take in future a totally different tone. In fact, the Blackwood part[1] was put in to please some friends (especially one to whom I am much indebted for his trusting me with his drawings) and the booksellers. The title-page is booksellers' work too, and was put in in defiance of my earnest wishes. I let it go, for I considered myself writing for the public, not for men of taste, and I thought the booksellers knew more about the public than I. I was wrong, however, and will allow nothing of the kind in future.

[1] This refers to Mr. Ruskin's reply to the severe criticisms of Turner which had appeared from time to time in *Blackwood's Magazine*, and to a review of *Modern Painters* in the number for October, 1843.

'But it seems to me that the pamphleteer manner is not confined to these passages: it is ingrained throughout. There is a nasty, snappish, impatient, half-familiar, half-claptrap web of young-mannishness everywhere. This was, perhaps, to be expected from the haste in which I wrote. I am going to try for better things; for a serious, quiet, earnest, and simple manner, like the execution I want in art. Forgive me for talking of myself and my intentions thus, but your advice will be so valuable to me that I know you will be glad to give it; especially as the matter I have in hand now relates not more to Turner than to that pure old art which I have at last learnt (thanks to you, Acland, and Richmond) to love.

'As soon as I began to throw my positions respecting the beautiful into form, I found myself necessarily thrown on the human figure for great part of my illustrations; and at last, after having held off in fear and trembling as long as I could, I saw there was no help for it, and that it must be taken up to purpose. So I am working at home from Fra Angelico, and at the British Museum from the Elgins. I passed through Paris in my return from the Alps, when I at last found myself *up* to admiration of Titian, and past Rubens (in matter of colour), and now therefore I think I shall do, when I have given a year or two to these pure sources. I don't think, with my heart full of Fra Angelico, and my eyes of Titian, that I shall fall back into the pamphleteer style again.

'Don't suppose, however, with all this, that I am going to lose Turner. On the contrary, I am more *épris* than ever, and that especially with his latest works, Goldau, &c. Monomania, you think. Possibly; nevertheless, I should not have spoken so audaciously as I have under the influence of any conviction, however strong, had I not been able to trace, in my education, some grounds for supposing that I might in deed and in truth judge more justly of him than others can. I mean, my having been taken to mountain scenery when a mere child, and allowed, at a time when boys are usually learning their grammar, to ramble on the shores of Como and Lucerne; and my having since, regardless of all that usually occupies the energies of the traveller, —art, antiquities, or people—devoted myself to pure, wild, solitary, natural scenery; with a most unfortunate effect, of course, as far as general or human knowledge is concerned, but with most beneficial effect on that peculiar sensibility to the beautiful in all things that God has made, which it is my present aim to render more universal. I think too that just as it is impossible to trace the refinements of natural form, unless with the pencil in the hand—the eye and mind never being keen enough until excited by the effort to imitate—so it is nearly impossible to observe the refinement of Turner unless one is in the habit of copying him. I began copying him when I was fourteen, and so was early initiated into much which escapes even the observation of artists, whose heads are commonly too full of their own efforts and productions to give fair attention to those of others. That it was politic to give expression to all my feelings respecting Turner might well be denied, had my object in the beginning been what it is now. But I undertook, not a treatise on art or nature, but, as I thought, a small pamphlet defending a noble artist against a strong current of erring public opinion. The thing swelled under my hands, and it was not till I had finished the volume that I had any idea to what I might be led. I saw that I should have to recast the whole, some time or other; and was too impatient to do *something*, to do so at once. So I let it go on as it was. The very end and aim of the whole affair was Turner; and when I let the second edition appear without alteration, it was because I found my views on many points altering and expanding so rapidly that I should never have got the thing together again until the whole of the following portions were completed. So I determined to let it alone, write the rest first, and then recast the whole. I think I shall have it too long by me to run the risk of flippancy of manner again, and the illustrations will render it unnecessary for me to run into caricatured description. I am going to Paris for some time, and then to Florence, before I put it finally together; chiefly to study the early Italian schools, for I want to bring the public, as far as I can, into something like a perception that religion must be, and always has been, the ground and moving spirit of all great art. It puts me into a desperate rage when I hear of Eastlake's buying Guidos for the National Gallery. He at least ought to know better—not that I should anticipate anything from looking at his art, but from his reputed character and knowledge.

'I shall be, as you will easily conceive, no little time in getting my materials together. In fact, I have to learn half of what I am to teach. The engravers plague me sadly, and I am obliged at last to take the etching into my own hands, and this demands much time. In fact, I ought to have good ten years' work before I produce anything; but the evil is crying, and I must have at it. I hope in twelve or eighteen months to see my way to a sort of an end; and however imperfectly (owing to my narrow reading and feeble hand in *exhibiting* what I feel), I think I shall yet throw the principles of art into a higher system than ordinary writers look for: showing that the principles of beauty are the same in all things, that its characters are typical of the Deity, and of the relations which in a perfect state we are to hold with him; and that the same great laws have authority in *all* art, and constitute it great or contemptible in their observance or violation.

'And now can you tell me of any works which it is necessary I should read on a subject which has given me great trouble—the essence and operation of the imagination as it is concerned with art? Who is the best metaphysician who has treated the subject generally, and do you recollect any passages in Plato or other of the Greeks particularly bearing upon it?

'Do you know Eastlake at all, or any man connected with the National Gallery? I hope you do all you can to put a stop to this buying of Guidos and Rubenses. Rubens may teach us much of mere art, but there is plenty of him in the country, and for Guido there is not even this excuse. We want Titians, we want Paul Veroneses. Our English school must have colour. Above all, we want the only man who seems to me to have united the most intense feeling with all that is great in the artist as such—John Bellini. I don't hope yet for Giotto or Fra Angelico; but if they would give us John Bellini and Titian I shouldn't grumble. I intend some time in my life to have a general conflagration of Murillos, by-the-by; I suppose more corruption of taste and quenching of knowledge may be traced to him than to any man who ever touched canvas.

'Pardon the villanous writing of this letter. I have been much interrupted, and have scarcely had a moment to myself, and I don't like to leave your kind one longer unanswered, or I would write rather more legibly.

'Ever, my dear Sir,
'Sincerely and respectfully yours,
'J. RUSKIN.'

To this letter Liddell seems to have written a long reply, and at the close to have desired his correspondent to drop for the future the formal style of address, and to call him simply by his surname.

An answer came from Mr. Ruskin, who was then living at Herne Hill, by return of post:

*October* 15, 1844.

'MY DEAR LIDDELL,

'You might think it affectation, were I to tell you the awkwardness with which I obey you, unless you considered the especially *child-like* position in which my good stars place me; for while many not older than I are already entrusted with the highest responsibilities that can demand or arouse the energy of manly character, I am yet as much at my ease as I was ten years ago, leading still the quiet life of mere feeling and reverie,

> That hath no need of a remoter charm
> By thought supplied, or any interest
> Unborrowed from the eye;

and in fact feeling scarcely any difference in myself from the time of impositions and collections, except in so far that I have discovered a great part of my time to have been lost, and made my way to a clearer view of certain ends which have been forwarded in nothing *but* vision; that I feel particularly ashamed of much that I have done, and particularly agonized about much that I have not done; that I should not now write letters of advice to Henry Acland, nor spend my time at Rome in sketching house-corners. But these changes of feeling render me, if anything, less disposed to unpupil myself than I was before; and therefore I obey you, though most willingly and gratefully, yet under protest, and only because there are better means of showing respect than mere matters of form.

'I could say more on this point, but I don't want to let your letter remain unanswered two days, and as I am going early into town to-morrow I must go on to some things I have to say about the points noticed in your letter. I am glad of your countenance in my opposition of studies, though I am a little afraid that such versatility of admiration—though it may make a good judge of art—makes a bad master of it. Nevertheless for my present ends it is better it should be so. But though I can turn, and am glad to be able to turn, to the most opposed sources of thought and characters of beauty, surely we ought to demand in each kind the perfect and the best examples. The world is so old, that there is no dearth of things first-rate; and life so short, that there is no excuse for looking at things second-rate. Let us then go to Rubens for blending, and to Titian for quality, of colour; to Cagliari for daylight, and Rembrandt for lamplight; to Buonarroti for awfulness, and to Van Huysum for precision. Each of their excellences has its use and order, and reference to certain modes and periods of thought, each its right place and proper dignity, incompatible. Any man is worthy of respect, in his own rank, who has pursued any truth or attainment with all his heart and strength. But I dread and despise the artists who are respectable in many things, and have been excelled by *some one* in everything. They are surely the more dangerous; for mediocrity in much is more comprehensible and attractive than the superiority in singleness, which has abandoned much to gain one end. Murillo seems to me a peculiar instance of this. His drawing is free and not ungraceful, but most imperfect, and slurred to gain a melting quality of colour. That colour is agreeable because it has no force nor severity; but it is morbid, sunless, and untrue. His expression is sweet, but shallow; his models amiable, but vulgar and mindless; his chiaroscuro commonplace, opaque, and conventional : and yet all this so agreeably combined, and animated by a species of waxwork life, that it is sure to catch everybody who has not either very high feeling or strong love of truth, and to keep them from obtaining either. He sketched well from a model, and now and then a single figure is very fine. He was not a *bad* painter, but he exercises a most fatal influence on the English school, and therefore I owe him an especial grudge. I have never entered the Dulwich Gallery for fourteen years without seeing at least three copyists before the Murillos. I *never* have seen *one* before the Paul Veronese.

'Next, with respect to Turner. I hope we are not opposed so much as you think. You know all my praise relates to his fidelity to, and love of, nature; it does not affirm in him the highest degree of solemnity, or of purity, in feeling or choice; and there is one circumstance which it seems to me has great influence on the minds of most men of feeling with respect to the works of the old masters as compared with him. On this subject—the creation of *pure* light and the sacrifice of everything to that end—I shall have much to say which (if it has not already occurred to you,—as it is most probable it should) will be more pleasantly read in print than in these hieroglyphics. Putting, however, this great source of power out of the question (and how much is involved in it I am not prepared to say), Turner will still appear rather in the light of a man of great power, drawing good indiscriminately, and therefore necessarily in very different kinds and degrees, out of everything, than of one devoting his energies to the full development of any particular moral emotion. He is rather the philosopher who perceives and equally exhibits all, than the ardent lover who raises some peculiar object by all the glories of imagination and with all the powers of his heart. His *powers* I think you never denied; at least when I first showed you my "Winchelsea" with the troop of soldiers at Oxford you said, "Yes, just like him, what no one else could do, but——." I am not quite sure what the particular "but" was; whatever it was, the *powers* were admitted. These powers then seem employed with a versatility which gives a result in art very much like what Don Juan is in literature, in everything but its want of moral feeling; a result containing passages and truths of every character, the most exquisite tenderness, the most gigantic power, the most playful familiarity, the most keen philosophy and overwhelming passion; and yet the whole will not produce on most men's minds the effect of a great poem. It does on mine; but certainly not to the degree which it might perhaps have done had there been less power and more unity. But it is great in its kind, and there is a system in both the art and the poem which may be reasoned out, and a great whole arrived at by reflection, as out of the chaos of human life and circumstances of its Providence. You must have felt this, I think, in looking over the "Liber Studiorum," in which you pass from the waste of English lonely moorland, with the gallows-tree ghastly against the dying twilight, to the thick leaves and dreamy winds of the Italian woods; from a study of cocks and hens scratching on a dunghill, to the cold, slow, colossal coil of the Jason serpent; from the sport of children about a willowy pond, to the agony of Rizpah.

'Turner, as far as I can ascertain anything of his past life, is a man of inferior birth and no education, arising at a time when there were no masters to guide him to great ends, and by the necessity and closeness of his study of nature withdrawn from strong human interests; endowed with singular delicacy of perception and singular tenderness of heart, but both associated with quick temper and most determined obstinacy, acting constantly under momentary impulses, but following out inflexibly whatever he has begun. Considering the little feeling for high art which, till within the last ten years, existed in this country, and the absence of sympathy with him in all but what he felt himself was the mere repetition of things bygone and which could not be bettered, we cannot but expect that there should be something to regret in his career, and something wanting to his attainments; and we must be content to receive the great and new lessons which he has read to us out of the material world, without quarrelling with the pettinesses and inconsistencies perhaps unavoidable unless where art is the minister to vast national sympathies and the handmaid of religion.

'I had much more to say, but my time is gone. I will attend to all you advise respecting the next book. I have not spoken about your kind defence of the present one, but cannot now. I think I shall be pretty sure not to use the language of any particular Church, for I don't know exactly which one I belong to. A Romanist priest, after a long talk under a tree in a shower at St. Martin's, assured me I was quite as good a Catholic as he. However, the religious language I shall use in what references I may have to make will be simply that of the Bible; and a few allusions to the doctrine of the Trinity and the general attributes of the Deity will be all I shall require. Thank you much for your reference to Vaughan about imagination, &c. Thank you also for your careful notes of the *errata* in the old book, which I shall take care to alter.

'If the only and single result of my labour had

been that which you mention, some rest to your mind in a period of pain, it would have been enough reward for me, even without the privilege which the close of your letter allows me, of continuing,
'My dear Liddell,
'Very truly and gratefully yours,
'J. RUSKIN.'

These letters, apart from their high intrinsic interest, show the common ground of artistic sympathy which, in distant days, had united Liddell and Mr. Ruskin; the profound respect with which Mr. Ruskin then regarded his senior (senior by only eight years), and the importance which he attached to his criticisms. It was a happy occurrence, therefore, that twenty-five years afterwards, when the great teacher was at the zenith of his fame, he was persuaded by his old friends, who had watched his career from those early times, to undertake the duties of a Chair which would bring him very prominently before the University, and give him an opportunity of instructing a large body of cultivated listeners on the topics nearest to his heart. The post was accepted somewhat diffidently.

'I was very grateful for your letter,' he wrote to the Dean in January 1870. 'I was beginning to feel great discomfort in the sense of inability to do—not indeed (for that I never hoped) what I would wish to do—but what with more deliberation I might be able to do. Your permission to give only seven lectures this spring will give me ease of mind, and, I hope, better power of thinking.

I am happy in the general thoughts of what may be possible to me; clear enough, for all practical purposes, as to what I have to say; and a *little* sanguine (yet not so as to be hurt by disappointment) respecting the effect of carefully chosen examples of more or less elementary art, put within the daily reach of all students, with notes enough to enable them to look at once for their main qualities. It is pardonable to be sanguine when I have you and Henry Acland to advise me and help me. I am well assured you know that I will do my best, and that not in any personal vanity.'

Dr. Woods has not exaggerated the deep impression which Mr. Ruskin's lectures, from 1869 to 1879, made upon the Oxford world; and his influence as a resident was exercised in many and various ways, some perhaps not a little Quixotic. He had rooms in Corpus, and his friendship with his near neighbours at the Deanery ripened into close intimacy. He would not indeed dine with them.

'I never dine out,' he wrote to Mrs. Liddell, 'tired or not. There is really nothing that makes me more nervously uncomfortable than the sound of voices becoming indecipherable round a clatter of knives.'

But he would often consult the Dean on matters where wide classical knowledge was specially needed; and there are letters from Liddell, written during the busiest days of his Vice-Chancellorship, discussing at great length, and illustrating by many quotations, the precise meaning of ἴον, and its identification with our 'violet,' and whether there was any Greek word answering exactly to our 'moss.'

Some years afterwards Liddell endeavoured, but without success, to persuade Mr. Ruskin to entrust the publication of his works to the University Press, and to allow them to be sold at reasonable prices.

'Many persons,' he wrote, 'wish to possess them, and cannot procure them except at a price which is prohibitive to all but the wealthy; moreover the profit of the large prices demanded goes not to you (as it ought), but to speculating booksellers or agents.' 'The speculating booksellers,' replied Mr. Ruskin, 'make no profit on my books, except on those which are out of print by my own wish. The others are perfectly accessible, venal to all men; the best of them for the price of a couple of bottles of good Sillery, and they shall not be sold cheaper. All my purposes in this matter are told at some length in *Fors*.'

# CHAPTER VII

DEANERY OF CHRIST CHURCH (*continued*)

THE Dean became Vice-Chancellor in Michaelmas Term, 1870, in succession to Dr. Leighton, Warden of All Souls College. No Dean of Christ Church had held the Vice-Chancellorship since Aldrich in 1692-4. Before that time it had not been uncommon for the two offices to be held together when occasion served. Owen and John Fell were conspicuous figures among the Vice-Chancellors of the seventeenth century. But the custom had fallen into desuetude, and Liddell broke through a venerable tradition in accepting the office. It was no light addition to his labours, and he was now fifty-nine years of age; but by universal acknowledgment he discharged the onerous duties for four years with unsurpassed dignity and efficiency. The Vice-Chancellor is in a very real sense the Head of the University. He presides over its public assemblies and its Hebdomadal Council; he is chairman of all committees and delegacies, and has a large share in the appointment of Professors, Examiners, and Preachers; he is the chief representative of the University on all occasions of public ceremony, except during the rare official visits of the Chancellor himself. Much influence and much patronage thus belong to the holder of this important office; and it is but natural that such power should not unfrequently be used during the short tenure of the office for the furtherance of the interests of the College of which the Vice-Chancellor of the time is Head, or for the advancement of political or ecclesiastical causes in which he is interested. Liddell brought to the work lengthened experience, thorough business habits, and familiarity with all academical questions; but he also brought that entire impartiality and clear sense of justice of which we have so often spoken already, and altogether declined to allow private friendships or personal predilections to influence his conduct. He distinctly raised the whole conception of the office, and laid it down amid universal regret, having won the profound respect of members of every party—a difficult achievement anywhere, but exceptionally difficult in the small world of Oxford.

No very important events occurred during his Vice-Chancellorship. The new Chancellor, the Marquess of Salisbury, had been admitted to his office just before, and had presided at the Commemoration of 1870. There was a momentary lull in the attempts to reform the institutions of the University; the Duke of Cleveland's Commission of inquiry into its revenues (the prelude to the Parliamentary Commission of 1877) began its investigations in 1872. But reform was then, as always, in the air. The University Tests Act of 1871 involved many changes in the statutes, to bring them into harmony with the new enactments; and on various questions connected with the examination statutes there were continual discussions, and some considerable alterations were made. One of the most important of these, affecting the Final Honours School of Literae Humaniores, came into force in 1873. There were also many debates and proposals in connexion with the school of Theology, a school only founded in 1870; and a division was made in 1872 between the schools of Law and Modern History, which had formed one school since 1853.

The Dean discharged his new duties with the utmost conscientiousness. He was very methodical in attendance at meetings and at University sermons; nothing could exceed his punctual fulfilment of all, even the most tiresome, routine duties.

'Nowhere,' writes Professor Max Müller, in an article already referred to, 'was his silent influence felt so much as when as Vice-Chancellor he acted as chairman of committees. There was a restraining influence in his very presence, people seemed ashamed of lowering themselves before him by selfish, ungenerous, or unacademic behaviour. No gossip was allowed in his presence, no insinuations were tolerated against anybody not present to defend himself;—no uncommon event at meetings, particularly when, at the same time, to disclose what is said on these occasions is considered dishonourable. If a debate had lasted too long, his question, " Is there anybody who wants to say anything else?" was generally sufficient to stop the flow of not always enlightening eloquence. As to any artifices of which chairmen are not always guiltless, such as proroguing a meeting instead of taking a vote, postponing a decision in order to secure the presence of a few more favourable voters—very harmless contrivances, it may be, in the eyes of so-called practical men, or men of business—the Dean would never have condescended to any of them. He knew of no "roguery" that was permissible in order to secure success. Every one who has had the privilege of sitting on committees with the Dean knows what a change his absence made, and how truly and widely his services, nay, his very presence, were appreciated, particularly after he had left Oxford.'

But he resolved to favour no party in the administration of his office. In making all appointments he took the utmost pains to find out the best men, and to dismiss all other claims but fitness. The selection of preachers gave him a good deal of trouble: his own knowledge of the foremost preachers in the English Church was naturally imperfect; he used to consult his friends, and especially Stanley; and one can remember the many questions asked, and the anxious desire to secure men of real merit, who would be likely to attract large congregations: the result being that divines of all parties, and from all parts of England, came up from time to time in answer to his invitation. Some, who travelled to Oxford to preach on a Sunday afternoon in Lent, were grievously disappointed at their audience at that untoward time: accustomed to address crowded churches, they found themselves in an almost empty building; and the Vice-Chancellor shared their disappointment. But he had the satisfaction of securing Jowett (then scarcely ever heard) to preach a remarkable sermon in 1871, when the church was full to overflowing; and Liddon and Stanley (as has been already mentioned) preached by his invitation on two consecutive Sundays in the same year. Dr. Pusey succeeded Dr. Stanley as preacher on the Jewish Interpretation of Prophecy. The present Bishop of Lincoln (then Principal of Cuddesdon) was followed by Mr. Stopford Brooke; and odd juxtapositions such as these showed the generous breadth of the Vice-Chancellor's sympathies, or at least his desire to give every party in the Church a hearing in the University pulpit.

One minor reform connected with St. Mary's was carried out at this period. Attendants at the sermons are familiar with the University Hymnal, in its dark blue cover; and perhaps, during some long sermon, have not been unwilling to peruse its contents and study the interesting notes at the end. But comparatively few will recollect its first appearance in the Summer Term of 1872, or the poverty-stricken selection of verses from the old metrical versions of the Psalms which the present volume superseded. In 1871 the University authorized the preparation of a new hymnal, and the Delegates of the Clarendon Press appointed a small committee to compile the book. The committee consisted of the Vice-

Chancellor, as chairman; Dr. W. Bright, Dr. Liddon, Mr. John Griffiths, Mr. Henry Smith, Mr. Wickham (now Dean of Lincoln), and the present writer. To these were added, as musical authorities, Dr. Corfe and Dr. Stainer. Each member of the committee sent in a list of the hymns which he considered most suitable for the special purpose of the book; and when these had been printed a selection was made, and the volume now in use exhibits the survival of what were deemed the fittest. The Dean took a lively interest in the discussions. To his own special choice and advocacy is due the insertion of some stanzas of Milton's hymn on the Nativity. It was objected that there was no tune to suit the metre, but Dr. Stainer replied with a promise that one should be forthcoming; yet the hymn has never (it is believed) been sung at St. Mary's. It was much wished that some Latin hymns should be introduced. Few, however, were really suitable, and in some which were selected changes had to be made. In the 'Ecce quem vates' Liddell's taste corrected the lines:

> Dexter in Parentis arce
> Qui cluis virtutibus

into the sonorous words:

> Dexter assidens Parenti
> Summa nactus robora.

And in the 'Dies irae' he suggested the more rhythmical 'Crucis *explicans* vexilla' instead of *expandens*; the line being an almost necessary substitute for the original 'Teste David cum Sibylla.'

One can remember many delightful criticisms on modern hymnody which fell from the Dean's lips: they were the ripe judgment of a master of the English tongue; and the many warnings on the score of orthodoxy which were uttered by the otherwise silent mentor of the committee, Mr. Griffiths. The notes were compiled chiefly by Dr. Bright. Great care was exercised to bring the text, in every case, as near as possible to the original; but it was not thought advisable to press this principle too far. The committee declined to substitute for the familiar opening of our Christmas hymn the far nobler original:

> Hark, how all the welkin rings,
> Glory to the King of kings;

although in 'Rock of Ages' they retained the strange expression 'When mine eye-strings break in death.' The doxologies and 'Amens' of modern hymnals were deliberately omitted. The volume is not without its blemishes, but it has for many years fulfilled its purpose well; and Liddell, who selected the type and binding, was greatly pleased with it.

It was during this same busy period that the Dean, in 1875, completed his twentieth year of office; and his portrait, painted by Mr. Watts, was presented to him at the Gaudy in the summer of 1876, as a gift from members of Christ Church. It was arranged that Liddell's former pupil, Earl Granville, should make the presentation; but, to the Dean's great disappointment, he was not well enough to attend. His place, however, was taken by Mr. Gladstone, and none who were present on that occasion are likely to forget the eloquent words with which he spoke of the Dean in proposing his health. To Liddell himself the ceremony was not a little trying:

'I had,' he writes, 'to sit under a shower-bath of praise from Mr. Gladstone. He delivered a really magnificent oration; but I felt very uncomfortable under it, and made a very lame acknowledgment. It was quite *miraculous* (nothing less) to hear the torrent of eloquence he poured forth for more than half an hour.'

It is interesting, as illustrating the great orator's extraordinary facility of speech, to add that only a few hours before, one of the Censors (the present writer) had, at Mr. Gladstone's special request, furnished him on a few sheets of note-paper with a list of the chief topics on which it would be proper for him to enlarge: and each in its order came forth, elaborated in the magnificent periods of the speaker.

This mention of Mr. Gladstone recalls another visit of a very different kind, which he paid to Oxford fifteen years afterwards. He came on this later occasion not to Christ Church but to All Souls: not as an orator, but as a simple student; and very delightful his visit was to all concerned. Liddell thus describes it in a letter to his son, who was then travelling in India:

'I did not in my last letter tell you about Mr. Gladstone's visit to Oxford. It was very surprising.

## Mr. Gladstone at Oxford in 1890

He wrote to Sir William Anson, saying that he should like to occupy rooms in All Souls (of which college he is an Honorary Fellow) for ten days or a fortnight, having some work on hand for which he should have to visit the Bodleian. No one would believe it at first. He seldom or never goes anywhere without Mrs. Gladstone; and how was he to live alone in college rooms, without her solicitous attentions? However, he came, stayed for about ten days, and seemed supremely happy. Politics were excluded altogether. I asked him to dinner, and invited some known scholars and *literati* to meet him. One day he dined in the common room, another at our club; three days in All Souls Hall, and where on the other two or three days I do not remember. He made himself very agreeable, and talked to every conceivable person on every conceivable subject. Mr. Goschen says it was the most remarkable episode in a most remarkable life. One night Mr. Gladstone went to the Union. He declined to take part in any debate, but said he would give them a kind of lecture on certain recent discoveries of Assyrian antiquities as bearing on Homer. One of these was that the Assyrian Hades had seven gates, through which the mythical hero Ishtar had to pass. Now, he said, Homer speaks of an Ἀΐδαο πυλάρτης, which is interpreted *gate-keeper*; so that it is clear Homer had the seven Assyrian gates in his mind. Q.E.D. He can persuade himself of anything. He values this discovery so highly that he has sent me a note of it for insertion in the Lexicon. By the way, I am ungrateful, for he paid the very highest compliment to the Lexicon.'

Liddell's experience as Headmaster of Westminster made his advice especially valuable in relation to all Public School matters; and though he avoided, as far as possible, engaging himself to the performance of duties which would call him away from Oxford, he could not escape them altogether. He was for many years on the council of Cheltenham College; and his official connexion with Westminster gave him a permanent place on its new governing body from its creation in 1869.

At Cheltenham he was one of a distinguished group of men who had been selected to co-operate with the local governors of that college. Lord Redesdale was chairman of the council; and it was accustomed to meet, not at Cheltenham, but in Lord Redesdale's room at the House of Lords.

'There were half a dozen men of mark,' writes the present Dean of Wells, 'among the council, besides the excellent chairman Lord Redesdale, a very hard man to convince of the goodness of a bad case, and a most kind friend to the college and to me. These were Dr. Liddell, Dean of Christ Church, Dr. Thompson, Master of Trinity, Sir Michael Hicks-Beach, Lord James of Hereford, Bartholomew Price, afterwards Master of Pembroke, and my own contemporary, W. L. Newman, whose solid intellect broke down under pressure of overwork in the early seventies. The Dean was excellent at business. His questions at a council meeting were few and piercing, his view clear, his solution practical. He brought to its deliberations exceptional gifts, exceptionally required there.'

## 'Election' at Westminster School

The connexion between Westminster and Christ Church was, as we have seen, a very ancient and a very close one; and the Dean, by venerable custom, went every year to the school to elect boys to studentships, now called scholarships, at Christ Church. He was accompanied by an examiner, usually one of the Censors or Tutors, who also had the status of an elector. At Westminster he was lodged at the Deanery, and there met his brother potentate, the Master of Trinity College, Cambridge, bent upon a like errand, and accompanied also by an examiner. In old days the visit began on the eve of Rogation Sunday, and lasted till the following Wednesday afternoon. Its duration has now been curtailed, and the date altered. Before the railway to Oxford was opened the journey was performed by road, and the Dean of those days could not return to his home at Oxford before Thursday afternoon. It was his duty to preach the University sermon on the Thursday morning, Ascension Day; but this duty was in his absence always performed by one of the students. With the completion of the railway the return was, of course, easily effected on the Wednesday; but so anxious was Dean Gaisford to observe the ancient tradition, as to the impossibility of his earlier return, that to the end of his life, though safely back in Christ Church on the previous night, he was careful not to appear in public till Thursday afternoon.

The few days spent at Westminster were a pleasant episode in each Summer Term. There were dinner parties, and stately processions on the Sunday to the Abbey, where 'High' service was twice performed, and the electors sat in dignity, dressed in full canonicals; and on the two following days there were processions through the cloisters to the big school, which was decorated for the occasion with ancient tapestry. The electors sat at a horse-shoe table, also covered with tapestry, the Dean of Westminster presiding. There they had to listen for several hours during two days, while the candidates for election were examined 'viva voce' by the Oxford and Cambridge examiners alternately. On the Monday evening there was a banquet to the electors in the college hall, and epigrams were recited by the Queen's Scholars. On the Wednesday there was again 'High' service in the Abbey, and at the conclusion the boys assembled in the college hall, and the Headmaster entered and read out the choice of the electors,—and many a boy's destiny for life was then decided for better or for worse. It was a leisurely and dignified proceeding, and had many good points, but it has been much shortened of recent years, the examination being now largely on paper. Dean Stanley used thoroughly to enjoy his sessions, with the Dean of Christ Church on one side of him, and the Master of Trinity on the other (each had precedence of his brother chief in alternate years) at the table in hall or school, and talked delightfully to them all the time.

This annual visit to the school kept up an interest in Westminster on the part of the Christ Church authorities, who fully recognized the value to their college of the prosperity and good management of the school. It was very important that its boys should be well taught, and their numbers well maintained. The question of the removal of the school into the country had been seriously considered, as we have mentioned, during Liddell's Headmastership, and it was again discussed under his successor. In 1860 a large meeting of Old Westminsters was held in the schoolroom, under the presidency of Dean Trench, to consider the matter, and Liddell was asked to attend and speak. He gave his opinion, in no uncertain tones, in favour of removal, declaring that he saw no way by which its ancient prosperity as a boarding school, and its legitimate place among the leading Public Schools of England, could be maintained unless it was moved into the country. 'Even if an angel from heaven were to come down, I do not believe the school's fortunes could be retrieved, so long as it remains in London.' Many Old Westminsters present at the meeting were offended at so outspoken a declaration. They were very reluctant to approve of so radical a change as removal into the country, though indeed few of them sent their sons to the school. It was found impossible, without the support of the main body of Old Westminsters, to carry out such a scheme, and it was definitely abandoned. But there is no doubt that Liddell's forecast was largely justified; the boarding houses have now for many years past become quite an insignificant part of the school: the increase in numbers—and that not very large—has come from the increased proportion of day-boys.

When the school—under the provisions of the Public Schools Act—acquired its own property, and was made independent of the Chapter, a governing body was created for it, upon which various interests were represented. The Dean of Christ Church was an *ex officio* member of the new body, and Christ Church also sent one elective member. Liddell was for many years regular in attendance at the meetings, and though he never spoke much his authority was very great. One important question came up from time to time, the expediency of retaining the college with its forty Queen's Scholars in the enjoyment of their ancient autonomy within the college building. It was thought by some that to hamper the chief prizes of the school with the obligation to reside within the walls of college, at a time when the boarding element of the school was dwindling, was seriously to diminish the value of the scholarships, and unduly to restrict the competition for them. It was urged that the Queen's Scholarships—the chief prizes of the school—should be offered to general competition, without this restriction of residence in the college. To this proposal Liddell ultimately gave his full adhesion; he had for long been favourable to it, but doubted the wisdom of carrying so great a change without evidence of a strong backing of public sentiment in its favour. The question has been settled—at least for a time—by a compromise. The forty Queen's Scholars still exist within their college fortress; but there are now twenty more scholars, of whom this obligation of residence is not exacted: so that clever boys who are desirous of living at home and attending the school as day-boys may yet enjoy the dignity of a Queen's Scholarship.

Both at Cheltenham and at Westminster Dean Liddell had to perform the duty (perhaps the most arduous duty that belongs to governors of a school) of selecting a Headmaster. To this task he brought the same inflexible justice which he showed on every occasion. No consideration of personal friendship, or college claims, would influence him for a moment in preferring one whom he deemed a less worthy to a more worthy candidate. He would be even a little suspicious of such claims, and look with the utmost readiness on the merits of candidates who were strangers to him. It was a grand and a rare impartiality, and gave to his final judgment a unique weight and authority.

He may be contrasted in this respect with a brother Head, who was always firmly convinced that members of his own college were of pre-eminent merit. 'They have not taken our man at ——,' said one of his Fellows to him after an election to a Headmastership. 'Have they not?' said the chief, 'then they have made a *very great* mistake. He was by far the best of the candidates. By the way,' he added a few minutes afterwards, 'can you tell me who were standing for that Headmastership? I have never heard their names.'

It will perhaps be a matter of surprise to the reader that no reference has been made to Liddell's own sermons throughout his long tenure of the Deanery. It was certainly a matter of regret with those who remembered the excellence of his preaching during the years of his residence as Tutor (as has been previously mentioned), that after his return to Oxford as Dean he seldom preached before the University. Sir Henry Acland, one of the few persons now living who heard those earlier sermons, still cherishes the most enthusiastic admiration for Liddell as a theologian, insisting on his richly-stored mind, his well-balanced judgment, his uncontroversial temper, and wide charity. He instances particularly a sermon on John vii. 17, in which the phrase 'If any man will do his will' was discussed with elaborate care and thoroughness. Other men of the older generation fully confirm this estimate. Even in the last year of his life he received an urgent request from Dr. A. S. Farrer, Canon of Durham, that he would publish some of the sermons which he had preached more than half a century before at Whitehall or at St. Mary's. And Mr. Goldwin Smith, in recording his recollections of Liddell in those distant days, dwells on his high reputation as a theologian, and expresses his disappointment that the promise of that time was not fulfilled in later years.

'There was, I think,' he writes, 'a certain turn in the course of the Dean's life and interests. In the midst of the theological fray at Oxford between the Oxford school and its opponents, he preached one or two very able sermons of a liberal and philosophic kind, and raised the expectation that he was going to be, as he well might have been, a theological leader in that line. But he seemed afterwards to turn aside and to devote himself entirely to Classical pursuits, and to the production of the Lexicon which has been such a blessing to all scholars. Perhaps it was that his serene mind abhorred controversy, and foresaw that if he gave himself up to theology in those days, controversy must be the result. Still, by some of us the Lexicon, excellent as it is, was not accepted as a full indemnification for the disappointment of the hopes of light and leading with which we had been inspired.'

Whatever cause may be assigned, it is undoubtedly true that after Liddell's return to Oxford in 1855 he rarely preached before the University except on Good Friday and Christmas Day, when it was his duty to do so. But his words were always well worth hearing. In Michaelmas Term, 1867, he delivered a very remarkable sermon on the philosophic basis of the doctrine of the Real Presence. It attracted wide attention, and was published 'in deference to opinions which the author is bound to respect.' He preached indeed not unfrequently in the Cathedral, after the introduction of morning sermons in 1869. It was his custom to address the undergraduates on the first Sunday of each Term; and on these occasions he would deal with current events in the political and religious world, and with incidents connected with the common life which they shared together as members of Christ Church. He was occasionally persuaded to print his discourses for private circulation; and a special interest still attaches to those which narrated the history of the Cathedral church, and described the demolition and partial reconstruction of the shrine of St. Frideswide. But there is no doubt that, as he grew older, he shrank more and more from theological discussions; and indeed, as some of his later letters indicate, ceased to interest himself in questions which even in a remote degree trenched on theological controversy. Moreover, distaste for the attempt to solve matters insoluble was an abiding element of his character. In almost the last letter which he wrote to Sir Henry Acland (Christmas Eve, 1897), he refers to 'my old dislike of speculation in things we cannot know—"Die Kerle die speculiren," Goethe says.'

THE DEANERY, CHRIST CHURCH, FROM THE GARDEN.

# CHAPTER VIII

### HOME LIFE

The chief events of the Dean's long reign at Christ Church have now been briefly sketched, and an attempt has been made to give a faithful picture of some of the many phases of his busy public life. But the picture needs to be completed by a short description of his home life during the same period.

When he came back to Oxford from Westminster, his family consisted of one son and three daughters, the youngest of whom was quite an infant, having been born in January of the previous year. Two daughters and three sons were born at the Deanery, and one of them, Albert Edward Arthur (whose names indicate his two godfathers, the Prince of Wales and Arthur Stanley), died in infancy, as has been already mentioned, in May 1863. For many years therefore the home life involved, for the parents, the care and training of their children, and all the delightful interests which gather round the life of a young family. The reminiscences of this period are full of charm; and the apparent contrast between the public and private life of the

Dean will perhaps surprise many who dealt with him only in official relations.

The home life, as recalled by those who knew it best, was a very simple and happy one. He tried to be with his children as much as was possible amid the business of the Term, and of an evening was accustomed to hasten up to the drawing-room as soon as dinner (not so late then as now) was ended, that they might have their hour's reading before bed-time came between 8 and 9. He shared their enjoyment of good tales of adventure, and some favourite books he read over two or three times to different detachments of his children. The first book of his choice was *The Children of the New Forest*; and as soon as they were old enough to appreciate Scott he would read some of the Waverley novels, selecting *Ivanhoe* to begin with, and then his own special favourites, *The Antiquary* and *Old Mortality*. He was intensely fond of Scott, both of his novels and of his poetry; the 'swing' of the verses had a peculiar charm for him; and the listeners learnt to share his taste. Then, after the children had gone to bed, he was accustomed to work for an hour or more, correcting the Lexicon; and when they grew older, and sat up till a later hour, he would delight in listening to their music as he went on uninterruptedly with his work.

His children cherish with loving remembrance those early days. However pressing the calls upon his time might be, he still found leisure to be with them during some part of every day. Their first thought, when family prayers were over in the morning, was to arrange the hour for a ride with him, which generally they took in turns. They consulted the Letts's diary which many will remember hanging by his fireplace in the study, and found there a list of his engagements for the day; and according to these the time for the ride was fixed. On Mondays, when the Hebdomadal Council always met at one o'clock, a morning hour was necessarily chosen, involving the additional pleasure of a respite from lessons. The high ground about Bagley Wood and Foxcombe, or the forest glades of Wytham Park, were their usual resort. And as they rode, their father taught them to know the different forest trees, and to notice the clouds and shadows and all the beauties of nature, or would tell them tales from history, or talk of the books he was reading aloud to them; and, as they grew older, would discuss various questions of the day.

In holiday time he was able to be much more with his children, and shared in all their interests. After Christmas Day (on which festival it is the Dean's duty to preach in the Cathedral at Christ Church) the whole family were accustomed, so long as his father was alive, to go down to the grand-parents' home at Charlton Kings; and then would come all sorts of Christmas amusements, and the Dean would help to prepare charades and compose parts for them to act. He was always expected to enter fully into their pastimes, and nothing was complete without his co-operation and approval.

In 1861 a small plot of land was bought near Llandudno, in order that a suitable house might be built as a holiday home. It was called Penmorfa, from the spot on which it stood, and was first inhabited in the long vacation of 1865. It was a delightful home for nine consecutive summers, till the growth of Llandudno, and its invasion by excursionists, robbed it of its privacy and quiet. The spot chosen for the house was a singularly beautiful one, and at that time quite retired. It was close by the shore, at the south-east corner of the Great Orme's Head, facing due south. The view extended over the Conway estuary, first to the lower heights of Penmaenbach, Moel Llys, and Penmaenmawr, with the ridge of Tal-y-fan bounding the amphitheatre between them, and then beyond to the loftier summits of Foel Fras and Carnedd Llewellyn. To the west lay an expanse of shallow sea, with Anglesea behind; and on a fine evening, when the tide was out and the sun set over the island, there were wondrous colours thrown on the hills, or reflected on the long stretch of wet sands. The place had been selected on account of the surpassing loveliness of the scene; and at that time, and for many years afterwards, the Great Orme's Head was untouched by a carriage road, and was a wild and little frequented headland, scored by rough paths and sheep-tracks, and still containing some rare plants to reward the search of botanists. Here the long vacations were spent by the children and their parents in unclouded happiness; there were endless walks and scrambles on the Great Orme, picnics, and drives, and lessons in sketching, when their father would suggest views and teach them how to use pencil and brush. And instead of late dinner, there was a common high tea in which the children joined, one of them always sitting next their father unless some tiresome guest usurped the coveted place. Sometimes if the day had been hot, and the moon was near the full, the walk would be postponed till late, and a ramble by moonlight over the Great Orme was a rare and special treat.

Visitors came and went. Among them was Mr. (now Sir William) Richmond, who spent eight weeks at Penmorfa engaged in painting 'The Sisters,' the exquisite picture of the three eldest daughters. Mr. Gladstone also came; and one day in the midst of a walk round the Great Orme he suddenly stopped, and clung to the Dean, declaring that he could not bear to look down upon the sea from the height which they had reached. They were on a steep and rocky path, and advance or retreat was equally difficult. The path became worse as they clambered down, the Dean leading Mr. Gladstone along, with eyes closed, while the rest of the party formed a sort of buttress to protect him on the seaward side. They were all thankful when the lower ground was safely reached.

Liddell's own tastes were of a very simple kind. He was abstemious, and scarcely touched wine. He was very regular in his hours, and never worked late at night. During the Oxford Term, he was always at morning chapel. He never smoked, and detested the pollution of the fresh air by the fumes of tobacco. He was in early life, and indeed for some years after he became Dean, a good walker, delighting in long walks : but Oxford engagements so greatly curtailed his leisure hours, that he found riding the best method of getting sufficient exercise in a short space of time. His favourite books were Shakespeare, Horace, Scott, and Boswell's *Life of Johnson*. They were always on his study table.

'I read Boswell's *Life of Johnson*,' he wrote, 'again and again with ever increasing pleasure. I think if I was allowed only one book (besides the Bible) to take with me to a desert island, that would be the book.'

The position of the Dean made it necessary that the Deanery should be a centre of hospitality, and throughout his long tenure of the office that hospitality was lavishly extended, not only to members of Christ Church and the wider circle of the University, but also to the frequent guests who visited Oxford. Mrs. Liddell's social duties made a great demand upon her time and strength, and many generations of Oxford men will recall with gratitude the refined courtesy and generous welcome shown to all their guests by host and hostess. The Dean indeed was not quite at his best if he lacked congenial neighbours at the table. He used to confess that he had no 'small talk,' and was sometimes not a little irresponsive in ordinary conversation. The undergraduates, who were conscientiously asked to breakfast at the Deanery, were often painfully nervous in his company, and he seemed to share their feelings. But with friends whom he liked, and with whose tastes he was in sympathy, he was the most delightful of companions; full of accurate information, and ready to pour it out, on subjects of art, or history, or politics. He was a careful student of passing events, both domestic and foreign; keenly interested in all the great movements of his time; profoundly distrustful of Mr. Gladstone in his later developments; cherishing warm admiration for some of the statesmen of the older generation, especially Sir Robert Peel. He used sometimes to say that no deaths had inflicted so great loss upon England in his time as the deaths of the Prince Consort and Sir George Cornewall Lewis. He was full of bitter sorrow when the news of Gordon's death arrived. In answer to a birthday letter from his eldest daughter he wrote:

'I ought not to reply to your affectionate words in so sad a strain. But really, just at present, my heart is woe for Gordon, and the feeling touches all my thoughts. It is the saddest, most dismal event that I have lived to see. When your Uncle Charles heard of it he burst into tears, and my feelings were close akin to his. What a true hero! I was sure he would never be a prisoner. Better that he should die sword in hand than that he should fall into the hands of those savages.'

As the years passed on, there came to the home at the Deanery the inevitable alternations of joy and sorrow which life is sure to bring. There was the proud satisfaction of the parents when their younger son won a scholarship at Eton, and afterwards crowned a brilliant career at Christ Church by gaining a First Class in the Classical School, and a Fellowship at All Souls College. On hearing of his son's success in the Schools in July 1888 he wrote:

'You can imagine—no, indeed, you hardly can imagine—the delight which we all felt on receiving Lionel's telegram announcing the news of your success. Never was success better deserved.... And now, my dear boy (I must still call you boy), you are fairly launched on the sea of life. You begin with good auspices, and I have no doubt that, so far as your own efforts go, as has been the beginning, so will be the whole course of your life. I cannot expect to see much of your future career. But I have seen enough of it to make me feel ready to depart in peace and in confidence. We are, indeed, very happy in our children. So long as my life is spared, your career will be, as it has been, one chief cause of happiness and contentment. Your mother will add her greetings to this imperfect expression of my own feelings.'

There were three happy marriages, and delightful visits to the new homes of their son and daughters in Hants and Fife, with all the affectionate interest taken in the grandchildren whom they loved to have near them. The Dean's letters to his married daughters are full of simple kindly goodness; every detail of their lives he wishes to hear of; and, as often as he can, he contrives to be with them.

But there were heavy—very heavy—bereavements also. His intense affection for both parents made him feel very deeply the loss of his mother in 1871, and of his father in the following year. Then in June 1876 came the crushing blow of his daughter Edith's death at the age of twenty-two, following close upon the joy of her engagement to be married, and coming with a startling suddenness after an illness of three days. The sorrow was so profound, so sacred, that it must not be dwelt on, even at this distance of time. But one may be allowed to quote a letter which Sir James Paget, who had been called in to advise on the case, addressed to Sir Henry Acland immediately after hearing of the death:

'This is surely the saddest thing that we have known among all the sadnesses that our calling has brought us to the sight of—a very tragedy. Nothing seems wanting for the perfection of sadness, and one cannot discern, in any of this world's hopes, a gleam of consolation. May God grant peace and comfort in the sure hope of heaven's joy. It seems very hard to be unable to stand aside for a time, and let life run by, while one might try to learn wisdom from these sorrows. But it cannot be; the work must be done, and, much worse, the pleasure must be worked out.'

A window at the east end of the south choir aisle

at Christ Church, called the St. Catherine's window, enshrines his daughter's memory; and her grave is just beyond it, in the quiet greensward which fringes the church. The inscription below the window tells the tale:—

> ✠ Sacra memoriæ EDITHÆ
> Henrici et Lorinæ Liddell filiæ,
> Quæ, juveni constantissima fide
> Vix quinque dies desponsa,
> Morbo correpta subitaneo
> Animam Deo reddidit
> Junii die xxvi° A.D. MDCCCLXXVI.
>
> Ave dulcissima, dilectissima Ave.

The wound was long in healing. A rest in retirement at Holnicote brought back in some measure the needed calm and physical strength; but the memory of those days was always fresh. From Holnicote the Dean wrote a few lines to his old friend Scott:

'Many thanks—such as an aching heart can render—for your kind letter. We are here for three weeks or thereabouts: Sir T. Acland has most kindly lent us this quiet and beautiful place to rest in; and we are all better, though what some of us had gone through, both in actual watching and still more in terrible anxiety, cannot soon be overcome.'

The death of Mrs. Liddell's aunt, Lady Smith, in 1877, at the remarkable age of 103 years and 9 months, and of her mother, Mrs. Reeve, in 1879, brought more sadness to the house; but perhaps few deaths affected Dean Liddell more deeply than that of his very dear friend Arthur Stanley, which occurred after a short illness in July 1881, at the comparatively early age of sixty-five. Liddell's affection for the Dean of Westminster, who was less than five years his junior, has already been mentioned; the two had been drawn together in many ways for many years, and were closely united in sympathies, religious and political. Liddell heard the news of his death when he was staying with his daughter, Mrs. Skene, at Pitlour, and wrote at once to Mrs. Liddell, who was then at Oxford:

'Alas! alas! and so my worst fears are realized; and our dear, dear friend must be taken to his last rest in that Abbey which he loved so well, and which owes so much to him. Ah me! Out of my own dear family no death could so rend my heart. Is there any one in England whose loss would be felt by so many, by people of so different conditions, creeds, and opinions? There was an all-embracing, loving kindliness in his nature which disarmed enmity, and made even those who most differed from him regard him with affection. It is a public loss, of which we can scarcely estimate the effect or the amount. I cannot, I cannot bear to think that I shall never again press his hand, or be greeted by his friendly smile, or listen to the charm of his words. What a fatal year! Not to speak of our own family loss—Rolleston, Coxe, and now our dear Stanley gone! *They* indeed were delivered from a state of hopeless disease, and they lived long enough in misery to make their nearest and dearest pray for their release. But he—how sudden has been his departure, how little expected, how crushing to those who loved him! Yet better so, than that he should have suffered a lingering and hopeless illness, and died after such a struggle as our poor friend at —— is making. Peace be with him, as it assuredly is with him. "Let me die the death of the righteous, and let my last end be like his."

'I cannot pass, on this paper, from thoughts of our beloved friend to those business matters which must claim attention while we are left on earth to minister one to another. Presently I shall be more collected, and will write a few lines respecting what we can and may do this summer.'

Next day he wrote again, having received by telegraph an urgent request to preach the funeral sermon on Stanley in Westminster Abbey:

'The telegram arrived about 3 p.m. yesterday. I answered: "Most reluctantly I must decline. The distance and the heat I could not well bear." And I have written in detail to-day. I COULD not have got through a sermon in the Abbey—I am sure I could not. Alas! if it were not for you, my dearest, and my beloved children, and one or two others, I feel as if life were at an end for me. All with whom one had sympathy falling one by one. It is a sad privilege to survive.'

It will be well to add in this place—as the matter affected Liddell's private rather than his public life—that on Stanley's death he was offered the Deanery of Westminster, and was very urgently pressed to take it. It was difficult to resist a pressure which implied an appreciation of his exceptional fitness for the post, and a gracious desire that he should accept it, on the part of those whose wishes were almost equivalent to a command; but Liddell, while feeling very deeply the honour paid to him, was conscious of his own inability at the age of seventy to undertake the very arduous duties of a new post, including the obligation of preaching sermons to vast congregations, and of guiding the services, and superintending all the varied matters of business connected with the rule of the great Abbey. It was a position rendered far more difficult than it would otherwise have been, from Stanley's splendid work as Dean; it was one which for Liddell had no attractions: his experience had not fitted him for it; he had never liked Westminster as a residence in former days, and was convinced that his health would break down if, at his now advanced age, he were once more to live there. His decision was quite clear, and was formed without any misgivings, and there is no doubt that it was a right one. He had yet strength for ten years more work in the familiar world of Oxford; if he had been transplanted to Westminster he would, in all probability, soon have sunk under the burden of the novel and uncongenial duties which would have faced him there.

Liddell's health, however, had been for many years satisfactory. The weakness of the chest, which had assumed so alarming a character in 1856, had yielded to the prescribed remedies. After two winters spent in the island of Madeira—'that island of the Atlantic (as he alluded to it in a sermon more than thirty years afterwards) which by its equable climate and gentle air seems to realize the description given by the great lyric poet of Greece of the islands of the blest,'—he returned to work with health fully restored. Except for crippling attacks of sciatica, painful and depressing at the time, he rarely ailed, and all the duties of his post were discharged year after year with unfailing regularity. In 1865, however, he met with a troublesome accident in Switzerland. He had been detained in Oxford that summer later than usual, owing to the contested election for Mr. Gladstone's seat at Oxford, which was then lost to Mr. Gathorne Hardy.

'It is very vexatious,' writes Liddell from the Sheldonian Theatre; 'the University is disgraced. To think that Oxford should reject Gladstone, and that such a constituency as Westminster should have returned Mr. John Stuart Mill!'

After this annoying business Liddell started for Switzerland in company with Dr. Acland and one of Acland's sons, and made for Engelberg. There, while descending a steep path, he slipped on a moss-covered stone and turned his left foot. He was with difficulty brought to the hotel, being quite unable to walk, and having to wait on the mountain until dark, when a *chaise-à-porteurs* reached him. At Engelberg he was a prisoner for a week, and then travelled by easy stages to Paris, where M. Nélaton, the Emperor's surgeon, visited him and discovered that the small bone of the leg was broken. It was properly set at once, and in time Penmorfa was reached, and the comforts of home obtained. Happily no permanent bad consequences resulted from the accident.

In the severe winter of 1880-1 Liddell endured a strange and most unpleasant experience. On January 18 he was travelling to Oxford from Bournemouth, in company with Mrs. Liddell, his youngest daughter and two sons, when on reaching a cutting near Radley station the train came to a standstill in a deep snow-drift. It could not be extricated, and the passengers were detained for nearly twenty-four hours in the carriage, without food, drink, warmth, or light. He described the event in a letter to Mrs. Skene :

'You really have no need to distress yourself about us. Strange to say, we have none of us suffered materially from our Arctic experiences. I do not think I can remember such a day as Tuesday the 18th, with Tuesday night and Wednesday morning. The wind howled, and was so furious that the heavy railway carriages shook and rocked under its force. The snow drove in swirling eddies all round and round. It drove into the carriages through every crevice; we had no light, for no lamp was in the carriages; no warmth, for the hot-water tins were cold as ice; no food to create inner warmth. Twenty-two hours without food at that temperature was indeed a great privation. Your mother and Vio were our great comforters. They retained their spirits, and to some extent their warmth, through all. I being held fast by the gout was a helpless piece of goods, I fear, but I hope I did not add materially to the difficulties. I should not have cared half as much if I could have got about. I think I suffered most in being carried by soldiers for about 200 yards from our carriage to the station, the snow driving furiously in one's face, and the poor fellows staggering with my weight through the deep snow. I wonder how they got me along at all. You would have been amused to see the motley party assembled about eleven on Wednesday morning in the little third-class waiting-room at Radley station, a stoker handing round tea from a kettle, and afterwards coffee in a bedroom ewer; all drinking in turn from the same tin can.'

It is a matter of surprise that no lasting bad effects resulted from this rough experience. The Dean soon recovered from the shock and fatigue, and within a few weeks was able to discharge his multifarious duties with his accustomed regularity.

# CHAPTER IX

RESIGNATION OF THE DEANERY, AND AFTER-LIFE

So the time passed on, every year adding authority and dignity to the venerable Dean. Honours came to him from various quarters. At Stanley's death he succeeded to his post of Professor of Ancient History at the Royal Academy. He became a Trustee of the British Museum, and received the Hon. Degree of LL.D. at Edinburgh. His duties at Christ Church were still discharged with unimpaired efficiency; nothing was neglected or delegated to others; and those who shared in the government of the House wondered at the readiness with which he threw himself into the discussion of the many and various proposals for changes and improvements which emanated from the governing body. He had none of the conservative instincts which are so commonly found in elderly men: he welcomed reforms to the last.

'Only a few months before his resignation,' writes Mr. Sampson, then Senior Censor, 'Sadler and myself and one or two others raised the question of what Christ Church did for poor men, and the "Extension" question generally (out of which the College at

Reading grew). We had a large committee, and held long meetings, and the Dean was as wise and generous and far-sighted as ever. There was none of the natural inertia and *non possumus* of old age, but he was kindly and hopeful, as though he were planning out a bit of work of which he would be able to see the issue.'

But the burden of his office grew heavier with advancing years; an exceptionally severe attack of sciatica in 1887 permanently impaired his walking powers; and Liddell had often averred, both in public and in private, that he would not consent to retain the Deanery when he was no longer able to perform its duties efficiently. 'I have spoken to my medical adviser,' he once said at the Gaudy, 'and have made him promise to tell me as soon as he thinks that I am becoming in any way unfit for my post: and as soon as that is told me I shall resign.' The audience thought perhaps of the Archbishop and Gil Blas; but the statement was made in all sincerity, and the promise faithfully observed. In the summer of 1891 the final resolution was come to, and resignation was determined upon. He wrote to Lord Salisbury on August 8 :

'DEAR LORD SALISBURY,

'I have waited for the prorogation of Parliament, when you will be in some measure freed from the pressure of business, before I communicate to you a purpose which I have deliberately formed. It is, to resign my office of Dean of Christ Church.

'You will believe that it is not without many

searchings of heart that I have come to this conclusion. Christ Church has been my home (barring nine years at Westminster) for more than sixty years. But it is my affection for the place that induces me to take this step. I am now in my eighty-first year, and feel that my work ought to be committed to younger and more vigorous hands. I will not say that I am unable to perform the routine duties of my office. But I am conscious of various infirmities incident to advancing years, and I cannot now take such part in academical and other business as ought to be undertaken by a person in my position. It cannot indeed be long before I must of necessity make the vacancy which I now propose to make voluntarily. But I wish, if I am permitted, to walk out of the Deanery rather than be carried out. This will be best for the college and myself. I have the satisfaction of believing that I leave the college in full efficiency, and that there never was a better or more devoted set of officers in charge.

'At Christmas then I propose that my resignation shall take effect. I announce this purpose to your Lordship beforehand, that you may have time to consider whom you will recommend to be my successor.

'Meantime, in the interest of the college, it will I think be expedient not to let the matter be generally known. But this I leave to your better judgment.

'I have the honour to remain,
'Dear Lord Salisbury,
'Yours very faithfully,
'HENRY G. LIDDELL.'

And so at the end of 1891, after a reign extending over thirty-six years and one term, he retired from his high office. He had taken a comfortable house situated among the pine woods of Ascot, with sheltered lawns and gardens, and a wide range of fine open country around, affording pleasant drives in all directions. Here he spent the remaining six years of his life, with his wife and unmarried daughters, in the enjoyment of well-earned and dignified repose.

He was never idle, even in these years of leisure. His faculties were happily quite unimpaired. He seldom used spectacles, except when persuaded to wear them for reading of an evening. His hearing remained perfect, and his mind as vigorous as ever. He still worked, as has been recorded, at the Lexicon, making many corrections throughout, and compiling a few pages of *addenda* and *corrigenda* for the final edition, which was published in the year before his death. He delighted in reading modern literature, and especially good biographies. He enjoyed the society of his neighbours and welcomed their friendship, and showed a kindly sympathy with all their doings. His advice and assistance were continually sought for in matters of business, and he was always ready to give the help of his wise counsel and ripe experience, and found himself chairman of various small committees to promote local objects. He took as keen and lively an interest in the discussion as to the remodelling of a golf club as he had ever taken in matters of academical importance; and busied himself eagerly in the establishment of the Nursing Home in South Ascot, of which Mrs. Liddell is now President. He was often consulted as to the appointments to Oxford Chairs; and he retained to the last one or two ties with the University. He was made an Honorary Student of Christ Church, and was still a Curator of the University Galleries; and one of the last visits that he paid to Oxford was to take part in the election of a successor to Professor Wallace in the Chair of Moral Philosophy which he had himself occupied half a century before. One matter disturbed him a little in 1892: the urgent request which came from his old friends, Sir John Mowbray and Mr. Vere Bayne, that he would allow them to place his statue in the niche on the north side of Kill-Canon. This proposal was genuinely distasteful to him. To Sir John Mowbray's first letter on the subject he replied:

'I feel deeply the high honour which you and Mr. Bayne propose to bestow upon me, and I thank you both with all my heart for your kind—too kind—appreciation of my services to Christ Church. . . . But I must ask you to forgive me if I demur to accepting this honour. Some time since, my kind friend Dr. Liddon, as I heard, proposed himself to place an effigy of me in the niche you mention. At that time I entreated that nothing of the kind should be done either by him or others. I have not changed my opinion. In the last few weeks I have received gifts and addresses far exceeding my expectation and, I fear, far exceeding my deserts.

I am more than grateful for the good opinions expressed of me, and I would fain hope that the honour you propose may at least be deferred. After a time people will perhaps take a different view of what is due to me, and may think that enough has been done. You will not, I am sure, think that I undervalue your kind proposal. On the contrary, I value it so highly that I think it goes beyond what I deserve.'

To this Sir John Mowbray sent a reply, stating fully the grounds of the request, and Mr. Bayne joined with him in asking for a reconsideration of the adverse decision: but Liddell still pleaded that he might not be pressed ἵστασθαι λίθινος. So the matter rested for a while; but the governing body of Christ Church backed up the request by the unanimous expression of a hope that Dr. Liddell would not withhold his consent to the execution of the statue; and in the end he was persuaded to waive his objections, and the statue (the work of Mr. Dressler) was put into its place in October 1893.

He was fond of occupying some of his spare moments in writing to old friends; and several characteristic extracts from his letters are worth recording. Sir Thomas Acland, his senior by two years, was engaged in writing a work (published subsequently under the title of *Knowledge, Duty, and Faith*, and containing a summary of philosophical principles as taught by great thinkers, ancient and modern), and he wrote in February 1894, asking for Liddell's judgment on some points:

'I wish I could help you,' he replied, 'but the summary of contents was too brief and general to enable me to form any conception of the substance of the treatise. And with regard to your account of Logic, I despair of saying anything worth sending. I fear I share Mountague Bernard's opinion that, after forty, Metaphysics become distasteful. I have so long discontinued any study of Speculative Philosophy, and am so ignorant of what has been said or written by moderns, such as Herbert Spencer, Lotze, &c., that I *could* not give any judgment worth a farthing. I fear the present generation care little for such things, and that any attempt to popularize them would meet with small encouragement. I only wonder at your energy in continuing to pass speculative thoughts through the filter of your brain.'

A few random quotations from his frequent letters from Ascot to Sir Henry Acland may be added:

'You say you are "almost broken-hearted" at your want of religious depth in faith and love. This is one of your self-tormenting thoughts, which I have often attempted to combat. Dismiss such dubitations from your mind whenever they arise. As to love, I am sure that there cannot be a more loving nature than yours. To feel yourself "broken-hearted" for want of love is a proof in itself how warm and real is the sentiment in you. As to faith, I suppose you mean that the *old* provinces of faith are being invaded by conviction of new facts inconsistent with their maintenance. Must this not be so? It is a question whether, *after a certain age*, it is worth while, as a matter of duty, to go into such questions. I, for instance, do not feel the least inclination to read the Gifford Lectures by (I forget his name), if he attempts to solve transcendental questions by abstract reasonings. The *history* of religion *must* be interesting. The *philosophy* of religion *may* be barren and provoking. I have been reading *Scenes of Clerical Life*, by George Eliot. I never read a tale more profound and striking than "Janet's Repentance." How different all our religious squabbles and doubts would be, if such questions were treated as she or Arthur Stanley treated them. But perhaps the tale would excite you too much. I did not know she was so powerful, and so completely fair to all varieties of religious thought and feeling.'

'Have you read Max Müller in the *Fortnightly* on Christianity and Mohammedanism? A great deal of it is very striking and very humiliating. . . . His references to the theological points in the Koran are very remarkable. He falls back upon the character of Christ as the point in which there can be no comparison. I have always felt this. If all dogmatic Christianity crumbled away, there is the Rock which never can be moved.'

'How can it be that men engaged in active life should not be "entangled with this world"? Whatever else Jesus Christ was, he certainly was a man: one to whom "nihil humani alienum erat"; one who consorted rather with publicans and sinners than with spiritual teachers; one who rather approved of our trying to do our duty in that state of life to which we may have been called, than our trying to solve insoluble problems, and shaping our life accordingly. I will look back to my sermon on the

Atonement. It is very flattering to have a discourse remembered for forty years! I fear I do not myself remember its tenor very accurately. Old Gaisford said he never remembered a sermon "after Wednesday."'

'I sympathize with the anti-gambling people. If horse-racing could be practised without betting and swindling and all its vile concomitants, well and good. But this I fear is impossible. It is no use for Lord Derby, or the Duke of Portland, or Lord Rosebery, to run their horses "square," without betting. The wretched subordinates, and all who follow in their train, bet and court ruin. Ought I to let my house for the races? I never doubted it before, but I have some qualms.'

'Do you mean to subscribe to the Huxley memorial? If so, I think you had better join the committee. It is quite true what you say about Christianity. But I think the true Christian *spirit* is best evinced by recognizing what is good in every man and every system.'

'I have been delighted by reading *The Relief of Chitral*, by the two brothers Younghusband. I have also been reading Lord Roberts' *Forty-one Years in India* with the greatest satisfaction. If you have not read it, pray get it without delay. It is a simple, unpretending record of good, hard work, and makes one proud to think that we have such men. Incidentally we learn much of others of even greater note, especially John Nicholson, who was a true hero. . . . These are the sort of books that give me pleasure. Philosophy and, I must add, theology have no delights for me.'

'How fast the leaves are falling! Old George Richmond and old George Anthony Denison gone in one day. They were both honest, genial, lovable men; Denison perhaps too positive and too sarcastic to deserve the last epithet. He was very violent, but transparently honest; and that covers a multitude of shortcomings. To you, of course, the death of George Richmond is far the most heart-touching. And indeed the character and manner of the man must nearly touch all who knew him. The notice in the *Times* is fair, but not enthusiastic. Well, we are all going the same way, and our time for "crossing the bar" cannot be far removed. . . . I have been reading *Manning's Life*, a painful book. I think we are better off at home than under a supposed infallible guide, who seems only to irritate and promote disunion.'

'What a curiously obscure poem is Keble's *Sunday after Ascension*! Who could imagine that "down" in line two means "thistle-down"? And then one is not disposed to be grateful to earth for fostering such down as produces thistles. The rest is more and more involved and obscure. Then one turns to *Whitsunday*, and lo! all is clear, simple, and bright as crystal. I remember Hawkins of Oriel saying to a young lady who was ecstatic over the *Christian Year*—with his chin up and his eyes half-closed, *more suo*,—" Do you understand him?" She might have answered, "Many things I understand and love; other things are like sayings of St. Paul, —hard to be understood." But I must confess that the clear and beautiful passages are far less numerous than the obscure. I have lately found a copy which was given me by Henry Jeffreys in 1834. That was the tenth edition.'

'I have no doubt that Ireland is "dear, romantic, and green." But in what respect is it "misunderstood"? It has been the prey of parties who did not try to understand it, but merely used it for their own purposes. Since Pitt's time, to the present day almost, this has been going on, and no doubt this game of shuttlecock has complicated the task of its honest rulers fatally. It is very surprising that the elections to small offices should be so entirely one-sided: anti-Catholic in the north, anti-Protestant in the greater part of the island. But why did the Catholics choose Wolfe Tone and Lord E. Fitzgerald (both, I believe, Protestants) for their chiefs at the end of the last century? And why in one day did they submit to Parnell so implicitly, while now they are divided into *three* Catholic sections? I confess it is hard to understand such things; and if that is what you mean by "misunderstood," I am with you: but I do not think this *is* what you mean. You mean, do you not, that the English do not understand them? Is not this due to the priests? In Carlow, where I have stayed, the same repulsion does not exist, at least not to the same extent as you found it in Mr. Trench's country. And if you speak to Livingstone you will find a very different state of things in that part of the west in which he lives.

'I think it is a pity that our Irish Church did not avail itself of the opportunity to make some greater alterations in the Liturgy. The high doctrines of the sacraments might well have been relaxed, and with such relaxation much of the sacerdotal stiffness of Pusey, &c., might have been abated.'

'I do not think that it can be fairly said that Judaism was the parent of Christianity. It was in distinct opposition to the *prevailing* Judaism that Christianity asserted itself, resting rather on Gentile tendencies than on Jewish. St. Paul cast aside Judaic principles altogether; and St. Peter was instructed to do the same, though he followed his instructions rather imperfectly.'

'As to your worry, I will tell you what I used to do about disagreeable matters. I never opened a letter arriving late in the day, for I could not afford to lose my sleep by speculating on how I should reply to a perplexing question. If the letter or question was future or contingent, I thought it over *in the day-time*, and wrote a draft letter. This I put in my desk, and let it lie there till it was wanted. This enabled me to put the thing aside; for having written my letter, so far as my information went, I found it useless to speculate, and so did not bother myself at night.'

On July 23, 1896, the golden wedding was celebrated at their Ascot home. It was a bright summer day, and many old friends from all quarters gathered together there to give their greetings and to show their affectionate regard for the Dean (as they would still call him) and Mrs. Liddell.

Among the numerous presents was a picture sent by Mr. Hamilton Aïdé, accompanied by the following words:

'I hope it is not inappropriate to ask your acceptance of "A Golden Sunset," or at least the attempt to portray one, in which the grey mists that troubled the city were being absorbed in the tranquil glory of the sky. Such I believe is the evening of your married life, and such may it continue, for your family and friends.'

Dr. Liddell replied :

'Allow me, in my own name and that of my wife, to thank you most sincerely for your beautiful symbolical drawing. So long as I live—it cannot be long—I shall look on it with delight, though I feel that the golden glow will gradually fade into darkness. I only hope that the twilight may be short, and that I may "cross the bar" before the glow has quite vanished.'

That hope was fulfilled. He lived for eighteen months longer, without experiencing more than the gradual failure of power which accompanied advanced years. The end came as he had desired, quite suddenly and painlessly, on the evening of January 18, 1898, and next day the big bell in Tom Tower announced to all Oxford that their old Dean had gone to his rest.

His body lies, as he had desired that it might, close by the grave of his daughter Edith, in the peaceful precincts of the cathedral at Christ Church, under the shelter of the southern wall of the sanctuary. A Cornish granite cross marks the spot, and upon the wrought-iron gate leading to it, through the Slype, from the eastern cloister, are placed his armorial bearings. Within the church, beneath the memorial to his daughter, is fixed a brass with this inscription:—

> Dilectissimam juxta filiam sepultus est
> Henricus Georgius Liddell
> Hujusce Ædis Alumnus MDCCCXXX—MDCCCXLVI
> Decanus MDCCCLV—MDCCCXCI
> Academiæ ornamentum fautor litterarum
> Ecclesiæ Cathedralis in pristinum decorem restitutor
> Qui post labores otio tandem perfructus
> Efflavit animam
> Januarii die XVIII° MDCCCXCVIII.

In the long series of rulers of Christ Church Dean Liddell will always hold a distinguished place. Other famous Deans will naturally challenge comparison with him. Prominent among them is John Fell, who came after the tumult of the Civil War and the desolation inflicted upon Oxford under the Commonwealth. Fell was a man of large views and imperious will; a divine, a scholar, and a wise patron of learning. To him is due the restoration and completion of the chief buildings of the college. But he was over-masterful and arbitrary; his rule belonged to an age when the sword had been scarcely sheathed, and rough and ready methods of enforcing authority and guiding opinion were adopted and approved.

Dean Aldrich, who came almost immediately after Fell, was a man of peace and culture; scholar, architect, musician, philosopher: illustrating his office in all sorts of ways, but happiest among his books and with his incessant pipe; 'humble

THE GATE IN CHRIST CHURCH CLOISTERS LEADING TO
DEAN LIDDELL'S GRAVE.

and modest to a fault,' as Hearne describes him, yet making others happy by his gentle and kindly sway.

Another great name is that of Atterbury; but Atterbury was only for a short time Dean; his fame at Christ Church is principally associated with his life as a student. He was a restless, overbearing chief; and Smalridge, who succeeded him at Carlisle and Oxford, complained that his first duty at both places was to quench the fires which his predecessor had kindled.

Cyril Jackson was a grand personage; perhaps the most remarkable and the most successful in the long line of Deans. He knew how to win and retain the confidence of the great families of England; Christ Church was never more famous or more popular than in his time; and he took a lively and helpful interest in the work and careers of his undergraduates, encouraged them to do their best, followed them in their after-life with generous sympathy, and did not forget their merits when occasion came to recommend men for promotion. He evoked the enthusiastic loyalty of members of Christ Church by his splendid loyalty to their House, and his statue in the library is a fitting memorial of their deep affection for him.

Of Dean Gaisford's sterling merits it will not be necessary to speak: his work, and the character of his rule, have been already described.

Dean Liddell, as we have seen,—if this brief memoir has not failed in its purpose—may worthily rank with the greatest of his predecessors, in regard to learning and intellectual power. His devotion to Christ Church was unsurpassed; his services to it were singularly great and various; and his majestic bearing, high authority, and unswerving rectitude raised him to a very lofty position among the rulers of Oxford. Humble and reverent, not caring for or seeking praise, he lived a long life of singular integrity; he might have been assigned a higher place than any of his predecessors, if he could have thrown off his shyness and reticence, and allowed himself to show and express how warmly he shared the interests of those over whom he was set, how keenly he rejoiced in their successes, and how eagerly he desired to encourage their efforts and to repress with a strong hand the idleness and extravagance which in every generation are apt to prevail among the wealthier undergraduates of our Universities.

Assuredly it may be asserted that as his term of office was unequalled in duration, so it was unequalled in importance. He witnessed and guided the transition from the old to the new Christ Church; and has left a lasting memory of a rule marked by august dignity, by strenuous labours, and, above all, by dauntless equity.

# INDEX

ACLAND, Sir Henry W., 28, 30, 45, 50, 79 *n.*, 117, 130, 151, 196, 210, 212, 215, 246, 257, 262.
—— Sir Thomas Dyke, 258; his work, *Knowledge, Duty, and Faith*, 270.
Aïdé, Mr. Hamilton, 276.
Albert, H.R.H. Prince, 97, 100, 120, 176, 255; appoints Dean Liddell Domestic Chaplain, 53.
Aldrich, Dean, 231, 278.
Anglesea, 252.
Anson, Sir William R., 239.
Arnold, Dr., 35, 97, 119.
Ascot, 268.
Athol, Duke of, 23.
Atterbury, Dean, 87, 279.

Bagley Wood, 251.
Bagot, Bishop, 135.
Bamborough Castle, 154.
Barnes, Dr., 135, 183.
Bayne, Rev. T. V., 164, 168 *n.*, 269.
Baynes, R. E., 168 *n.*
Bernese Alps, 83, 84.
Billing, Mr., 154.
Binchester, 1.
Biscoe, Rev. Robert, 14, 24.
Bishopton Grove, 2.
Blomfield, Bishop, 10, 53.
Boldon, 2.
Boyle, Dean, extract from his *Recollections*, 56.

Bradley, Dean, 21.
Bright, Dr. W., 183, 236, 237.
Brooke, Rev. Stopford, 235.
Brown, Rev. W. L., 30.
Bruce, Colonel, 178, 179.
—— Lady Augusta, 190.
Buccleuch, Duke of, his Sanitary Commission, 100.
Buckland, Dean, 62, 64, 87, 91, 95, 100; letter on Dean Liddell's postponement of the meeting of school, 118–20.
Bull, Dr., 59, 136, 182; his preferments, 136 *n.*
Burgon, Rev. J. W., 193.
Burton, Dr., 26; his death, 32.

Cambridge, 27.
Canning, C. J., afterwards Earl Canning, 7, 18, 19, 20, 21, 56.
Cardwell, Dr., 210.
Chamberlain, Rev. T., 155.
Charlton Kings, 251.
Charterhouse School, 3–10; system of teaching at, 6.
Cheltenham College, 240.
Cherwell, the, 197.
Christ Church, Oxford, 13, 134; Chapter, 135–7; students, 137; report of the Royal Commission, 141; system of private nomination to studentships abolished, 143; appointment of

a body of Referees, 144; Act of 1867, 145; alteration of the Deanery, 147; of the Cathedral, 149, 151; Latin Prayers, 152; sermons, 153; work of restoration, 155-9; the Chaplains' Quadrangle, 160; the Great Quadrangle, 161; the Chapter House, 163; list of Censors, 168 *n.*; number of undergraduates, 175; abolition of differences of rank, 175; class of undergraduates, 181; new Governing Body in 1867, 194.
Clarke, Sir James, 48.
Cleasby, Mr., 205.
Clerke, Archdeacon, Sub-Dean of Christ Church, 135, 167.
Cleveland, Duke of, his Commission of inquiry, 232.
Clifford, Mr. Charles, 140.
Cockerell, Professor, 51, 208.
Coleridge, Sir John T., 144.
Conway estuary, 252.
Conybeare, Rev. C. R., 123.
Corfe, Dr., 152, 236.
Cosin, Bishop, motto over his Library at Durham, 26.
Coxe, Rev. H. O., 259; appointed Bodley's Librarian, 200.
Cramer, Dr., 122.
Curtius, Georg, 80.

Dalhousie, James Ramsay, afterwards Marq. of, 17.
Dampier, J. L., 125.
Dasent, Sir George, 205.
Deane, Mr., 161.
Denison, Ven. George Anthony, 19, 274.
—— Henry, 17.
—— Stephen, 17, 18, 48; his estimate of Dean Liddell, 57.
Denmark, Crown Prince of, at Oxford, 176.
Desart, Earl of, 150.
Dindorf, 78.

Douce, Mr. F., 209.
Dowdeswell, Dr., 15, 158.
Doyle, Sir Francis H., 17, 21.
Dressler, Mr., 270.
Drisler, Professor, 80.
Dufferin, Lord, 153; *Letters from High Latitudes*, 153 *n.*
Dunlop, Andrew, 14.
Duppa, Dean Brian, 151, 157.
Durham, G. W. Kitchin, Dean of, 80, 168 *n.*, 176, 180, 198, 203, 207.

Easington, 20, 22.
Edinburgh, 22.
Eldon, Earl of, 209, 212.
Elgin, Earl of, 19, 178.
Eliot, George, *Scenes of Clerical Life*, 272.
Ellacombe, Rev. H. N., on Dean Liddell's first University sermon, 52 *n.*
Emlyn, Lord, 150.
Engelberg, 262.

Farrer, Dr. A. S., 246.
Fell, Dean John, 154, 161, 231. 278; his statue, 164.
Fellowes, Mr. Thomas Lyon, 12, 57.
Felpham, 139.
Fisher, Mr. Herbert W., 177, 179.
—— Mr. Joseph, 210, 214.
Fishlake, Mr., 68 *n.*
*Fortnightly Review*, extract from, 72 *n.*
Foxcombe, 251.
Frewin Hall, 176.

Gaisford, Dean, 13, 16, 18, 24, 51, 59, 60, 66, 241, 279; his hostility to the first Oxford University Commission, 128; his death, 131; appointed Regius Professor of Greek, 139.
Gardner, Mr. Percy, 213.
Gell, Mr. Lyttelton, on Dean

## Index 283

Liddell's services as Delegate of the Press, 201-5.
Gibraltar, Bishop of, 134, 168; on the changes in Christ Church, 145.
Gildersleeve, Professor, 80.
Gladstone, Rt. Hon. W. E., 15, 141, 255, 262; his speech on presentation of Dean Liddell's portrait, 238; visit to Oxford, 239; at Penmorfa, 253.
—— Mrs., 239.
Glenlyon, Lady, 23.
Goodwin, Professor, 80.
Gordon, General, his death, 255.
—— Mrs., extract from her *Life of Buckland*, 88.
—— Rev. Osborne, 150, 168 *n.*, 176 *n.*; on Dean Liddell's work as Professor, 53.
Goulburn, Dr., 193.
Graham, Sir James, 63.
Granville, Earl, 26, 237.
Grenville, Lord, 139.
Griffiths, Rev. John, 236, 237.

Hamilton, Walter Kerr, 17.
Hampden, Dr., his appointment to the Regius Professorship of Divinity, 32; opinions, 33; action for damages against, 38.
Hardy, Mr. Gathorne, 262.
Harrison, Benjamin, 17.
Harvey, Rev. H. A., on Dean Liddell, 47.
Hawkins, Dr., Provost of Oriel, 274.
Hawkshaw, Sir John, his scheme for the drainage of the Thames Valley, 197.
Heidelberg, 27.
Herkomer, Mr., his appointment to the Slade Professorship, Oxford, 213.
Hermann, Godfrey, his Review of Göttling's *Hesiod*, 25.
Heurtley, Dr., 137, 185.

Hicks-Beach, Sir M., 240.
Hinds, S., Bishop of Norwich, 125.
Holland, Rev. H. S., 168 *n.*
Holnicote, 258.
Howley, Archbishop, 137.
Hussey, Rev. Robert, 182.
Hymnal, University, 235-7.

Icelandic Dictionary, publication of, 205.
Iffley Lock, proposed abolition of, 197.
Irvine, Rev. Andrew, 6.

Jackson, Dean Cyril, 139, 141, 279.
—— J., Bishop of Lincoln, 21.
—— W., Bishop of Oxford, 139.
Jacobson, Dr., 136, 143, 183.
James of Hereford, Lord, 240.
—— Rev. B. F., 89.
Jeffreys, Rev. Henry Anthony, 17, 25, 275.
Jelf, Dr., 21, 136.
Jeune, Very Rev. Francis, 125.
Johnson, Rev. G. H. S., 125.
Jowett, Rev. Benjamin, 74, 140, 185 *n.*, 197.

Keble, his Sermon on *National Apostasy*, 41; his *Christian Year*, 274.
Keys, the verger, 149 *n.*
Kildare, Marq. of, 150.
Kingsley, Rev. Charles, 186.
Kynaston, Rev. Herbert, elected High Master of St. Paul's, 51.

Lansdowne, Marq. of, 96.
Leighton, Dr., 231.
Leopold, H.R.H. Prince, at Oxford, 177.
Lewis, Sir George Cornewall, 255.
Lexicon, Greek-English, publication of, 57, 65, 76; origin, 66; Preface to the first edition, 69-71, 76; arrangement, 72;

progress, 73; reception, 77; abridgement for schools, 76; number of editions, 78.

Leyden, Dean Gaisford at, 25.

Liddell, Albert Edward Arthur, death of, 186, 249.

—— Arthur, his death, 129.

—— Charlotte, 83.

—— Edith, her death, 257.

—— Harriett, her death, 48.

—— Henry George, his birth, 1; parents, 1; at a private school, 2; Charterhouse, 3-10; religious instruction, 9; confirmation, 10; hatred of school, 10; reserved disposition, 12, 169; matriculates at Oxford, 13; life at Christ Church, 14; elected to Fell's Exhibition, 14; nominated a Student, 15; member of the club 'Ten Tribes,' 17; his friends, 18, 25, 30; Long Vacation, 19; gains a Double First Class, 21; in Scotland, 22; his first stag, 23; returns to Oxford, 24; studies Divinity, 26; pupils, 27, 39, 47; duties of a College Tutor, 28; artistic tastes, 30, 46, 50; on Dr. Hampden's appointment, 32-6; attitude towards Dissenters, 37; on the suit of Hampden v. Macmullen, 38; his Ordination, 40, 49; memories of Cardinal Newman, 42-44; on the preaching of Newman and Dr. Liddon, 44; death of his sister Harriett, 48; appointed Greek Reader, 51; Select Preacher, 52; elected White's Professor of Moral Philosophy, 53; Censor and Whitehall Preacher, 53; Domestic Chaplain to H.R.H. Prince Albert, 53; style of his sermons, 55; congregations, 56; publication of the Lexicon, 57, 65, 76; engagement, 58; appointed Headmaster of Westminster, 60; marriage, 64; Preface to the first edition of the Lexicon, 69-71, 76; severe labour, 74, 79; mode of life, 75; on Ruskin's criticism, 81; his first visit to Switzerland, 83; at Westminster School, 86; reforms, 89; difficulties of his position, 94; system of periodical examinations, 99; strain on his powers, 101; literary style, 102; sermons to the boys, 103, 112; his austere demeanour, 105, 169-72; gift of teaching, 106; the challenges or examinations for admission, 107; epigrams, 109; moral tone of the school, 110; his love of *exact* truth, 111; special school services, 111; his prevention of the boat-race, 116; effect of the outbreak of fever, 117; letter from Dean Buckland on postponing the meeting of school, 118-20; his *History of Ancient Rome*, 121; on Vaughan's lectures, 123; his labours on the first Oxford Commission, 125; friendship with Stanley, 125, 183, 189; death of his son Arthur, 129; appointed Dean of Christ Church, 131; on the Professorship of Greek, 140; refusal to act as Commissioner, 146; alterations of the Deanery, 147; restoration of the Cathedral, 149, 151, 156-9; supervision of the work, 154; illness, 155; services, 159; other important architectural works, 160-5; his statue, 164, 269; enforced absence, 167; mode of discipline, 168; on Father ——, 174; on the Prince

## Index

of Wales' matriculation, 177; his delight in Stanley's appointment at Oxford, 182; death of his infant son, 186; sorrow at Stanley's appointment to Westminster, 189, 191; on Stanley's marriage, 190; Vice-Chancellor, 191, 231; his influence as chairman, 194; interest in the work of drainage, 195; the Thames Valley scheme, 196-8; services to Oxford, 199; Curator of the Bodleian Library, 200; Delegate of the Press, 201-5; on the publication of an Icelandic Dictionary, 205; Curator of the University Galleries, 208-14; on Ruskin's appearance, 215 *n.*; criticisms on *Modern Painters*, 216; letters from Ruskin, 216-22, 222-8; influence as Vice-Chancellor, 233; his interest in the compilation of the University Hymnal, 235-7; his portrait, 237; on Mr. Gladstone's visit to Oxford, 239; Council of Cheltenham College, 240; on the removal of Westminster School, 243; impartiality in selecting Headmasters, 245; his sermons, 246-8; his home life, 249; simple tastes, 253; favourite books, 254; hospitality, 254; death of his parents, 257; of his daughter Edith, 257; of Dean Stanley, 259; declines the Deanery of Westminster, 260; health, 261; accident to his foot, 262; caught in a snowdrift, 263; various honours, 265; letter on his resignation, 266; retires to Ascot, 268; extracts from his letters to Sir Henry Acland, 271-6; celebration of his golden wedding, 276; his death, 277.

Liddell, Rev. Henry George, 1.

Liddell, Hon. Henry T., 22, 23.
—— Mrs., 9, 129, 132, 149, 229, 254, 259, 263, 269, 276; her illness, 100, 117; death of her infant son, 186.
—— Robert, 4.
—— Sir Thomas, 1.
—— Thomas, 2.
Liddon, Dr., 191, 235, 236, 269; style of preaching, 45.
Lincoln, E. King, Bishop of, 235.
—— E. C. Wickham, Dean of, 236.
—— Lord, 18, 19.
Llandudno, 252.
Lloyd, Rev. C., 168 *n.*
Longley, Archbishop, 144.
Louise, H. R. H. Princess, 165 *n.*
Luke, Mr. G. R., 180.
Lushington, Dr., 193.
Lyon, Charlotte, 1.
—— Hon. Thomas, 1.

Macdonald, Mr., 211.
Macmullen, Rev. R. G., his action against Dr. Hampden, 38.
Madeira, Island of, 167, 261.
Manchester, Jas. Fraser, Bishop of, 194.
—— Duke of, 38.
Marshall, Rev. Geo., 39, 168 *n.*; his help in the work of the Lexicon, 74; his abridgement of, 76.
—— Rev. James, 89; on Dean Liddell's work at Westminster, 94-101; on his literary style, 102; on his sermons to the boys; 103; on his *History of Rome*, 121.
Melbourne, Lord, 32, 33, 35.
Mildert, Bishop Van, 2, 16.
Mill, Mr. John Stuart, 262.
Mowbray, Sir John R., 147, 164, 269.
Müller, Professor Max, 272; on Dean Liddell's Greek Dictionary, 72 *n.*, 80 *n.*; on his influence as Vice-Chancellor, 233.

Nélaton, M., 262.
Newcastle, Duke of, 18.
Newcastle-on-Tyne, 2.
Newman, Cardinal, 33, 37, 41; his pamphlet, *Elucidations of Dr. Hampden's Theological Statements*, 34; his influence, 42; sermons, 43; style of his preaching, 44.
—— W. L., 240.
Newton, Sir Charles T., 27, 30, 133, 140, 151.
Nicholson, John, 273.
Nuneham Park, 164.

Ogilvie, Dr., 137, 185.
Orme's Head, Great, 252.
Owen, Dean, 231.
Oxford. University Commission of 1850, 125; Commissioners, 125; recommendations, 126, 127; Commission of 1877, 145; establishment of non-collegiate students, 198; University Galleries, 208; collection of pictures, 209; work of cataloguing, 210; classes, 211; lectures of Mr. Ruskin, 211; appointment of six additional Curators, 212; University Hymnal, compilation of, 235-7; Tests Act of 1871, 233.

Paget, Sir James, on the death of Edith Liddell, 257.
—— Mr., afterwards Dean, 171.
Palmer, Archdeacon, 202.
—— Sir Roundell, 144.
Palmerston, Lord, 131, 134, 139, 140, 160.
Passow, F., his Lexicon, 67.
Pattison, Rev. Mark, 202.
Peel, Sir Robert, 35, 56, 63, 100, 255.
Penmorfa, 252.
Phipps, Colonel, 114, 115.

Powell, Rev. Baden, 125.
—— F. York, 206, 207.
Price, Rev. Bartholomew, 240.
Prothero, Mr., his memoir of Dean Stanley, 190 n.
Prout, Rev. T. J., 168.
Pusey, Dr., 27, 33, 41, 135, 136 n., 185, 186, 235; on the reform of the constitution of Christ Church, 143; on a Roman controversialist, 172; on the death of Dean Liddell's infant son, 187.

*Quarterly Review*, extract from, 68 n.

Radley station, 263.
Randolph, Dr., 51.
Ravensworth, Baron, 1.
—— Earl of, 22, 27.
Rawlinson, Rev. Geo., 210.
Redesdale, Lord, 240.
Redmarshall, 2.
Reeve, Mrs., 258.
Rich, Rev. J., 62.
Richmond, George, 274.
—— Sir William B., 253.
Rigaud, Rev. Stephen J., 89.
Ripon, 3.
Roberts, Lord, *Forty-one Years in India*, 273.
Robinson, Alfred, 202.
—— Sir J. C., 212.
Rome, 85.
*Rome, History of Ancient*, 121.
Rost and Palm's *Greek-German Lexicon*, 80.
Ruskin, Mr., 30; his opinion of Dean Liddell, 30, 81; on the Cathedral of Christ Church, Oxford, 150; appointed first Slade Professor of Fine Art, 211; his lectures, 211, 229; appearance, 215 n.; letters to Dean Liddell, 216-22, 222-8.
Russell, Dr., Headmaster of

## Index

Charterhouse, 4; the 'Bell and Lancaster' system, 5.
Russell, Lord John, 114.
Ryle, Bishop, 27.

Salisbury, Bishop of, 202.
—— Marquess of, Chancellor of Oxford, 232; letter from Dean Liddell on his resignation, 266.
Salwey, Rev. Herbert, 168 *n*.
Sampson, Rev. E. F., 168 *n*., 265.
Sandford, Rev. C. W., 168 *n*.
Saunders, Rev. Augustus Page, 19, 22, 60.
Schneider, Professor, 67; his Greek-German Lexicon, 68.
Scott, Dr., Headmaster of Westminster, 117.
—— Mr. G. Gilbert, 155, 159.
—— Rev. Robert, 25, 27, 84, 140, 258; his share in the work of the Lexicon, 65; accepts the college living of Duloe, 71; his death, 78.
Scrope, *Deerstalking*, 24 *n*.
Selborne, Lord, 145.
Sewell, Rev. William, 66.
Sherbrooke, Viscount, 22.
Short, Rev. Thomas Vowler, 13.
Shotesham Rectory, 12.
Shuttleworth, Dr., 33, 34.
Smalridge, Dean, 279.
Smith, Mr. Goldwin, 124, 125, 178, 246; his lectures to the Prince of Wales, 179.
—— Henry J. S., 202, 236.
—— Lady, 258.
—— Dean Samuel, 13, 16.
Sneyd, Rev. L., 138, 208.
Somerset, Lord Fitzroy, 30.
—— Lord Granville, 63.
Southchurch, 2.
Stainer, Dr., 236.
Stanley, Dean, 88, 235, 242; Secretary of the Oxford University Commission, 125; friendship with Liddell, 125, 183, 189;

appointed Regius Professor of Ecclesiastical History, 182; his influence, 184; sermon on the evils of controversy, 185; letter on the death of Dean Liddell's infant son, 186; preface to his *Collected Essays*, 188; Dean of Westminster, 189; marriage, 190; nominated Select Preacher, 192; death, 259.
Staverton Vicarage, 136.
Stockton, 2, 20.
Strathmore, Earl of, 1.
Studley Royal, 3.
Sunderland, 2, 20.

Tait, Archbishop, 125.
Talbot, Edw. Fitzroy, 31.
Talboys, Mr., 66.
Teesdale, Major, 178.
'Ten Tribes,' 17; list of members, 17.
Tennyson, Hallam, Lord, letter from Dean Liddell to, 20.
Thackeray, W. Makepeace, 8.
Thames Valley, the work of drainage, 196-8.
Thompson, Dr., Master of Trin. Coll., Camb., 204.
—— Rev. H. L., 168 *n*.
Thynne, Lord John, 89.
Trench, Dean, 243.
Trill Mill stream, 165.
Twisleton, Hon. Edward, 144.

University Galleries, 208.

Vaughan, Henry Halford, 17, 20, 21, 27, 35 *n*., 37, 66, 127, 130; Professor of Modern History, 123; his lectures, 123; resigns the Professorship, 124; appearance, 124.
Veitch, Dr., *Greek Verbs, Irregular and Defective*, 80.
Veysie, Rev. Daniel, 16.
Vigfússon, Gudbrand, 205; his

Icelandic Dictionary, 206; his death, 206; memorandum in Bishop Gudbrand's Bible, 207.

Wales, H. R. H. the Prince of, placed under Dean Liddell's charge at Oxford, 54, 176; his matriculation, 177; attends lectures, 179.
Wallace, Professor, 269.
Warner, Rev. W., 168 n.
Watkinson, Mr., 4.
Watts, Mr., his portrait of Dean Liddell, 237.
Weare, Rev. T. W., 60, 90.
Wellesley, Dr., 210.
Wellington, Duke of, 112.
Wells, Dean of, 240.
Wemyss, Earl of, 28, 131, 151; on Dean Liddell, 46.
Westminster School, 60, 86; condition of, 61; teaching staff, 61; reforms, 89; construction of new rooms, 91; life of the boys, 93; food, 93; restoration of the Play, 96; question of its removal, 98, 120, 243; movements checking its prosperity, 97–101; system of periodical examinations, 99; effect of the outbreak of fever, 100, 117; examinations for admission, 107; moral tone, 110; Latin Play, 113; the boat-race, 116; elections to scholarships, 241-3.
Whickham, living of, 12.
Williams, Hervey Vaughan, 96; his death, 112.
—— Mr. Justice Vaughan, 130.
Williamson, Dr., 116, 119; resigns the Headmastership of Westminster, 60.
Wilson, Rev. J. M., 183; letter from, 122.
Wood, Sir William Page, 144.
Woods, Dr., on Dean Liddell's services as Curator of the University Galleries, 208-14.
Wordsworth, Charles, 17, 27.
Wykeham House, 177.
Wytham Park, 251.

York, Archbishop of, 63, 192.
Younghusband, *The Relief of Chitral*, 273.

www.ingramcontent.com/pod-product-compliance
Lightning Source LLC
Chambersburg PA
CBHW030014240426

43672CB00007B/948